ALASKA CALLING

A memoir

Marilyn Cochran Mosley, Ed.D

Suzanne & Meleana

This book is written by a good friend of mine. I met her in Ft Yukon. She live on Vashon Island. Some of my pictures are in here & a story or 2. Hope you enjoy this Alaska Adventure.

Love,

Aunt Marylu

ISBN 9781731046628

Additional copies of this book are available by mail:
Marilyn Cochran Mosley
P.O. Box 1883
Vashon, WA 98070
(206) 463-4751

Printed in the United States by:
Amazon

Marilyn heading to Arctic Village

MAP

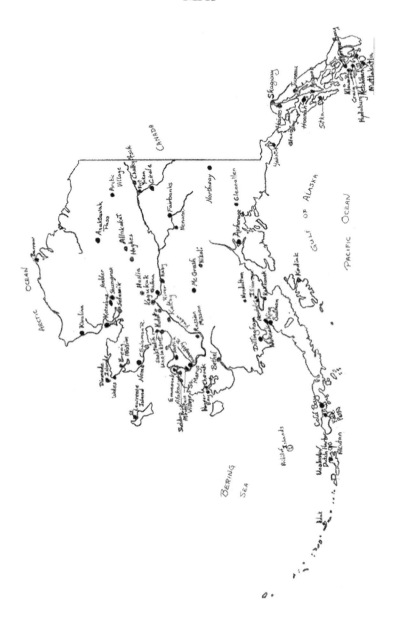

(Original Map by Rob Mosley)

Books by Marilyn Cochran Mosley

Dachshund Series

Dachshund Tails North
Dachshund Tails Up the Inside Passage
Dachshund Tails Down the Yukon
Dachshund Tails Rescued
Once Upon a Dachshund Tail
Cruiz'n to Dixie with Dachshund Tails
Dachshund Puppy Tails
Dachshund Tails Then and Now
Island Dachshund Tails

Other

Alaskan Ferry Tales for Children (editor)
Adoption in Peru

ACKNOWLEDGMENTS

I want to give a special thank you to the following individuals who read various drafts. Rhealee (Smokey) Snowden of Vashon Island repeatedly encouraged me to write the story of my Alaska years after hearing bits and pieces in conversations with me. She just kept saying "write it down." Every so often she would remind me to keep writing. My good friend, Marian Brischle, also of Vashon Island, was an early reader and made some excellent suggestions. She also read the final draft.

To get first-hand knowledge of life in Alaska I asked my boss Twyla Barnes to read the manuscript. She initially hired me to work as a school psychologist for SERRC (Southeast Regional Resource Center) in 1983. She is now retired and living in Vancouver, Washington. Twyla was both excited and very encouraging when I first mentioned the project. She provided a number of insights and was full of questions after reading the draft.

Roxie Quick, another Alaska connection now living in Washington State, after reading the manuscript was very instrumental in helping me sort out Native names and villages as well as the overall readability of the final draft. She spent a number of years as principal in Bering Strait School District, a year in Fort Yukon, and another year in Juneau.

Marylu Martin, a counselor in Galena's private school and also in the Yukon Flats School District and a good friend, read parts of the manuscript and provided several photos for the book. She is now retired and lives in Moses Lake, Washington. When we get together, we tend to reminisce about the experiences we shared.

Heidi Barnes is a designer transplanted from Alaska, living in Washington State. She first read a draft of the book in order to get a sense of what might be appropriate for the cover design. On the subject of art, Rob Mosley (Bob's oldest) son, created the two maps that appear in this book many years ago for two books I previously wrote. I added a number of place names on one of the maps. Finally, Marilyn Ingram, a friend when the two of us met at the age of three in Oregon, took the picture for the back cover.

The cover photo was a picture taken from the air by me while flying over the Chugach Mountains near Anchorage.

A special thank you also goes to my copy editor Dr. Roberta M. Meehan of Phoenix, Arizona, who is fascinated by Alaska, having spent one summer in Fairbanks teaching at the University of Alaska. Rumor has it that her two dachshunds, Tilly and Molly, added a few barks to keep her on track as she went through the manuscript.

A grateful and heart-filled thanks go to Melissa McGann for rescuing the manuscript from the clutches of a poltergeist in my computer at the last minute. She is dedicated founder of the book booth at Saturday Market on Vashon.

TABLE OF CONTENTS

Hooper Bay

ALASKA CALLING
INTRODUCTION

The shiny, black feathers of the raven standing in front of me were in sharp contrast to the recently fallen snow all around it. I stopped the car to watch the raven. Initially I thought it might be injured, but then it suddenly slid head first down a two-foot embankment, stood up, gave a quick shake and hopped back up to the top, and slid down again. I followed this prankster as it repeated the slide several more times before I moved past it, parked my car, and went into Juneau's airport terminal. I had a plane to catch. I was on my way to work, although I wouldn't be "on the job" for several more hours as I first had to fly by small plane to a village in "Bush" Alaska (most parts of the state that are off the road or ferry system) where I would be working in a local school—today, tomorrow, and the next day.

I thought back to my thirty-three years going to Alaska. Beginning in 1973 I was a casual visitor along for the ride but soon became hooked by its dramatic and diverse terrain of wide-open spaces, water ways teaming with life, snow-covered mountains, as well as forested landscapes with their abundant wildlife along with the small isolated native villages, logging camps, and fishing communities. In 1983 I accepted a job that was to become far more than just a paycheck, and continued until I retired in 2006.

That fun-loving raven I watched so long ago as it played in the snow without a care in the world pulled at me. Many other memories also surfaced. I can still smell the wood smoke wafting up from the chimneys of log cabins' fires as I walked in the snow through Tanana between its school and where I was staying. Above me the Northern Lights danced on that chilled night as they did on other cold, wintery nights in other villages. The snow crunched beneath my boots. I had just finished another day of testing kids and meeting with teachers and parents.

I have always enjoyed sharing my stories with friends and family including my raven tale in Juneau that probably happened the first winter I worked up there. I suspect they find some of my tales unreal or at best a bit difficult to imagine. I decided to put a few of those experiences down in a book for my family, my friends, and anyone else who might be interested.

I visited many more communities than are mentioned here, but these stand out in my memory. Some of the chapters have been written in great detail as they occurred. Others are from the hastily written notes I kept as well as from letters and post cards to both my husband Bob and to friends. Still others are from faded memories I treasure and want to share.

I want to add a word about flying in Alaska as it can be dangerous, more so than flying in the Lower 48 for several reasons. Inclement weather, remote and rough terrain often with no prepared landing strips, and few navigational references all play a part to the unwary. Bob, my husband, didn't like to fly instruments in Alaska because as he put it, "There is ice in those clouds." Judgment and common sense were also very important. Risk-takers as I think of them were another factor, and there seemed to be more of them taking to the air than elsewhere. Bob used to say, "There are old pilots and there are bold pilots, but there are no old, bold pilots." I encountered all of these situations at one time or another

The adventures that follow are not in a strict chronological order because some of them are from undated notes. Others are a compilation of several trips over a span of years. I have identified dates where known. The earlier stories include the first flight I made to Alaska and occurred before I began working in the 49th State. The time period occurred over a seven-year period. Incidents from the six-week research-gathering trip taking me over 13,000 miles in 1980 for my dissertation are also included as are several mini vacations during the summers when I traveled in Southeastern Alaska, mostly by boat. The third part covers a span of 23 years while I was working in Alaska.

PART I

1973 to 1979

Introduction to Alaska

Juvenile Bear Across from Chatham Cannery

CHAPTER 1

The Arctic Circle and Beyond

"Clear!" Bob's voice rang out across the Fairbanks airport as he started the plane. No one was near enough to hear except for me sitting in the co-pilot's seat. The 1948 Beechcraft Bonanza's single engine caught on the first try spinning its propeller with authority. The abruptness of the engine's roar quickly quieted to a steady hum after a few moments. Its vibration surged through me with anticipation. I loved to fly. Besides I was in Alaska. It was early summer in 1973 when my future husband, Bob, and I took off on that sunny day from Fairbanks.

Our intention was to go to Fort Yukon, or "House on the Flats" as it was translated from the Gwich'in language. It was 145 miles north. From there we planned to head down to spend the night in Central, a small community where hot springs were located, and enjoy soaking in the hot mineral waters.

Fort Yukon was above the Arctic Circle and we were full of adventure.

It was my first visit to Alaska. I didn't know then that it was the beginning of many visits to come. The trip happened some ten years before I was hired to work as an itinerant school psychologist traveling into the remote communities of Alaska, otherwise known as "Bush" Alaska.

Bob was on his annual business trip to Alaska meeting and working with building materials' business managers and owners. I was along for the ride. Flying and seeing Alaska were high on my list of things to do. I had never been to Alaska before, but it had captured my imagination from the books I had read as a child.

Nothing really happened on that trip, nothing that is, except an insatiable hunger to return that for me was monumental. Little did I realize at the time that this flight was the early beginnings of what was to become an amazing career and one in which I would spend years flying all over the state going from one village to another assessing kids' learning problems, meeting with parents and teachers, and making recommendations for individualized school programs for the students.

The trip had actually begun the previous week when we had flown in the Bonanza from Vashon Island in the State of Washington where I called home. We had already visited several communities in the southeastern part of the state before going north to Fairbanks in order to meet with two of Bob's customers. Finishing early left us with free time. A spur-of-the-moment decision found us heading to the northern Athabascan village of Fort Yukon.

The population of Fort Yukon was roughly 600 people. The surrounding area had been occupied for thousands of years by cultures of indigenous people. In historic times the Athabascan-speaking Gwich'in people had settled there. Fort Yukon itself was founded as a fur-trading outpost in 1847 by the Hudson Bay Company. Surprisingly enough, it had only been an established native village since the 1940s.

The northerly aboriginal peoples living on the North American continent at its northwestern limits were known as the Gwich'in. They were part of a larger family of aboriginal people called Athabascan. Only the Inuit Eskimo lived further north.

That day in 1973 when Bob and I chose to go to Fort Yukon was perfect for flying. The air was smooth and visibility was excellent. Shafts of sunlight streamed in through the plane's windows adding warmth to our sense of contentment as we headed northeast over the White Mountains. We didn't have a care in the world. The continuous hum of the engine was like music to my ears.

Beyond the small range of mountains named by the prospectors because of their composition of white limestone was the "Flats" and it was well named. Below I could see nothing but treeless tundra, miles and miles of it. Minutes passed as the landscape appeared all the same. Finally, in the distance and well ahead of us sprawled the Yukon River twisting and turning like a lazy snake. My eyes traced its meanderings as we flew closer and I could see small islands here and there on the river with some of them no more than sand bars. I followed it with my eyes until it just disappeared into the horizon. Its flood plains spread out as far as I could see.

From the very first moments I saw the Yukon River, it held a fascination for me. Thirteen years later Bob and I took our 17-foot canoe 200 miles down this same river along with our family of seven dachshund dogs. We paddled from White Horse to Carmack; both communities were in the Yukon Territory in Canada. We didn't even get into the Alaskan part of its 1,980 miles that emptied into the Bering Sea on the Yukon-Kuskokwim Delta on that occasion.

Fort Yukon's airport was easy to spot from a long distance out. My eyes searched along the river's shoreline as we neared the village. I noted the river widened. Tiny islands along with a few sand bars were evident particularly at the point where it changed directions. The village was on the north side of the Yukon River at an elbow in the river that marked its northern apex before it bent and twisted in a southwesterly direction toward the Bering Sea. The smaller Porcupine River flowed into it just west of the landing strip.

The runway was long, some 5,000 feet to be more precise. While it was made up of gravel and dirt, it appeared to be in good condition. Bob set up an approach for landing and announced our intentions to anyone within hearing distance of our radio. We weren't expecting anyone to answer as we had not seen any other air traffic since leaving Fairbanks. Surprisingly we heard the distinct voice of another pilot acknowledging us. He said that he had us visually. He added that he was well behind us and would wait until we cleared the runway before landing.

A smooth landing was followed by taxing in and parking near a building that served as a terminal but looked more like an old single-story warehouse or more probably a WWII hangar converted into a terminal. The "Passenger Entrance" sign was displayed over its one visible door. Once out of the Bonanza I watched the other plane land. It was a commercial plane from Wein Airlines and looked like it was carrying quite a bit of cargo. Tourists, I later learned, visited this village in order to say they had crossed the Arctic Circle. I suspect that's what motivated Bob and me to fly up here in the first place.

The community from the air had seemed sprawled out. We walked around the airport after landing kicking up dust with our boots until we reached a road behind the building that led to the village. We stopped and just stood there looking and did not go any further. I guess we were content to say we had been there and didn't venture beyond our vantage point at the edge of the airport. It didn't look that terribly interesting.

I gazed down the road for several minutes and wondered. Dust swirled around with any movement at all as everything was dry and various shades of brown. There were a few houses visible along both sides. They had long since lost their paint if they ever had any. A four-wheeler, also known as an ATV (all-terrain vehicle), was coming down the road towards us. I did a double take as it went by us when I realized a boy of maybe ten or eleven years old was driving. Three other kids all smaller that he was clung to the seat behind him laughing as he bounced through a pot hole in the middle of the roadway. Dust stirred up into the few nearby trees and sifted slowly back to earth almost like lazy snowflakes falling once the kids had passed.

I had no idea at the time that I was looking into a crystal ball when I saw those kids; I was seeing my future when I gazed down that road. That was Bob's first and only trip to Fort Yukon. Instead he turned around and walked back towards the plane. To him it was just another village. He was an accountant and mainly interested in credit.

It was prudent to buy more fuel, but we didn't see any readily available. It wasn't the kind of airport where a gas tanker rolled out to the plane nor were there any pumps visible that we could park next to and fuel up. We walked into the airport's one building trying to find someone to sell us gas. Private planes didn't buy fuel here except in emergencies. Well, we did and as a result paid almost double the price of gas in Fairbanks and topped the two main tanks then filled one of our reserve tanks. Fuel, I was told, was shipped by barge up the Yukon River before freeze-up, and quite naturally it was expensive. It was kept in oil drums stored at the airport. We realized we should have loaded up in Fairbanks before our little sight-seeing journey.

By this time Wien's commercial plane had landed and its cargo unloaded. The pilot saw us and walked over to our plane.

He introduced himself and asked where we were from as he did not recognize our yellow and white Bonanza. While the inside of the Wien airplane was being physically converted from a cargo ship to a passenger carrier, we sat in its cabin drinking coffee and talking to its crew.

I brought up the subject of flying north of Fort Yukon. The pilot wasn't too positive about our flying into the Brooks Range or the North Slope beyond. He told us about some of the dangers in the mountain range with its unstable air and quickly changing weather conditions. I looked at Bob and he looked at me. We knew exactly what we were going to do as the challenge beckoned to us like a moth drawn to a flame. Besides, we now had three full tanks of gas.

Goodbyes were said as we walked back to our plane. We noted that several passengers boarded the commercial airliner. Once the doors closed it started up and headed for the runway. We spent time looking at our air charts before we taxied out. Minutes behind the now airborne Wien plane we took off and headed north while it headed south with several tourists who proudly held onto their certificates that said they had crossed the Arctic Circle. Fort Yukon was all of eight miles north of it!

The warmth of the sun continued to find its way into the cockpit, but with it a chill as I stared out at the emptiness around us. There was no airplane chatter from other pilots as there were no planes even within radio distance from us. I looked down at the wilderness below. There were no villages or even cabins, and certainly no roads. We were hundreds of miles north of Fairbanks and completely alone. Fort Yukon was behind us, and it was north of the Arctic Circle.

I found myself frequently glancing at the red flickering light on the plane's transponder as we approached the Brooks Range and began flying into it. Someone's radar screen was tracking us, or at least I hoped so. That brought a little comfort if indeed they were tracking us. I only hoped that if there were an engine failure or other emergency and we dialed the emergency number of 7777, the person watching the radar would pick up our location before we disappeared into the mountains. Different from those early pioneers who didn't know what radar was, yes. But I suspected they had the same pit in their stomach flying into the unknown that I had at that moment. It was definitely an adrenalin rush.

I stared out the window at what lay below us. The peaks were rugged, nothing but granite with ice and snow on the higher ones. I closed my eyes for a brief moment and then quickly opened them to see if I was in a dream. Nothing had changed. Mile after mile seemed all the same. I thought about sheep, bear, caribou, wolves, and all manner of small furry critters living below us. I wanted to see them, get close and personal and take pictures. But, of course, there was no place to land. The only sound was the continued hum of our single engine. The propeller never faltered.

Finally, we flew out of the mountains and found ourselves above another flat plain. Beyond was the Beaufort Sea—nothing but white, frozen white, as far as I could see. Clouds started to form as we banked the plane and headed back into the range of mountains. We checked the air charts for Arctic Village and decided to head for it since we were this far north. Arctic Village is one of the most remote Native villages in Alaska, and far away from the noise and turmoil of mainstream society. It was still early in the afternoon. This small isolated community was 100 miles north of Fort Yukon and was the northern border of the Venetie Indian Reservation with its southern border at Venetie. And, I thought to myself, Fort Yukon was remote.

Flood plains near the east fork of the Chandalar River were evident once we were out of the mountains. The tundra below also boasted of wooded hills full of stunted spruce trees.

In the years that followed I spent many a flight looking for caribou among the small trees and was often rewarded, but that day we didn't see any. We easily found Arctic Village.

The runway was bumpy, and to our discovery the town was at least a mile away from the airport. Jumping out of the plane once we landed and shutting the engine down I looked around beyond the airstrip. Building supplies and a few 50-gallon oil cans were stacked up near the end of the runway but nothing else.

The nearby tundra was full of vegetation including lots of little three-to-four-foot bushes, probably high bush cranberries I thought to myself. Peaks from the Brooks Range were not too distant from where I stood. The air smelled of drying grass and leaves, and in the back ground was the warmth of the sun as it splashed across my face.

The Formidable Brooks Range

Out of nowhere, one of the villagers came up from beyond the airstrip and started talking with us. We walked along listening to him and asking questions as he headed towards the village. "Surveyors are in town," he volunteered. Then he added, "Airport is being enlarged." We learned that we were the only other visitors the village had. He continued talking about the community. He told us about the caribou that migrated through it, when they arrived and where they fed.

This village was much smaller than Fort Yukon with maybe 90 to 100 people living in it. Bob always liked to talk while I was curious about what we would find.

Evidence, I later learned, from various archaeological investigations indicated that the Arctic Village area may have been settled as early as 4500 BC. Around 500 AD the Athabascan speaking Gwich'in peoples (often called Neets'aii Gwich'in or "those who dwell to the north") came into the area staying in seasonal hunting and fishing camps. It wasn't until around 1900 that the village became a permanent settlement.

Time passed quickly as we walked with the man all the way into town where people came up to us because we were strangers. Visitors were a rarity to the inhabitants. We didn't meet the surveyors. A blind woman walked up and touched my hands laughing in delight because I was different. Our "guide" left us at that point.

I felt I had gone back in time into another world. A musher spoke to us. He started talking about his third-place dog team and pointed out his dogs. They were tied up around his house barking as we walked by. Two bashful school girls came up and started giggling when I tried to talk with them. One of them pointed out the post office when I asked where it was.

We walked over to it and found ourselves in someone's kitchen. One corner had the traditional postal bars framed in a window from which to do business. I wanted to mail a post card from this remote spot. The cook set her kettle down and walked behind the bars where she hand-cancelled the plain post card on which I had scratched my address.

Evening was not far away as we hiked back to the airport. The time of year, however, meant we had lots of daylight left, almost twenty-four hours of it to be exact at this latitude. Nearby we passed a small lake bed with trash piled high. In it were washing machines and various other symbols of civilization. The rusted ones were in the middle as were empty beer bottles and all those other things one finds in today's world.

Climbing back into the Bonanza we took off for Circle Hot Springs. This time we bypassed Fort Yukon.

I wasn't to see either of these communities again until seven years later when I was doing research for my doctoral dissertation. Then it would be several more years before I returned as a school psychologist to work with the kids in the school district, going to both of the villages we visited that day as well as to Central where the hot springs were located and where we stopped for the night.

Central's airport was gravel and in poor condition. After making one pass Bob set up for landing and guiding the plane down onto the 936-foot runway. Once stopped and when I opened the door a hoard of insects descended on us. Getting out of the plane we fought off some of the largest mosquitos I have ever encountered. Fortunately, they didn't like me. Bob wasn't so lucky. They dive-bombed and attacked with every pass. One could almost hear them call, "fresh blood, fresh blood, come and get it" as they circled his bald head and lined themselves up for it time and time again. We ran for the nearest building with mosquitos trailing right behind us and attacking at every chance they had.

Later that evening we added our names to the hundreds of signatures already on one of the beams in the local bar at the Steese Roadhouse where we spent the night after taking a refreshing dip in the hot mineral waters and eating dinner. The next day it was back to Fairbanks.

Arctic Village

CHAPTER 2

Other Early Flights North

Between that first early summer flight I made in 1973 and my research-gathering trip in 1980 when we flew 13,000 miles and visited over 30 native villages, Bob and I made at least one trip a year and sometimes more to Alaska in the Bonanza. We covered much of the State including the southeastern part, Fairbanks and Anchorage, as well as western Alaska. If it was late summer, we occasionally encountered a little snow in the more northly communities as if Mother Nature was teasing the uninitiated.

Some of our flying was for pleasure, but most of the time these were business trips for Bob. With every one of those trips I was getting to know Alaska better and better as it was rapidly becoming a friend. Each flight was an adventure. The flying, the wilderness, the new experiences all served to whet my appetite, my passion for wanting to work in the "Great Land".

Bob was a credit manager for a wholesale building materials company with its headquarters in Washington. Every year he flew north because credit there was a decidedly different ball game than in the Lower 48. In his words, "The credit manager who did not visit his customers in Alaska could be in for a big surprise." To avoid those surprises, Bob visited.

The flying we did in and out of small communities was my introduction to Alaska. I didn't get my pilot's license until 1975. The air charts said a lot. I could see the villages were evident as yellow dots that were few and far between each other. Most of them had runways but not all of them did. Also evident was the occasional tiny dot with the word "cabin" written beside it. Most of the time I couldn't even find the cabin even though we were flying at a fairly low altitude.

One late afternoon we ended up landing on the Anchorage-Fairbanks Highway near Healy in order to meet one of Bob's customers at the local roadhouse to go over some business. Meeting finished we didn't taxi back to where we had touched down but took off from the parking lot where we had left the plane. Zing! I can still remember hearing the electric lines go overhead as the plane left the ground. We hadn't seen them. We were very lucky that evening. It would have ended badly had we hit those wires.

Other early trips included landing on St. Michael's soft sandy strip, walking three miles across tundra between the old and new town sites of Point Hope, riding on a three-wheel balloon-tired vehicle from the airport to the village of Savoonga on Saint Lawrence Island, as well as getting on the back of a snow machine to ride into Shishmaref located on one of the barrier islands on the Bering Sea. These trips were all in the interest of credit. They prepared me in part for the job I would eventually take in 1983.

Chevak and Hooper Bay in western Alaska as well as Alakanuk a little further north of the other two villages were three native communities I particularly remembered from those early flights. I was to visit all three villages much later as a school psychologist but in the winter months. We were there in the summer.

Chevak at the time was one of the most remote places I could imagine. It was located on a river inland from the Bering Sea. Hundreds of tiny lakes surrounded the area. The water didn't have anywhere to go as the land was flat—there were no mountains, no high places, no craters, just flatness as far as I could see. Following the landscape from the air I decided it must be what the moon's surface looked like.

The runway was soft. Bob was very careful not to put the nose gear down until we had slowed considerably. He usually landed like a duck sitting on the water but tended to really exaggerate on strips like the one at Chevak because of its soft surface. I glanced out the window when we stopped to see several Eskimo children running around naked. They were no more than toddlers but were having a great time playing. I shivered. While it was summer time I felt chilly enough to wear a light jacket when I stepped out of the plane and couldn't imagine being outside with no clothing for protection. I sank down a little with each step.

Half the people in the village or so it seemed were there to greet us and a number of them were on snow mobile machines even though there was no snow. They used them quite efficiently on the tundra. Incoming planes were a big social event for the villagers as people were looking for family and friends, mail, anything that was different from the routine of their daily lives. Several buildings were close to the runway. I realized these were people's houses. We spent all of an hour there while Bob looked up Peter Boyscout who had ordered some building materials for his "business."

I was to spend many nights in Chevak in later years working at the school.

Hooper Bay was our next stop on that particular trip and was only a few miles away but located right next to the Bering Sea, or at least the airport was. The strip was a long, asphalt one on which small jets could land. The wind almost took the door off as I opened it. I quickly grabbed my heavier jacket. The gusts off the sea cut right through me. We walked into town where we met Bob's one customer. The village was a little less than two miles inland from the airport so the wind wasn't as fierce as it had been out on the airport but it was still cold.

Business was finished. When we were walking back to the plane we were invited into one of the homes to look at Butterfly baskets, and found a woman sitting on a skin rug with the inside up cutting fish with a primitive tool. Much later I learned she was using an ulu, but at the time I didn't know what it was. The house was warm and a number of smiling faces greeted us. Nearby was a plate of fried walrus liver. In contrast to the ulu I saw an electric frying pan which had obviously seen a lot of cooking.

There were two entrance doors separated by a small area. One opened directly to the outside while the other led into the main house. Outside near the entrance a seal skin had been hung up to dry. While there was a well in town, it wasn't currently operating—why, I never found out. Instead people went out in six-wheeled snow vehicles and collected ice which they carried back to their homes and melted for water. I didn't get a basket on that trip, but years later I did from another woman I met.

We left the house and continued to walk back to the airport. A small jet had just landed from Anchorage. Several four-wheeled vehicles had picked up its passengers. A couple of the women wore long fur coats. I was surprised when Bob greeted one of the men who turned out to be an attorney he knew who was working for the Native corporation in Hooper Bay. He and the attorney stopped for a few minutes to talk with one another as we stood in the middle of the roadway. Bob knew him from his credit management days in Anchorage.

The last village we were to visit that day before returning to Bethel for the night was Alakanuk on the Yukon River. This village was strung out along part of the river for several miles. The airport's runway had partially washed away by recent flooding due to "break up" when snow and ice melted. The one road leading into town wasn't in much better shape. Several children were out playing and pointed the way. We began walking. It took us about an hour as we dodged mud holes before we reached our destination and met with Bob's customer. He showed us his store, which included a little bit of everything it seemed including, of course, building materials. The store was the only business in town as far as I could see.

We were given a ride back to the airport in a boat. Travel within the village it turned out was mostly by boat, and all of the ones we saw had motors on them. I later made several trips to Alakanuk but only two trips back to Hooper Bay. One of these trips during the winter was most memorable and appears in a later chapter.

It was time to head back to the southeastern part of the state that is a region sometimes called the "panhandle". It is a thin strip of land and islands between Canada's British Columbia and the northern Pacific Ocean. It contains the Inside Passage, a series of waterways largely protected from the Pacific by islands and provides a safer sea route up and down the coast.

We were in Anchorage so we flew just south of the Chugach Mountains over Prince William Sound and followed the coastline heading towards Yakutat. The snow-capped mountains reflected the blazing sun off the higher peaks. I took several pictures. One gave the impression that we were actually standing on the ground in the snow. I used it for a Christmas card that year and had an enlargement made that is now hanging in my house. It is the cover for this book.

Once we left the Anchorage area we were alone. There were no other planes in the air. Blue seas blended with the sky as sunlight danced on the waves below then crashed against the shoreline. Off to the right my eyes caught some movement in the deeper water. Suddenly a living creature breached out of the water causing the sea around it to spray thousands of water droplets in the air and leave a foamy sheen behind when the animal disappeared in an instant. Then I saw another monster, and yet another and another. I realized I was looking at a pod of Humpback whales, or at least I thought they were Humpbacks as other species also swam in these waters.

We circled to find several of them playing below us. Several stuck their heads above the water while others spouted jets of water upward. I took out my camera and started taking pictures. The sun reflected off their backs. A second one breached spouting more water. I held my breath as we continued to circle above them and I continued to take pictures. It was a beautiful sight to see them.

Between Yakutat and Glacier Bay

We finally left the scene and continued along the coastline. Somewhat later we landed at Cape Yakataga just for fun. Jumping out of the plane the two of us started walking along the beach. We hadn't gone very far when some very large bear paw prints visible in the soft sand cut our exploration short. Nearby was a pile of bear poop that looked all too fresh. Nothing was said. We both turned and retraced our steps back to the plane, took off, and continued towards Yakutat where we landed.

The next day we continued along the coast flying over Glacier Bay and then into Juneau.

I should note that when we were in Fairbanks other flights took us through the interior when we were heading for the panhandle or southeastern part of the state. When that happened, we flew east towards Northway following the Alaska Range. Once beyond Northway we were in Canadian airspace for a while before we flew through the pass crossing back into the U.S. and going to Haines and Skagway where we had friends.

On one particular flight from the interior I remember we had left late in the day. It was early in the fall so we didn't have the long days we normally had on our springtime Alaskan flights. We had left Fairbanks later than we intended and decided not to stop at Northway but continue on to Haines, a small community in Southeastern Alaska where we planned to spend the night.

That wasn't going to happen, however, not that night. It started out as a moon-lit evening flight with the moon playing tag with a few clouds and patches of snow below separating land from sky. We continued flying hoping visibility would stay good. As we approached the mountains there was some fog around particularly in the direction we were headed. Visibility started to deteriorate. We initially decided to gamble and it looked as if we were winning. Another half hour and we would be landing in Haines. Not knowing where the mountain peaks hid, however, created a dangerous situation for us. Now and then we caught momentary glimpses of the land below us. Neither of us wanted to hit one of those peaks.

My mouth became dry as I stared out of the window trying to catch sight of the ground. I swallowed. I blinked a number of times as I tried to spot anything in our flight path. We weren't high enough to avoid potential peaks that were in our path.

The fog was drifting in patches combining with clouds to become thicker as we flew through alternating shafts of moon light and into the spaces in between. Fields of snow below faded each time the moon disappeared. Below the Canadian wilderness beckoned. High peaks stood tall. With visibility deteriorating, Bob's voice echoed my thoughts exactly. "I'm turning around and heading back to Northway."

The last fifteen minutes through the pass were perhaps the most dangerous part of the trip. We had lots of fuel, so rather than carry our poker hand to its limits, we carefully turned with the light from the moon keeping us away from mountain tops and retraced our path back towards Northway. It was a good decision.

Bob was flying while I kept track of the air charts and the geography around us as much as I could see. The pass we had hoped to go through was on the Canadian-U.S. border just north of Haines. Once turned around we radioed ahead for a cabin and were told, "Go to the second door on the right. See you in the morning."

Northway is a sleepy little community near the Alaskan-Canadian border. The highway passed it along with the nearby airport with its lone restaurant and motel. The airport had been built in the 1940s as part of the Northwest Staging Route for Lend-Lease aircraft bound for Russia during World War II. We had stopped there on previous trips as it was on the main air route that connected Southeastern Alaska to the rest of the state that took us through Canadian airspace. We always had more than enough fuel so didn't have to land in Canada eliminating our need for Customs. Bob knew the man who owned much of the property in Northway so he always liked to stop.

Around 2:30 the next morning we landed at the airport and found our assigned room. The long runway had grass growing up through its pavement and had many years before seen its last military bombers.

Flying through the pass brought other memories to mind. On one such occasion Bob and I were flying from Southeastern Alaska to the interior when weather began to move in about the time we left Haines. Below the snow-covered mountains were evident. Rain became more aggressive and changed to a light snow making the ground barely visible. We found a hole in the overcast and climbed up through it to 13,000 feet.

We had some radio contact with the Northway station but it was minimal. We heard the radio's operator ask us to monitor the emergency radio frequency of 121.5. A plane was reported down on the route we were flying. "Copy that!" was Bob's answer. No additional details were given.

Further communication became impossible as nothing but static came through the ear phones. We had no idea if it was a small plane or a big one, or whether it was a private carrier or one of the commercial flights. The two of us listened intently concentrating on the radio's crackling. Then we thought we heard muffled voices on the frequency, but they were badly distorted. Then there was nothing but static.

Gulkana where we were heading was reporting 1800-foot ceilings with ten-knot winds. We were above the overcast at this point with no visible ground. At least we were well beyond the pass and out of the mountains. We flew for the next fifteen minutes with my eyes rotating between the compass and the directional-finder, when I spotted what appeared to be a river. Then I could see some ground. Mist hung in the air but it was thinning out. Spotting a hole in the cover we spiraled down like a corkscrew through it to within a thousand feet of the ground. I was quite happy about not having to make an instrument approach to Gulkana Airport, although Bob was instrument certified and often flew instruments in the Lower 48.

I thought about the downed plane and wondered if there actually was a downed plane. We never learned any more about it.

That evening we hitched a ride into Glennallen from the airport and spent the night there. Glennallen was on the pipeline route. We had stayed there before when it had been a sleepy little town where everyone knew everyone else. This time we found a lot of strangers with Texas drawls greeting us. Big trucks with heavy equipment were everywhere. Diesel engines blocked out all other sounds. The newcomers didn't know much about Alaska and didn't seem to care. They were there to make a fortune. Building the pipeline to transport oil from the North Slope to Valdez had become the new "gold rush."

Meals and other necessities were expensive, and finding an available room was hard to do. We made our way to the last motel room in town, but then it was questionable as to which room we really had. The first room we were given a key to had someone already in it. They were as surprised as we were when we walked in. We solved it by quickly staking claim on a vacant room we found somewhat accidently. By then we were ready for getting something to eat and settled for over-priced hamburgers in the nearby café. We left Glennallen the next morning after getting another ride to the airport and headed for Fairbanks.

Rock Oyster Pole—Ketchikan

CHAPTER 3

The *Morning Mist*

Sitka is located on Baranof Island and the southern half of Chichagof Island on the Alexander Archipelago of the Pacific Ocean and is part of the Alaskan Panhandle (Southeastern Alaska). It was once the capital of Russian Alaska until 1867. A dock there was a most unlikely location for a building materials warehouse but that's where the Calvins had developed their very successful business. Bob had a long history of working with them in the lumber yard's infancy. He became close friends with Larry and Maryann. When we were invited to spend a week aboard their new boat, the *Morning Mist*, we jumped at the chance.

Larry kept busy with the marina, commercial fishing, and their building materials business, and probably in that order, while Maryann kept track of the business end of things. I still remember standing on the airport's tarmac with the two of them and Bob as they burned the loan papers to celebrate their final payment to the bank. That was definitely a moment for celebration.

Bob and I had borrowed a much smaller motor boat from them in 1975 for our honeymoon. We had cruised north of Sitka in the salt water channel, fishing and camping aboard the boat at night. A small bay provided the remains of a long-forgotten cabin with only the stone chimney standing. Who had lived there was a mystery. I could only imagine. Looking at the chimney through the camera lens and finding it surrounded by wild beach grass made a memorable picture. The shoreline near it had provided us with fresh clams for dinner.

*Long-forgotten cabin chimney near
Fish Bay*

The water in front of the cabin had more than its share of fish. This was where we dropped the anchor. Crabs were visible below us but we didn't have a crab pot so concentrated on catching several fish with spinning tackle. That night while one of the larger ones was cooled down in a nearby creek for breakfast, some four-footed thief looking for an easy meal discovered it. By the next morning our fish was long gone. I wondered if the thief returned the next night looking for another free handout.

Larry and Maryann had the *Urchin,* a smaller boat than the *Morning Mist,* at the time and met up with us in Fish Bay not far from our "stone chimney". They motored around the small bay behind us fishing. A couple of whale on-lookers joined us as we circled. I suspected they were fishing as well and probably had better luck than we did, although Larry caught one very nice salmon.

Fortunately, neither of us smoked or we would probably have blown ourselves up as there was a leak in one of the spare gas cans that was full of gas. The tiny hole in the can wasn't discovered until the end of the trip when the Calvin's oldest son found the culprit gas can while helping unload the boat back in Sitka. The gas smell had accompanied us the entire trip.

The *Morning Mist* had been built in 1978 to Larry's

specifications by Delta Marine Industries in Seattle. Its length was 47.5 feet, which was slightly longer than the average commercial fishing vessel. It had a depth of 6.7 feet. Gross tonnage was 51, while net tonnage was 39. Larry was particular in every detail and had made several trips to Seattle to supervise its construction.

It was the following year when we were invited for a week of cruising in Glacier Bay. I had just finished a month of summer school in Seattle University's doctorate program. My work in the Central Kitsap School District on the Peninsula didn't start until after Labor Day so I had the time and was more than ready for a trip to the southeastern part of the state. As for Bob, he could always justify a trip. After all, he was visiting some of his customers in Alaska.

It was July 20, 1979 when Vashon Island disappeared behind us as we took off from its grass strip. Vacation time meant two weeks in Alaska. The first half was to be spent cruising with the Calvins on their new boat.

We dropped a friend off in Victoria, British Columbia, gassed up, and flew to Port Angeles to clear Customs back into the United States and then headed north over flying Canada on an instrument flight plan (IFR) to Sitka. The flight was smooth at 10,000 feet. Then clouds moved in obscuring the surface and dictated that we climb another 2,000 feet in order to remain above them as long as we were in Canadian airspace. The controller was quick to clear us up to 12,000 feet. More clouds caught up with us near the U.S./Canadian border. Occasionally we found ourselves between layers once in Alaska and headed for Sitka on the outer coast.

Clouds dictated an instrument approach into Sitka. Occasionally seawater was visible below us although we were still in the overcast. I was surprised by the low cloud layer as reports had indicated a 4,500-foot ceiling over Sitka. I don't like flying in clouds or fog as I don't have a sense of where we are in relationship to the ground.

The instruments we had in our plane were adequate but a far cry from those found in jet airliners. Below there was definitely an ocean swell that was visible as well as some small islands as we were cleared to land in Sitka. Once the airport was in sight, I breathed a sigh of relief as no instrument landing was needed. After an instrument flight I was always glad to have my feet on *terra firma*!

We taxied over to the area for small planes and parked. A quick call to our friends, the Calvins, was followed by unloading the plane. They were there in no time to pick us up. We headed for their home where we had a delicious supper that included fresh abalone. Before we ate I wandered into their "front yard" which was mainly covered with blueberry bushes that were loaded with fruit. I started picking as the berries were sweet and ripe. Once the meal was over the four of us headed for the marina and their boat. This was the first time I had seen it and I was impressed. That night and the next week were to be spent on board the *Morning Mist.*

The air smelled of damp and salt, and in the back ground there was the constant murmur of the tide. I quickly fell asleep that night content with the world. Those blueberries I had picked found their way into pancakes for breakfast the next morning along with broiled char, juice and coffee. My taste buds were stretched to their limits when lunch was served. First there were appetizers of pickled salmon (compliments of Larry's mom and oh so good) and nuts, followed by a cold beer, and cold cuts topped off with a delicious blueberry cake (also compliments of Larry's mom). I was reminded of Alaskan hospitality and how very special it was.

Dark clouds hung low the next morning. Plans for a 10 o'clock departure was delayed. The damp and smell of rain permeated the air. We left at noon despite the low visibility. But then this was Southeastern Alaska. Small planes flew overhead as we made our way up the channel towards Fish Bay and not far from where Bob and I had spent our honeymoon four years earlier. They were flying low up and down the waterway at probably 200 feet maximum due to poor visibility at higher altitudes. I was quite content to be on the water. The *Morning Mist* was equipped with radar, and Larry was an excellent mariner not to mention he had grown up in these waters and knew them like the back of his hand.

Several log bundles drifted lazily past us with the tide as we headed north. They must have separated from a large log raft headed for the mill. Salt spray, the forested growth along the banks, and the fresh air all called to me when we suddenly spotted a bear. That meant a stop.

The anchor was thrown out in a small nearby bay. Larry hoisted the canoe into the water. Bob and I jumped in behind Larry and started paddling across the bay with Larry giving directions. Leaping out I noted the bear's footprints suggested a much larger bear than I first imagined when I initially saw it from the boat. "A juvenile," Larry pointed out and then commented that it was "still pretty awkward despite its size." I'm not sure how he knew, but I didn't doubt him.

Our destination that evening was Chatham Cannery that had long since seen its last official activity. It was an old burned out and abandoned building covered with overgrowth in some areas when we saw it. Years later I met a woman who had worked in the cannery during its hay day. She reported all sorts of parties with lots of dancing and much fun among the workers. But now it was no more than a ghost of what it had been with only birds chirping and other wildlife calling to each other. We firmly secured the boat up to the lower dock. Apparently, it still saw a lot of use as it was in good shape despite the cannery's disrepair.

A ladder went straight up from where the boat was tied and led to the walkway above. Once on shore the cannery's caretaker, Frank Wright, greeted us. He and both Maryann and Larry knew each other quite well. I suspected they had been here many times before. I sampled a few fresh salmonberries straight from the bushes that were growing everywhere in and around the building and probably attracted bears. They were delicious, as members of the rose family and related to raspberries, wild strawberries, and thimbleberries.

Frank was full of stories and welcomed visitors. I mentioned the bear we had seen earlier, and he launched into one of his tales. "That bear is a stranger to these parts." He then added that there had been two cubs and a sow as well as a large male that was after the cubs the night before. I never did learn how the bear we had seen fit in with his story, but his comments convinced me there were lots of bears around the area.

His eyes lit up before I could ask as he began another bear story. "That mamma bear goes through the cannery nightly with her cubs. One time she startled some visitors who were fishing, so I decided I ought to scare her away to prevent any problems."

Frank's eyes danced with laughter as he continued, "So I took my 400-guage shot gun with bird shot in it and got her one evening in the hind quarters without hurting her. The next morning when I opened my front door I found her calling card—a big pile of 'bear shit' on my door step." Since then there had not been any problems between Frank and the bear, and "she still comes around regularly". Too bad we didn't get to see her, I thought to myself.

Frank went on to say that one evening he looked up to see the same bear and a cub standing on their hind quarters peering in at him through his cabin's front window. There were lots of hummingbird feeders there, and neither bear so much as touched any of the feeders. I guess they just wanted to get a good look at Frank.

Frank loaded us up with smoked salmon and frozen salmonberries for breakfast before we returned to the boat. We remained tied up to the cannery's dock that night. Bob and Frank took the canoe across the bay to fish with spinning tackle. No luck!

A whale got me up the next morning, but by the time I was on deck with my camera the one that had been spotted was "sounding". I didn't get a picture. Fishing gear went out a bit later. I did hook a large Coho salmon, but my luck was short lived. It jumped clear out of the water and knocked the hook loose. It obviously had practice with inexperienced fishermen before! Breakfast consisted of cereal, bananas and some of those salmonberries. I did catch a Coho later, and while it was much smaller than the one I had lost earlier it was large enough to keep and made a nice meal for us.

What a parade with Humpback whales and half dozen porpoises joining us as we headed for Glacier Bay; I struggled with my camera the whole time trying to get the perfect shot only to discover the light meter was broken. I did some guessing as to camera readings.

Humpbacks swim in circles around a school of herring blowing bubbles that forms a natural net that the herring won't go through. That's when the whale comes up from below in the center of the circle with its mouth open. I admired their ingenuity in fishing. I later learned that other ocean predators use the same hunting technique.

Larry and Bob took the canoe first going over to a small water falls catching a number of Dolly Varden trout that weren't trout at all but rather char. From there they headed on to Pavlof Lake before their return. Maryann and I had a good visit aboard the boat while they were gone. When we finally left the bay, a number of porpoise escorted us out using the bottom of the

Morning Mist to "scratch" their backs.

We made a run for Bartlett Cove and Glacier Bay that afternoon, then stopped at Pulaski Island for supper. The boat was adrift while we dined on delicious shrimp cooked in beer. A sudden grating sound from the bottom of the boat could be heard along with a slight shudder that ran the length of the keel. We were grounded on a sand bar but Larry didn't seem concerned. He slowly backed off the sand and then used a pike-pole to push until the boat cleared the bottom.

It was back to the cooked shrimp that soon disappeared, at which point we continued to Bartlett Cove some 30 miles away. Thick fog rolled in and wrapped around us obscuring much of the shore. At that point most of the navigation was by radar and compass. Once at our destination the crab pot came out. Five good-sized male Dungeness crabs found their way into it by the next morning.

The tiny museum at Glacier Bay's lodge had a nice satellite picture of the entire bay area. It gave an excellent overview. We purchased an updated chart of the area and then compared it to the one on the boat that was ten years old. It was immediately evident how much the glaciers had changed just in that small amount of time. They were obviously retreating. One of the most noticeable changes was Muir Glacier.

Don Close, one of park rangers, loaned me a spare light meter for the Glacier Bay part of our trip. I was most appreciative as I did get some nice pictures.

The sun materialized once we were in the actual bay. That was definitely a good omen. We headed straight to Johns Hopkins Glacier and took the skiff through lots of small ice bergs in order to get closer to the glacier. The water was alive with hundreds of swimming seals! One would pop up out of the water and then dive, only to be followed by several more. They were everywhere.

Like us, they stayed away from the face of the glacier for safety reasons. Falling ice could readily catch the unwary. The cry of terns was continuous as they flew overhead and along the cliffs screaming challenges to any and all intruders including us. Beyond wildflowers splashed their colors across the landscape much like one would see on an artist's pallet. I realized how much I missed the closeness of nature on our trips by air.

Mini icebergs were gathered to cool our fish down as well as our scotch! Thinking about the drinks being cooled by 10,000-year-old ice give or take a few thousand years definitely added something to the flavor. Bob, Maryann, and I stepped off the boat and out onto a fairly large and somewhat flat iceberg floating nearby. There was just enough room for the three of us to stand although I crouched down. Larry took a picture. The cold seeped right through the soles of my boots just in the few minutes I was on the ice. I still treasure that picture.

We dropped anchor just outside of Teacup Harbor as the harbor itself was quite shallow. This time all four of us took the skiff and went ashore. Footprints of a recent bear visitor were immediately evident. The bear was no longer present. Three different shades of Indian paintbrush named for the clusters of spiky blooms that resemble paintbrushes dipped in bright red or orange-yellow paint and a multitude of other wild flowers I didn't know by name covered the shore and beyond. Vibrant colors surrounded me emitting sweet perfume. I breathed it all in wanting the memory to stay with me.

Bob, Maryann Calvin, and Marilyn Standing on iceberg
Glacier Bay

Two oystercatchers were spotted on our way back to the *Morning Mist*. There was no mistaking these shore birds with their bold dark plumage, bright yellow eyes and long, improbably thick red bills. They were fun to watch walking along the beach. The female flew up then ran along the ground as if wounded, obviously trying to draw us away from her young.

My eyes traced her route backwards where I spotted one half-grown chick as well as her mate. The adults were an awkward looking pair of birds with morning promised another beautiful day with crisp air, blue sky, and wonderful their red beaks and a circle around their shinning eyes being otherwise black.

The next morning promised another beautiful day with crisp air, blue sky, and wonderful sunshine. Once on shore a short walk yielded wild strawberries hiding beneath the underbrush. I started picking a few berries then attempted to scare up the ptarmigan Larry had seen. Instead I ran across a dozen or more grouse. I watched as they scurried in many directions. They were quick and escaped my camera lens. The berries I had picked did find their way into my mouth and the sweetness from the wild fruit was not just tasty but absolutely exquisite.

This time we headed between Margerie and Grand Pacific glaciers where there was solid ground and then climbed to the top of a sluffed-off area from the Grand Pacific. We were actually on the edges of the glacial ice, and after walking about ten feet Maryann decided she had had enough. Rivers running underneath the ice could be heard. She definitely had a point as none of us wanted to push our luck by falling through rotten ice. We turned around and headed back the way we had come and back to the skiff and on to the *Morning Mist*.

Frequent gunshot-like sounds erupted that afternoon as the boat drifted in front of Margerie Glacier—the glacier was talking to us! It was full of activity with glacier ice breaking off continuously or "calving" as it is formally called.

We anchored at Reid Glacier later. Two iceberg visitors came by that night and nudged the boat gently. They weren't very big although large enough to make their presence known as they rocked the boat. We stopped at Strawberry Island the next morning where we found lots of strawberry plants but no berries.

Back at the lodge I returned the light meter. A quick lunch

on board was followed by a run to the outside coast line. The going was a bit rough. Taking one of the inlets on the north western part of Chichagof Island we ended up at Klag Bay and dropped anchor for the night.

Bob and I took the small motor boat to an old mine and fished as they were jumping everywhere. They weren't interesting in biting. Instead they seemed to be bent on teasing us. On our return to the *Morning Mist* we ran out of gas so rowed the remaining distance. Larry in the meantime had caught one sockeye in a float net.

Larry took Bob and me along with our fishing poles up to a small water fall the next morning. Hip boots for the trip were needed, so I borrowed the smallest pair available but found them to be several sizes too big making walking in streams and over moss-covered rocks no easy task. Reaching our destination, we found the water was high, and once again the fish outsmarted us. We came back empty-handed.

Lake Anna was also on the agenda and meant taking the canoe overland between a small lake and the salt water. Lots of sea cucumbers and sea urchins were evident on the salt water side. On the other side of the lake a pair of loons greeted us with their eerie calls echoing across the mirror calm water. And, yes, there were more bear tracks visible and these appeared fresh. Chichagof Island is one of three islands in Southeastern Alaska noted for its brown bear population. It has the largest population of bears per square mile of any place on Earth so I guess seeing the tracks should not have been a surprise.

We continued with the canoe and crossed over to where there was an outlet with a water falls. Sockeye salmon were all around trying to navigate the falls while we tried to catch them by hand. Bob caught the first two then I managed to get a couple. He then tried to pick up one that was apparently dead on the rocks. What a surprise when it started swimming off. He still managed to catch it!

Sadly, the week came to an end. We left the falls mid-afternoon without lunch. Anchoring at High Water Island for supper we found our way back to Sitka's marina.

That evening after saying goodbye to the Calvins, Bob and I walked through the Sitka National Historical Park that is the site of Russia's defeat of the indigenous Tlingit people and has a trail dotted with totem poles.

Leaving the trees behind us we continued through the town passing Saint Michael's Cathedral, a Russian Orthodox Church that had been built in 1842 when Russia owned Sitka, a reminder of its Russian past. We had once attended mass there, or at least most of it as it was a very long service. The original church had burnt down in 1966 but had since been rebuilt. From there we headed to the marina where we climbed into bed for our last night aboard the Morning Mist.

I was to work at Mt. Edgecumbe High School, a boarding school across the bridge from Sitka, years later but never in the Sitka Borough Schools. Nine years later Bob and I returned to Glacier Bay in our own boat with our two kids and our family of dogs. The trip did not go as smoothly as when Larry was skipper, but that's another chapter later in this book.

We left Sitka the next day and made the short flight over to Skagway following the route we had just taken aboard the *Morning Mist*, at least, as far as Chatham Strait. From there we headed north. It probably took us an hour. It was the 30th of July.

Building Materials Warehouse in Sitka

CHAPTER 4

Hiking the Chilkoot Trail

Skagway's airport can be downright dangerous unless one understands the tight constraints of the path needed for landings and takeoffs. Bob had landed at this airport a number of times. Skagway, I might add, is a very windy place. When we arrived, the wind was blowing fairly hard and in the wrong direction making a straight-in landing out of the question.

The wind generally blows from the south during the summer and can be wickedly strong and gusty. Winds turn around in the winter and blow from the north. The airport is situated in a north-south direction and against the west side of the valley next to the Skagway River. We flew north directly toward the mountains and made a tight right 180-degree turn at the last minute and lined up with the runway in order to land into the south wind.

Once on the ground we walked over to Benny and Bea Lingle's back yard a couple of blocks away. We had carried a sockeye salmon over from Sitka and barbequed it that evening for supper. The next day the four of us climbed into "Penelope", an old yellow Dodge pickup truck with a bad universal joint, and took off for the Yukon Territory. The truck was Bea's pride and joy.

Benny and Bea were customers of Bob's as well as good friends. Benny owned the air service in addition to the hardware store that sold building materials. Since he was a pilot Bob and he had hit it off from the first time they met. Bea was a cancer survivor and after the doctors sent her home saying there was no more they could do for her, she swore off house work, stopped worrying, and made little explorations into the wilderness oftentimes taking her grandchildren on day trips. She also painted driftwood showing cartoon Eskimo children for the tourists as a hobby. I have three of her pieces.

Penelope, Bea's old pickup truck, carried the four of us right out of Skagway and across the Canadian border to Carcross, despite its bad universal joint. The local bar had closed just minutes before our arrival. We headed down to Lake Bennet and camped for the night then headed back to Skagway after visiting the sand dunes followed by a trip to the Ice Cream Parlor the next day. The weekend ended and Benny went back to work.

The following Monday started out innocent enough. Bob's two sons were working in Skagway that summer. His oldest son Rob had the day off so joined the two of us and Bea for a flight over to Lake Atlin where we rented a boat. Rob and his dad went fishing, while Bea and I wandered around on a small island looking for various plants and animal life. Once back in the boat the subject of the Chilkoot Trail came up. It was part of the Klondike Gold Rush National Historical Park.

Both Bob and Bea were all for hiking it, and Rob thought it was a great idea although he had to work so couldn't go with us. I wasn't sure at all about it. I guess I could have said "no." But I didn't. None of us were back packers, but I have to admit I was curious.

I knew from reading that some twenty to thirty thousand people crossed the "Pass" between Alaska and Canada on their way to the Klondike goldfields in 1897-98. The Chilkoot Trail has been described as "the meanest 32 miles in history" by students of the gold rush. That same trail has also been referred to as "the most beautiful 32 miles in Alaska and British Columbia."

No one knows how long the trail had been used by the Indians before the first white men arrived at the Yukon headwaters after sailing north on the Inside Passage from Puget Sound and going over the pass. When they arrived, the Chilkat, a branch of the Tlingit nation, were trading with the Nahane Tribe, or Stick Indians living along the Yukon River. The Sticks trapped and exchanged pelts for fish oil and other sea products from the Chilkat, and the Chilkoot Pass, a narrow slash in the foggy and windy Coast Range, was the only practical route for the traders.

The following morning Bob and I scurried around getting camping equipment put together for the trip. Some planning went into it as well as listening to lots of opinions from the locals. That afternoon about 4:15 pm we took Chris's Taxi Service to Dyea, more specifically to the steel bridge that crosses the Taiya River eight and a half miles from Skagway along with 17 other hikers. There had been almost 100 people going ahead of us that day to the beginning of the most famous trail in the north.

Bea Lingle, Bob, and Marilyn

We let the other 17 hikers go before us. The first few steps amongst the willows on the trail and along the river were beautiful. About ten feet into the trees, however, the trail went straight up and up and up some more for about a quarter of a mile. We had to climb over large rocks, huge granite boulders to be exact. But then the trail leveled off after topping the ridge above the river. Another half mile of seeing huge boulders, windfalls, spruce, and brush evident all around us the trail dropped down by the river.

After several rest stops the search for a camp site became a priority. Nothing appealed to us so we continued for another twenty minutes on the fairly good trail. Then it changed to real muck and lots of water with mud as it had recently rained. Another quarter of a mile and we were exhausted. A small creek tempted us to camp beside it but it lacked that certain something. We continued, stumbling on over the well-defined trail for some time when we spotted the remains of a camp fire. We stopped and followed a little path that led us about ten feet off the main trail and dropped our backpacks.

What a surprise! Before us was the perfect camp site with a view of Irene Glacier. Included in our picture-perfect view were a water falls and the river right at our door step. The crush of water gave evidence to considerable authority. Sun light danced on the river. It was spectacular. Later Mark, one of the park rangers, came by and had a cup of white wine with us. He told us we had found one of best camp sites along the entire trail. He also said we had hiked about four and half to five miles from the head of the trail to where we were. It felt more like twenty-five miles as far as I was concerned.

The ground was very hard for Bob and me as we were used to the comforts of the *Morning Mist*. Normally when we camped we used camp cots but not wanting the extra weight for hiking we left them behind. Bea did not have any trouble as she had been camping all summer. The weather looked fairly good the next morning. Irene Glacier was right where we had left it the night before and so was the river.

I half expected it but did not see any signs of bears. We had carefully hung our food stuff from a tree limb away from our tents. Buttermilk hotcakes, eggs, and bacon served as breakfast. Bob tried a bit of fishing, but glacial water doesn't produce fish. He knew it but just liked to throw his line into any kind of water, imagining fish might be tempted by his bait. We left our beautiful camp site around 10:30 in the morning.

The trail led in and out of the timber. Devil's club made impenetrable blocks to potential side trips. I knew a scratch from one of its poisonous spikes could give trouble for days so was careful to stay away from any encounters. Ferns also graced the edges of the pathway. The forest smelled damp and earthy.

We arrived at Canyon City tired. It was around one in the afternoon and a good time for a little exploration of the area as well as a nice rest. A little side trip to the original town site led to an old boiler, remains of a cabin, a dog sled that had not transported anything for years, and other artifacts. All too soon we forced ourselves back on the main trail loaded down with packs hiking in earnest. We continued on the well-worn trail but quickly tired out. Along the pathway I found some deadly Amanita mushrooms and took a few pictures of them and other plants. Our goal was getting to within a mile of Sheep Camp that night.

We kept going passing several potential campsites because of the earliness in the afternoon. We knew the following day would be long and strenuous. We didn't find any camp sites, however, when we wanted to stop so had to keep going. We were kicking ourselves for not staying at one of the earlier spots. I remember telling first my left foot to move and then my right foot with neither one wanting to obey.

Exhausted, we dragged ourselves into Sheep Camp. The rain started coming down to the point of being serious shortly after our arrival. The hundred plus people who had left the trail head the day before were all there—too many for the area and for the trail. Bob finally found a potential camp site which entailed a walk across a river that was really only a small creek. Two narrow logs made sort of a bridge onto a tiny island.

Our tents went up in record time. Cocktails were followed by supper consisting of macaroni and cheese with a side dish of chicken-flavored top ramen.

Bob burnt his finger trying to light the stove the next morning. The sleeping bags were wet, and our muscles sore as we ate a breakfast of hash browns, eggs, bacon, and coffee, then went up to the lone cabin and built a good fire in an old cook stove to dry out sleeping bags and tents so we could pack them.

The hundred plus people had left, that is, all except one couple and a park ranger, one of several park rangers who patrolled the trail regularly. It turned out our group including Bob, Bea, and me, was the oldest group in age on the trail that day. The ranger sized us up, was friendly and provided what information he could. It was three and a half miles to the summit, which I was dreading. Following that, the next official camping area was 21.5 miles away and meant going in and out of snow on a wet, muddy trail. Oh, wonderful, I thought. At least my muscles were beginning to work more efficiently.

Leaving Sheep Camp was almost all up hill. We finally arrived at the "last half mile" of the pass and the "Scales," the historic rocky ledge where miners had to prove they carried the requisite weight of equipment and supplies to pass muster with the Canadian Mounties in order to enter Canada. Mounties no longer guarded the border.

The pass appeared to be straight over lots of rocks. Below were all sorts of abandoned equipment—80 years old! Above us were the remains of a Lake Amphibian airplane in which two fellows had tried to go over the pass at much too low of an altitude and couldn't turn back—they never had a chance.

Going around and over huge rocks was difficult for me and I didn't handle heights well. The air was also getting colder. Fog moved in and out of the pass. Once over the first part we could see a snow field and another rock climb. We sheltered ourselves behind some boulders to protect us from the wind. We rested all too briefly before continuing up and across more snow fields. Finally, we reached the summit. I guessed we were actually out of Alaska and in British Columbia at that point. The different trail markers were the only indication that we were in a different country. Snow, fog, and cold were about all that greeted us. Definitely there were no Mounties guarding the border and welcoming us to Canada.

We were neither prepared for the snow nor the cold although we all had good hiking boots and warm jackets. While it had been a tough climb for me it was worth it when the trail leveled out.

Fortunately, we were soon out of the snow. We stopped a few minutes at the rangers' house to chat. Back on the trail we passed Summit Lake and on to a second lake where we camped amid a field of spectacular wildflowers. There were blue lupine and other flowers I didn't recognize. I closed my eyes and inhaled deeply taking in the aroma that permeated the air.

The tents went up and Bob lit the burner. After several false starts and one stiff drink of scotch he had it going. All three of us got in one tent and cooked our meal—vegetable stew followed by beef stroganoff. Desert was mocha coffee with vodka. We slept with all our clothing on inside our sleeping bags. Even so my jacket somehow didn't get in all the way and got wet along with everything else by the next morning.

It was our wedding anniversary. There was an icy wind that morning. With my head bent I could still feel the sting against my face. Bea's comment was that the only two muscles that didn't ache were her upper lip and her lower lip. One could peel the dirt off of us. We were looking forward to getting to lower altitudes with a warmer climate. A hot shower and a warm bed were also on our wish list.

The hike out to Lake Lindeman was rough. Cold, wind, and rain were constant travel partners; however, once we reached a lower altitude the wind stopped making life slightly better. Hiking over Hog Back Ridge, however, was no fun—the Indians had told stampeders to use the lake while it was still frozen to avoid this ridge—they definitely had the right idea.

We passed through spectacular country, but it was so wet we didn't really appreciate it. Upper Cabin at Lake Lindeman had wall-to-wall fellow hikers jammed in it, so we decided to go to Lower Cabin that provided a more sheltered location although we didn't know it at the time. Historically I later learned that on the Canadian side of the pass trail re-development had started in the fall of 1967 when a Yukon Corrections crew marked out a route. The staff and work crews worked on it the following summer plus the next five years when Parks Canada took over all operations and maintenance in 1974. Upper Cabin was completed in 1968, and Lower Cabin in 1970 as shelters for the crews.

Bea ran into several local fellows she knew from Skagway who offered us hot coffee once we were at Lower Cabin. We dried out our tents, sleeping bags, socks, and had supper then went back on the trail. We found a little camp spot overlooking the lake that was infested with mosquitos, black flies and no-see-ums. I think they thrived on Cutter's bug repellant.

Bob tried his hand at fishing—no luck. We had an anniversary drink—Bea's remaining vodka, mocha coffee, and water. We went to bed on what Bob termed as the "hardest rock in British Columbia!"

By morning the rain increased to river proportions going through Bea's tent. The socks she had carefully dried out the night before were rung out before breakfast. Bob and I fared a little better as we had devised a rain fly. We began the big push to Lake Bennett right after breakfast in order to catch the 1:45 train. We did not want to miss it and spend another night on the trail and in more rain!

The trail went up and down, mostly up, or so it seemed. There was lots of marshy stuff to walk through. Then we got into sand that proved very tiring to already sore muscles. Bear signs were evident as we continued. We just kept walking ignoring them. We wanted to catch that train. We finally picked up the railroad tracks and walked the last mile to Bennett, only to learn the train had derailed so there was no train in either direction. We didn't know when the next train would make it—maybe the next day and maybe not.

The White Pass and Yukon Railroad personnel had planned for 500 tourists that were not coming because of the train derailment. We had all the hot coffee and helpings of a hot meal of stew, beans and cheese that we wanted as a result.

We decided to leave two of the backpacks at the station and have Bea's son-in-law who worked for the railroad pick them up later. Bob carried all our essentials and sleeping bags in the third pack, and we headed out on the tracks for an eight-mile hike to Log Cabin where the road intercepted the rail road tracks.

Bea called her daughter from Bennett to meet us there. All of the mosquitos and black flies we had met earlier joined us and had invited their cousins along for the hike. We arrived about 40 minutes early and waited for her daughter Dorothy. The view of Penelope coming down the road a little later to pick us up was a most beautiful sight.

Still tired we left Skagway the next morning and flew over the route we had just hiked in 20 minutes, then headed to Juneau for refueling with a little detour over Glacier Bay and then home.

Glacier Bay Area

PART II

1980 to 1982

Research and Beyond

Yukon River
(Photo by Marylu Martin)

CHAPTER 5

Research Begins with Helping Paws

One more bounce on the grass airstrip and we were airborne. It was August 14, 1980, and we had just taken off from Vashon Island's airport where I called home.

So began a flight in which Bob and I were to fly over 13,000 miles with our three dachshunds while I interviewed Native women and gathered information for my doctoral dissertation. My focus was on Native women's changing rolls since statehood in 1959 and the implications for education. Our plans were to camp under the wing of the airplane, stay with friends, and occasionally stay in hotels or whatever we could find while I interviewed Alaska's Native women.

I breathed a sigh of relief as we were finally on our way. My husband Bob and I headed north to Oak Harbor on Juan de Fuca Strait. The airport there afforded a paved runway and more importantly a place to fill all five of our gas tanks—two main wing tanks, one reserve tank in back, and two wing tip tanks. Each tank held 20 gallons. Once we refueled and took off, our climb out was slow because of the weight we carried with a total of 100 gallons of fuel plus everything else we had on board. I had packed the plane for a long trip. The early part of our route took us over water so it didn't make much difference as to how fast we climbed. There were no mountains in our path. Our three dachshunds, Otto Junior, Moose, and their mother Schnapsie curled up in the back seat and soon fell fast asleep.

"Inside Passage"
(Map by Rob Mosley)

"Seattle Radio this is 'Banana' 584 Bravo…we wish to file an IFR flight plan for Skagway, Alaska. We are a Beech Bonanza A35/uniform. Speed is 140 knots. Fuel on board is eight hours plus. Estimated time in route is six hours plus 30 minutes. We have emergency gear and an Emergency Locator Transmitter (ELT). Altitude is 10,500 feet. The Pilot's name is Bob Mosley. The address is Vashon, Washington. There are two souls aboard. We are yellow and white with brown trim." Bob's clear voice spoke into the radio. He often referred to his beloved Bonanza as a "Banana". I smiled. After all it was mostly yellow.

"584 Bravo, we copy and have activated your flight plan at ten minutes past the hour." The controller's response was clear and concise. We were on our way.

I had already made two earlier trips to Alaska that year in order to obtain background information. The first was to Juneau in order to meet with the Commissioner of Education, and the second to Fairbanks to attend the Women's Statewide Organization Convention. I also set up interviews with as many women as I could via letters and telephone calls. In my letters to the women I asked that they return the enclosed post card to indicate their willingness to participate. Dennis Wilt, Program Director for ACTION/Alaska, was instrumental in providing me with potential interviewees and their villages.

I was able to obtain Community Survey forms through Lois Bergerson, Chief, Nursing Section, Department of Health and Social Services. The information on these forms was invaluable and provided population numbers in villages as well as insights into most of the communities I visited.

We were to visit more than thirty villages as well as several larger communities. We covered Alaska's interior, the North Slope, western Alaska from Barrow to Tuntutuliak, the Dillingham-Bristol Bay area, the Alaskan Peninsula, and Aleutians as far south as False Pass, Kodiak, Anchorage, Fairbanks, and the southeastern part of the state.

Bob and I were both pilots—he had more than 6,000 hours flying time most of it in the Bonanza, while I had a measly 48 hours mostly in a rented Cessna 150. I occasionally made a landing or takeoff on those long, paved runways in the Bonanza, but on this trip Bob did all of them as many of the landing strips were marginal strips at best for which Bush Alaska is noted. Make no mistake we were headed for the "bush" or remote areas in the back country. The "bird" we flew was a 1948 Beechcraft Bonanza. Bob had owned it for 19 years.

Flying with our four-footed family was not a new experience for us. We had flown my black Lab mix Tiggy (Antigone) along with my Burmese cat named Tasha on camping trips around the Pacific Northwest in the 1970s. Both of them loved it. Later our golden retrievers as well as our dachshunds went on vacation trips with us both in the boat and by air beginning in 1975 when we first got MacDuff and later Kodi (Kodiak) in 1977. This trip, however, was too long of a trip for the goldens so we left them at home with our house sitters.

Bonanza 584B on Kodiak Island

The first day was a pretty typical flight as we headed north. The sun was out initially and the weather was ideal for flying. Both large and small boats were visible in the waterway below us. Fishing boats, sailboats, and even several kayaks were evident. The long-awaited moment had arrived. I could feel my heart pounding with excitement about the project as well as the flying. Bob was excited because he liked to fly, and as for the dachshunds, they slept once we were airborne. This was not their first rodeo.

We crossed into Canadian airspace in the middle of Juan de Fuca Strait and followed the Inside Passage north between Vancouver Island and the mainland of British Columbia, Canada, hugging Queen Charlotte Sound's eastern shore. As we burned up fuel we climbed higher and higher. An Alaskan-bound ferry slowly made its way heading in the same direction. With Alaska consisting of 663,268 square miles and over twice the size of Texas, much of it is without roads. The primary forms of transportation are by air or sea. We were following one of the main routes of its "highway system" some 10,500 feet above it. We soon passed the ferry as it was much slower than our air speed. It appeared to almost be standing still.

Once we left Port Hardy at the north end of Vancouver Island, there was less and less traffic in the passage below. Finally, only an occasional fishing boat was all that was visible, and then even the boats disappeared.

CHAPTER 6

Place of Caribou Droppings

The weather was "fickle" as we flew through the mountains. I distinctly remembered the Wien airline pilot's words so long ago on our first trip to Fort Yukon and Artic Village about the instability of weather in the Brooks Range. A local storm lived up to his words causing us to make a detour by flying near Bettles. Below the pipe line was readily visible despite the fact we were flying fairly high. We followed it for a while before we cut across several mountain tops and valleys finally following one right down to the airport at Anaktuvuk Pass.

The runway looked inviting from the air. Next to it on one side were buildings that appeared to be small individual houses. There was a school at the far end, distinguished by its larger size and its newness. We landed.

I had a name, Lilia Aghook, to find and interview. In a village with about 200 people I figured everyone knew everyone else so I asked the first person we met where she lived. The man pointed in the direction of the village to one of the houses. There we met Lilia and her family. She was one of the women who had sent her post card back to me indicating she would be more than willing to do an interview.

Once inside her home we were offered some caribou. I watched with interest as she used an ulu, or "woman's knife" that is an all-purpose knife traditionally used by Inuit, Yup'ik, and Aleut women to cut off chunks of cooked meat. She then cut off a fatty portion to accompany the meat. The fat was what provided the flavor. I enjoyed this sharing of meat. I watched Lilia as she worked; she was obviously very skilled in its use.

I remembered the ulu I had seen in Hooper Bay several years before, although the one in front of me at this point was a little different. I noted the handle was made from a piece of caribou antler. It was centered over a flat piece of metal that looked as if it might have been a recycled saw blade. The shape of the ulu ensured that the force was centered more over the middle of the blade than that of an ordinary knife. I suspected this made the ulu easier to use when cutting hard objects such as bone.

Later I was to receive an ulu as a gift while in Bethel. It was the same principle but the handle was definitely different as it was wooden with the blade bolted into it by two screws and I suspected was a commercial version for tourists and not one used routinely by Eskimo women.

Lilia told me she was 40 years old. I was surprised as she looked much older. Her life had been hard. She smoked cigarettes that I suspected added years to her appearance. As we talked I was beginning to gain confidence that I would get the necessary interviews for my project. She readily answered my questions and shared comments about her personal life.

She served us a very strong tea. It went well with the caribou I had eaten. The women I had met so far in Arctic Village and now Lilia enjoyed talking, wanted to share their lives, and I found them easy to communicate with. Lilia told me she had worked for the post office for eleven years, and then postal inspectors came through and fired her because they thought she was taking money. She pointed out that she only had a seventh-grade education and didn't know how to balance the books. Apparently, the new person hired was never on duty so it looked like Lilia might get her job back and maybe some more education and instruction in bookkeeping. Until the new high schools were built because of the decision of the Molly Hootch case a seventh or eighth grade education was all that was available unless a child left the village and went away from family and friends to attend a boarding school. If they did leave, there was no returning home for holidays or vacations like Christmas.

Lilia told us she used to make caribou masks. I was

interested in them and asked her questions. She said she could set up as many as 16 masks in one day, and then it would take her about a week to do the sewing on them. "Few people do this anymore." Her comment made me think that mask making with caribou skins was rapidly becoming a lost art. I was saddened by this.

Bob and I walked back through the village on the way to the airport and encountered two teachers out for an evening stroll. School had already started for the year. They had their husky puppy with them. He was on a leash. The dog was huge, and very friendly. He was not one of the typical village dogs at all, but a family pet that arrived in the village with the teachers. Despite his large size, Otto Junior was ready to have him for lunch. Bob had to pick all eleven pounds of Otto up.

Once back at the airport we set up our tent near the plane. Then Bob concentrated on making a fire. There were lots of rocks around, the kind that are uncomfortable to sleep on. I was very glad we had brought fold-up cots.

Some of the local villagers were curious about us. They came out to where the plane was parked. A man named Riley rode up on a three-wheeler with his daughter Cindy. He asked who we were. I mentioned that I was doing research and gave Lilia's name as someone I had met. He immediately volunteered to open his store up earlier than usual the next morning. Ahhh! He was a good salesman I thought to myself.

Four children also arrived. They must have been eight or nine years old. The three boys wanted to help Bob; they gathered some wood to keep the fire going. Helen, the only girl in the group, came over and sat down on one of the cots near me while I heated water to cook dinner. She was fascinated with the dogs. Her dark brown eyes sparkled from her rusty and rosy-cheeked face. She petted them and then started talking to them. Otto rolled over on his back for a belly rub while Moose curled up in a ball right next to her. Schnapsie jumped up next to Moose. Helen began telling them stories about her ancestors. I later sorted out some of the details by doing more background reading about the community.

Anaktuvuk Pass was named after the river of the same name meaning "place of caribou droppings." Many years ago there was a nomadic group of Inupiat called Nunamiut (Alaska's Inland

Eskimos) that lived inland in northern Alaska. They were nomads who followed the caribou herds instead of hunting the marine mammals and fish that the rest of the Inupiat who lived on the coast did. A decline in caribou populations around 1900 caused many of the Nunamiut to move back to the coastal villages. Several of the Nunamiut families moved back to the Brooks Range in 1938, and in 1949 the Tulugak (means Raven) branch moved to Anaktuvuk Pass. That's when Nunamiut peoples from other locations moved to the settlement as well. Now, I understood, it was the only Nunamiut village in existence. The villagers led a more sedentary lifestyle, however, than in earlier nomadic times.

Tales about the great migrations of caribou as they went through the village came to life as Helen talked. Her people had settled at this particular location as it was a place where the caribou passed. Her soft voice soothed the dogs. She continued to talk about the things hunters were supposed to avoid in order to ward off evil spirits and have a successful hunt. One "should never hide," she said. "It was bad luck." She continued to gently stroke each of the dachshunds as she talked.

All too soon the kids left. Later that evening Helen's dad came by on a three-wheeler. He wanted to buy one of the dogs for his daughter. We explained that the dogs were part of our "family" so we couldn't sell them. He understood.

I went to the local store the next morning while Bob went fishing—this time he caught three Grayling and I bought two caribou masks, one of them was for my Aunt Eloine, who had made a trip with Bob and me in the Bonanza several years previously one summer to Southeastern Alaska. Despite it raining every day, she enjoyed the trip tremendously and wanted me to pick her up a mask. The other one I kept for myself only to have moths attack it once I got it home.

I was sorry to leave this community as I felt there was so much more to learn. Unfortunately, I never had the opportunity to return to it unlike my return visits to Arctic Village in later years when I eventually worked in Alaska.

Bob applied full throttle as we raced down the runway then he gently pulled back on the yoke and we began to climb. We soon left the ground behind. He adjusted the gas mixture and retracted the wheels. There was a momentary glint from somewhere down below as we passed over the village. We continued to climb and took a northwest heading once out of the mountains. The sun beat down through the glass and soon Anaktuvuk Pass was no more than a memory as we set a course for Barrow. The land was flat. We were flying over the North Slope.

I was looking forward to visiting Barrow. It was considered to be a large Native village of over 3,700 people with only about 350 being white. Unfortunately, the woman I planned to see was on jury duty and couldn't do the interview. She talked her daughter into meeting with me. I did an interview of sorts with the daughter in the middle of the street. I didn't feel very positive about this interview, but the young woman did give insightful answers to several of the questions. Disappointed, I walked back to the airport. We left heading in a south-westerly direction following the coast line.

CHAPTER 7

Steel Mats on a Remote Barrier Island

Once Bob and I left Barrow our next stop was Kivalina, a village that was on a fragile barrier island near the coast line of the Chukchi Sea 83 miles above the Arctic Circle.

The runway was parallel to the sea. There was water close by on the other side of it as well. We landed in a 20-mph cross wind on World War II steel military mats that had been placed on top of the sand. The touch down went perfect, but when Bob taxied he veered off the runway just enough to put us right in the sand. We came to an abrupt stop. "No!" Bob yelled. "No! We're stuck in the sand!"

To say that we had come to a screeching halt was an understatement. Bob immediately shut the engine down while I opened the door. Sand blew up in my face. Below I could see our tire tracks had joined others that were now quickly disappearing with the blowing sand.

Just then I looked up to see a woman at the end of the runway running towards us and waving her arms. I jumped down to the ground and Bob followed about the time she reached us. "Are you the Mosleys?" she asked. That got my attention.

Janet Barr, the woman whose husband I had talked with on the phone in order to set up an interview, smiled as she asked the question. Our yellow and white Bonanza was unique in this part of the world. Having been told what our plane looked like, she already knew the answer.

Janet had an emergency message for us. I had left a rough

itinerary with our house sitters. It turned out that there was a plumbing problem. They wanted to know what to do and who to contact. Bob was later able to solve the problem over the phone. Of course, this was long before cell phones, and even had they been readily available I doubt we could have received a call in this very remote village.

I nodded "yes" to the woman's question as Bob pulled the nose gear bar out from the rear compartment after getting out of the plane. He attached it to the front wheel and tried pulling the plane back onto solid ground—it didn't budge.

While Bob continued to use the tow bar, Janet, as well as a 13-year-Stold girl named Rosie and two husky Eskimo men started to push and pull until our plane was freed from its sand trap and back on the mats. They had obviously had practice before doing this. Without their help, we would have had a very difficult time getting free.

Janet's husband, Samuel, was in Seattle where he had been hospitalized since May but he was returning home within the week. He was on the school board and the reason why I had contacted him. I found out he was also the "preacher" for the Friends Church in Kivalina. He and his wife Janet had five children, all adopted. They also had the only telephone in the village. With the Bonanza back on solid ground, or I should say on a mat that wasn't moving, we followed her to her house along with our three dachshunds. Her son greeted us with a big smile when he saw the dachshunds.

Sammy, Jr. contributed to the dogs being good and staying out of mischief. He was on the floor laughing with all three crowding around him for attention. Otto rolled on his back with Sammy rubbing his tummy.

Janet occasionally dropped bits of fish that also kept their attention. She insisted we eat supper with them and fixed a marvelous meal including Arctic Char. She had us back the next morning for eggs with cheese, sourdough hotcakes and coffee. In addition to Janet, her daughter Theresa agreed to be interviewed after breakfast. Theresa loved to cook and baked some cookies in the meantime.

This tiny and isolated town of Kivalina cannot be reached by a road but then most of the places we visited couldn't be reached by roads.

I learned that the Iñupiat peoples of the region had hunted the gigantic bowhead whales for generations from camps on top of the sea ice that stretched out from the town's icy shores. In recent years climate change had thinned the ice so much that it was becoming too dangerous to hunt the whales in this manner.

It may soon be too dangerous to live in the community at all with less sea ice to protect the barrier island from the powerful waves that washed across the village not to mention washing away the sand. I knew that Point Hope, another village on the same coast, had moved three miles back in recent years for the same reason. Bob and I had visited there on an earlier trip.

That evening the wind picked up to about 30 knots. Darkness overtook us before we got back to the plane. Since there were building materials stored right on the airport, Bob was able to find several 50-pound cans of roofing tar and tied two to each wing to keep the plane from rolling or worse turning over in the wind. That would be more than adequate with the Bonanza being low winged. We pitched our tent behind some additional building materials that were secured and stacked up. They protected us a little but not a whole lot.

The dachshunds were put in the plane for safety. They refused to leave its interior until the tent was up then dove into it and tried to get into our sleeping bags with me not far behind. The wind brought stinging sand. All three had short hair, and besides a sudden gust of wind could catch a little dog off guard and send it sailing into the lagoon.

Sammy, Jr. took us to the store the next day. I bought two whale bone masks, a bone figure of a man on one side and woman on the other, and a baleen boat. One of the masks was made by Sammy's father. He told us that one day when he was sad, his father said, "Come, we'll make a mask together." When it was finished, Sammy said he was "no longer sad." It was a funny looking mask with fur on top of the head. The rest, of course, was all whale bone. While I was interviewing the women, Sammy took Bob down to where he could fish.

I was sorry to say "goodbye." The weather, however, was deteriorating rapidly, and we needed to get going and away from the coast line. Serious rain started to fall as I threw everything including the dachshunds into the plane, but not before I took a picture of Sammy in the airplane with the dogs. He was going to be nine years old in September.

Sammy checks out the plane with dachshund's help

CHAPTER 8

Drying Fish and Wire-Chewing Mischief

We took off in a 20-knot cross wind at about a 45-degree angle to the runway. I was very glad for all Bob's expertise in flying as we left the ground. We headed for Kotzebue where we refueled while our dachshunds took care of business. The weather calmed down considerably once we were away from the coast. We flew to Ambler some 138 miles northeast of Kotzebue.

Bob had a headache so stayed in the plane with the dogs and promptly fell asleep. That was a mistake as boredom set in as soon as I left. Once in the air the dogs usually go to sleep but parked on the ground it's a different story. They can and do get into mischief.

I hitched a ride in a pickup that happened along and was going into town. The driver was friendly and liked to talk. He told me he worked in Kotzebue during the summer months for a packing company and collected unemployment during the winter. He said he "got a job for the past 15 summers." He told me that some of the men like him "go outside" to either Kotzebue or Fairbanks in search of seasonal work such as joining one of the firefighting crews while others stayed right in Ambler and collected food stamps. He volunteered that his wife was the local post mistress. That was a lot of information for such a short ride.

Ambler was located on the north bank of the Kobuk River 45

miles north of the Arctic Circle. I walked down to the beach and spent a couple of hours talking with Katherine Cleveland. She was cutting fish for hanging on the drying racks at the time along with several other women all doing the same thing. She told me that her father owned the local store. Her mother supervised the turning of the fish while they were drying and cooked for the family. I could see that the fish was cut a certain way and hung in the air so wind and dry air cured it. The "flies are wiped off daily" as it was processed. I was curious and asked why they cut the fish the way they did. Katherine said that it was, "what my mother showed me, and her mother showed her."

Katherine was the bi-lingual teacher for grades 7 through 12. Her comments suggested she was from a very traditional family. She felt strongly about parents who did not talk to their children in their native language. "It's the parents' fault. That's why the kids don't know their own language."

The man who had driven me to the town volunteered to drive me back to the airport. He told me that he had been born in Ambler. I asked him what the most important changes were in Ambler since he was born. He didn't need to think long at all before he said "sewage, water, and electricity."

Ambler was permanently settled in 1958 when people from Shungnak and Kobuk moved downstream because of a variety of fish, a plentiful supply of wild game plus spruce trees in the area. It was a beautiful place. I understood as I loved to see those little spruce trees as they were all over. None of them were very tall, but then the winters were long and dark so no wonder. There were only 215 people living in Ambler at the time I visited including 28 non-native individuals. This was slightly less than in Shungnak where we flew next.

When I returned, Bob had awakened and gone fishing. We cooked the three grayling he caught at the airport while the dachshunds chased imaginary critters in the tall grass. Tiny no-see-ums attacked their undersides until I rubbed musk oil on them—it worked. They were delighted to get out of the plane and run.

Later we flew up the Kobuk River to Shungnak 30 miles away. The fall colors were emerging everywhere. The flight was beautiful. The next woman who had responded to my request for an interview was Sally Lee Custer. Instead I met her mother who steered us down to the fishing area where she thought Sally was. It was an incredibility steep and sandy bank. I made it without falling only to find she wasn't there so I had to climb back up. Sally's younger sister found her helping an older sister with fish. The older woman worked in school all day and came home tired.

At last I caught up with Sally, who looked just like her younger sister. She was a very articulate woman who explained that they were getting fish ready for hanging on the drying racks. She was quick to show me how they did it. I noted that it was much the same way as I had observed in Ambler. Sally beamed as I took more pictures.

The two villages were very similar both in population and in their traditional life style. The way they cut their fish supported this in addition to the comments made by Sally as well as the women in Ambler. But then the people left Shungnak historically to move to Ambler for "greener pastures". Namely, there was more variety of food available—both fish and wild life—and because of the availability of trees that I suspected went into their housing. When I checked the population of Shungnak, I found it to be 225 individuals with only 10 non-native people.

Back at the airport we let the dachshunds run around a bit. They left their mark as they had done at every airport where we landed. I could just imagine some bear or other critter coming across the "we were here" scent and wondering what it was that had been there.

We discovered a "silent" radio on our approach to Kotzebue. We didn't know it at the time but the dogs had chewed on the radio wires in the plane as well as a roll of toilet paper while Bob slept at the Ambler Airport. Bob flew the pattern to alert the tower we were landing without radio contact. There were no other planes in the immediate area, although Kotzebue has regular jet service connecting it with the outside world.

Once on the ground it was fortunate that it started to rain distracting Bob who was ready to hang all three dachshunds up by their tails. Actually, he threatened to shoot the "little buggers" with our emergency rifle in the back of the plane when he discovered tiny teeth marks all along the wires. I covered the rifle up hiding it with other belongings just in case he was serious. We camped that night on the Kotzebue Airport pitching our tent in the rain, which was becoming an all too familiar occurrence.

CHAPTER 9

Ferry Service Only

Once our radio was repaired we headed for Selawik where I discovered the village could only be reached by boat from the airport. That certainly eliminated uninvited guests. When asked if we had "permission to go to the village," I could honestly say "yes," and was very thankful I had set up appointments before leaving the Lower 48. I gave Nancy's name as well as my own. Her adopted son Davey and his friend picked us up in their boat and ferried us across to the village.

We met Nancy Starbuck, a most remarkable woman who had 17 grandchildren. She told me that permission from the City Council and the mayor had been needed for me to interview her. That surprised me.

She was very welcoming, and served us coffee, pilot bread, dried pike, and salmon berries. Nancy had a pace maker as a result of a heart attack four years earlier. I found her to be a woman with tremendous spirit, and immediately liked her.

The jail and a pool hall were right next door to her house. An interesting combination I thought to myself and could only imagine what went on within earshot of her tiny home.

Selawik had a population of 560 people although initially the village did not appear that large from the air. The water around the village was misleading as to its size. Its location was at the mouth of the Selawik River where it empties into Selawik Lake. It is about 112 miles southeast of Kotzebue. I later found out it is near the Selawik National Wildlife Refuge, a breeding and resting area for migratory waterfowl. The name comes from *Sillvik*, or "place of sheefish" in Inupiaq. It is part of the Northwest Arctic Borough.

As I went through my interview questions, Nancy volunteered a lot of additional information about herself. Obviously, she enjoyed talking and was pleased to have someone from the outside fly in to visit with her. She said that she was "always discouraged to do men's hunting but did it anyway" because she "loved to hunt." She was very proud of the guns she had. I smiled at this remark. I could only imagine this woman in her younger years out on the tundra with rifle in hand stalking a caribou or maybe looking for a fine goose to roast.

The winter months were very cold for her, so much so that her blankets on the bed froze to the wall. She blamed inadequate insulation for her house. The prejudice I had heard about in the villages for being a woman living by herself raised its ugly head as she talked. Single women regardless of the reason were often considered second-class citizens. This was the first time I had actually talked with someone experiencing it. I wondered about her children and where they were. Not in Selawik, I suspected. I wondered if her adopted son who picked us up in a boat could help. He seemed to be quite positive towards her. Her other children were living in different communities and away from her.

Nancy Starbuck, Four-Footed Friend, and Marilyn Selawik

Nancy talked about her daughters and expressed concern about her older girl going into the Army. Another daughter she said went to school in Anchorage but fights erupted between her and the two roommates because they bought clothes for themselves while the daughter bought food. I wondered if the two roommates were interested in education or had other agendas for being in Anchorage.

She felt the man, Dennis Wilt, who had helped me set up appointments in the Bush might be able to help her. I thought of him as well and left her with his contact information. Maybe he could do something in the way of getting better insulation for her house before the coming winter months.

Nancy expressed concern about the young people in the village. She said they were being trained for a life they would never have, for example, the boys were trained to be auto mechanics but there were no cars in Selawik. I wondered why a class wasn't focusing on small engine repairs, specifically boat motors, instead. I spent almost three hours talking with her. She was full of surprises and told me she was a carpenter and a painter then showed me a table she had made. It was well done.

At the end of our visit she gave me a slice of jade almost six inches in length from Jade Mountain located in the Kobuk Valley above Ambler. Her son worked there and apparently was involved with mining jade from the mountain. She insisted I take the piece and showed me where the mountains and valleys as well as the trees could be seen if one used a bit of imagination while looking at the piece. I traced the river with my finger as she pointed out the Jade Mountain and the water coming from it. I have this piece of jade sitting on my desk to this day and remember that wonderful afternoon we shared.

CHAPTER 10

Nome and the Last Train to Nowhere!

After another boat trip across the moat followed by a quick dog walk, we climbed into the plane and headed for Nome. We barely made it with 15 minutes to spare before we would have had to pay a call-out charge for gas as the pumps would be closed for the evening. It was expensive enough without an additional fee so I was happy about that.

Nome is located on the tip of the Seward Peninsula and faces the Bering Sea. Bob and I had visited this community on an earlier trip in connection with his work. I was to make many trips to Nome in later years, one of those years (1991-92 school year) I visited the community once every month during the winter.

Surprisingly enough, I didn't have any women in Nome to interview. It provided a good reprieve for the schedule I had set for myself. Actually, it's about 50 percent Native. I just did not have the contacts there at that time and thought of it as a white community. Wrong! Later when I started working in Nome I realized it very definitely had a strong Native population.

Bob Reddaway, who owned the local lumber yard, was an old acquaintance of my husband's. He invited us to camp in his warehouse. That definitely beat putting the tent up in a rain storm. We borrowed his Blazer the next day and drove out on the road to Council City. It was one of the three roads leaving Nome. None of the roads were very long, no more than 72 miles at most. We headed for Solomon to see the "last train to nowhere." The train had long since been abandoned and was part of the deserted railway equipment from Council City. It included an old barge that had been beached and dated back to 1870.

Bob went fishing and caught a salmon as well as six white fish.

Schnapsie, our female dachshund who was with us, entertained herself by going after a fur coat—an ermine changing colors from brown to winter white. I first noticed her when she started to dig under the deserted barge, straight into the critter's home but initially I didn't know what she was after. Soon, however, an ermine appeared above her on the deck of the barge watching Schnapsie's excavations with keen interest. I kept an eye on her and snapped several pictures when this very curious little fellow suddenly disappeared under the deck.

Schnapsie soon disappeared as well. That's when I became concerned. I could hear a discussion between the two animals. It was definitely not friendly. There was no way I could get to her if she needed help. Schnapsie finally emerged for a brief moment, and I grabbed her much to her displeasure. It was back to the vehicle where Otto and Moose had already been incarcerated because of their own mischief.

The road went along the coastal flats, grasslands, and wide, sandy beaches, following the coastline of the Bering Sea northeast for about 30 miles before it had turned inland. Since we had use of the Blazer for the day, we continued on to Council City. We were almost at the road's end when the weather soured. There were old log cabins that were mostly abandoned and a few trees there but I didn't see any people. The "City" was a misnomer. We didn't explore much heading back to Nome because of the weather. A brief stop part way to Nome was made at Safety Sound as it was a major birdwatching area. Once we pulled over I readily could see why bird watchers loved it as there were marshes and little water inlets all around. It wasn't a day for birds, however, so we continued our road trip.

That night, we had a chef from one of the local restaurants prepare the salmon, and ended up with baked stuffed salmon for dinner. The recipe included Ritz Crackers, onion, peppers, pimento, celery, and lemon butter with garlic over the top and then baked. Delicious! The cook told me not to use anything but Ritz Crackers, because "anything else just isn't the same." He definitely had a winning combination of ingredients.

We spent a second night in the warehouse, but not before we saw a can-can show in town, a new addition to Nome's tourist attractions that brought back the gold rush era. Gold had been discovered on Anvil Creek in the summer of 1898. News of the discovery reached the outside world that winter. By 1899, Nome had a population of 10,000. I found that hard to believe as I looked around the town with its 2,300 people. It still had board sidewalks even in 1980 when we landed and very muddy streets when it rained.

Gold had been found in the beach sands for dozens of miles along the coast as well. That spurred the stampede to new heights. Thousands more people poured into Nome during the spring of 1900 aboard steamships from Seattle and San Francisco. A tent city on the beaches and on the treeless coast reached 30 miles in length, from Cape Rodney to Cape Nome by 1900. Nome averaged 1,000 newcomers a day in June of that year. Unbelievable! I thought to myself.

Once back at the airport Schnapsie started digging for Parki squirrels (Arctic ground squirrels) right by our plane. She, I realized, was determined to get a fur coat. This time both Otto and Moose joined in the hunt as well. They found a hole and started digging. The squirrel ran out a back exit to another hole. Otto spotted him and the chase was on. Schnapsie went right down into the hole and completely out of sight. Fortunately, I had seen where she had disappeared.

Bob reached down a full arm's length into the hole and retrieved her by her tail. When he let go, she went right back down just like a rubber band that had been stretched and suddenly released. No way! Bob was determined to get her back.

Once all the dogs were loaded in the plane as well as our supplies, we decided to fly out to Gambell on Saint Lawrence Island. I didn't have any one to see out there, but it would be interesting. Bob knew a man from there through business connections. We arrived above the island after a scary flight over much water with our single-engine plane. Had we lost an engine we would have only been alive for a few minutes at the most in such frigid water.

We could see Savoonga, a neighboring village from the air, but Gambell was obscured by fog, so we had burned up a lot of gas for nothing. We made a 180-degree turn and headed for White Mountain back on the mainland.

CHAPTER 11

Villages Along the Yukon

A different Alaska greeted us once we landed at White Mountain. It was a beautiful village down along the Yukon River. We were no longer in the Arctic. The airport was at the top of a hill. I didn't think much of it walking down to the village but climbing back up I knew why its name had "mountain" in it. It was a short walk, I guess, but definitely uphill. I had an appointment with Enid Lincoln and found her with ease when I asked where she was. Her responses provided me with a number of good comments about the changing roles of women.

While in the village I also met the mayor and we briefly discussed education—he wanted a strong program in the basics, and "if there was a bad teacher in the system, the program would still allow for kids to learn." Simple enough, I thought to myself, but experience told me it wasn't as easy as it sounded.

Near the coast the villages along the Yukon were Eskimo. Once the river turned north they were Indian village—Athabascan to be exact. White Mountain was close to the coast and is an Iġaluiŋmuit Iñupiut village, with historical influences from and relationships with Kawerak and Yupiaq Eskimos. That's one of those names I never mastered.

Yukon River Near White Mountain

It was dark when Bob and I arrived back at the airport after walking up the hill from the village, but a full moon gave us plenty of light to cook and make camp. That night we actually slept in a little six by eight-foot building with a couple of windows, roofing materials, and an electric waxing machine stored inside. It turned out to be a nice little shelter. I think Bob and the dachshunds appreciated it. I know I did. The local cemetery was close by and conjured up all kinds of thoughts.

It was August 27, 1980, when we left White Mountain and headed for Kaltag.

The village itself was located on an old portage trail that led west through the mountains to Unalakleet. The Iditarod Race, I knew, went right through this village and followed the trail to the coast. Historically the Athabascans had seasonal camps in the area and moved as the wild game migrated. It was named by the Russians for a Koyukon man named Kaltaga.

I found and interviewed the one woman in Kaltag who had agreed to meet with me. She had four daughters in Fairbanks, one of whom was a teacher. She told me that her son had just been taken to Tanana on an emergency flight for combining two bottles of pills with alcohol. The manner in which she told me was almost as if it were a common occurrence. There were lots of references to drinking in Kaltag.

We began the interview sitting on a pile of lumber when her husband came by and said we should go to their house. He followed us, served us hot tea and then left. I found their home was a small log cabin heated by a wood stove. In the corner of the room I noted there was a large television set.

Bob and I walked around the village after I completed the interview. One of the men we met while there told us that a lot of fish had been caught that year, but there was no fish buyer. This had to be heartbreaking for the fishermen and their families.

Much later I was surprised to learn that Kaltag was a Koyukon Athabascan area used as a cemetery for surrounding villages. There had been a smallpox epidemic in 1839 that killed a large part of the population in the entire area.

I was to return to this village many years later following a bad airplane crash shortly before I arrived. A couple of the teachers had been involved. Several people were killed, and one high school boy who survived was burned on his hands and in bandages when I met him for testing. But that was all in the future.

Our next stop was Galena where we had friends, Bev and Max Huhndorf. We had visited them in past years. Bob knew them because they sold building materials and had traveled to Seattle. I will never forget that first trip when we had stayed with them. I discovered a complete set of Shakespeare in their living room, and just wasn't expecting it in this Athabascan community! They owned the village store and were leaders in the community including making attempts at cleaning up the Yukon River by encouraging residents to go to the dump rather than throwing refuge into the river.

When Bob and I arrived this time, I noted the store that had its beginnings in their home on our first visit had greatly expanded. Bev and Max had finished their house that was just a few steps away from the original cabin. They now had indoor plumbing and a lot of modern conveniences.

Another surprise greeted us when we landed at the airport in the form of an eight-year old dachshund named Skeeter who was the official airport dog or at least he belonged to the airport managers. He had had the sole attention of air travelers and local residents for those eight years, so I think he was somewhat put out at having my three dachshunds descend on him! People came in just to see three of these long low riders in one place.

Skeeter with his nose out of joint spent the rest of the afternoon roaming around outside looking somewhat rejected. I think he tried to ignore the fact that the three canine visitors were still in the office and worse they were lounging on his favorite couch getting all sorts of praise and attention. I had to chuckle when he went into hiding.

Rosie Yaeger and her husband worked at the airport and were the first people we met after landing. She ran the office while he managed the air service. Rosie drove me out to a salmon processing area where we picked up a number of salmon heads for her dogs. She introduced me to ten full-grown racing and mushing dogs plus four puppies. The pups were worth about $1,000 each because of the father that was "a well-known lead dog worth at least $5,000" she said.

I found it most interesting visiting the dogs while she started cooking the salmon heads by boiling them in a large container of water on an open fire. Another person was there to help her with the feeding of the dogs. I understood that he stayed there a lot of the time. We went back and picked up more heads. After that we headed for the airport flight station, but not before taking a quick tour of the dump to see if any bears were there—none were present as it was too early in the day.

Once back in town Bev gave me several women's names in Nulato as well as Holy Cross with comments, "Indians are never included in surveys." She convinced me! "Okay, I promise we will go back to Nulato." It was 45 miles west of Galena between Kaltag and Galena. "Eventually, we will go to Holy Cross." I promised.

That evening we attended a potlatch (a ceremonial feast with the distribution of gifts) and met a number of the white community but very few natives were present. Bev commented on the low attendance of natives, although her mother was there, as well as a few others. The potlatch wasn't what I think of as a traditional one.

Later in the evening Bev reminisced over past years when they were traveling all the time, being "gypsies," and using dogs to travel with, and now the dogs were only used for racing. She and her husband grew up in the village, moved to Fairbanks and then returned to the village because they didn't want their sons to grow up in the city with all its problems. The younger one wanted to become a pilot and was most interested in Bob's plane. Sadly, the other son had a bad accident on a snow machine after drinking too much one evening. While suffering a TBI or brain injury, he fortunately survived. Years later I met both boys who had grown into young men. The one had become a pilot and worked for the local air service while the older one was helping in his parents' store.

I was curious about the airbase that was a main part of Galena. During World War II in 1941 and 1942, a military air field had been built adjacent to the civilian airport. The two facilities shared the runway and flight line facilities. The air field was designated as the Galena Air Force Station shortly after the split of the U.S. Air Force from the United States Army.

Before that the Koyukon Athabascans had seasonal camps in the area and moved as the wild game migrated. There had actually been twelve summer fish camps located on the Yukon River between the Koyukuk River and the Nowitna River. Galena was established in 1918 near an Athabascan fish camp called Henry's Point, and it became a supply point for nearby lead ore mines that opened in 1918 and 1919. Later during the 1950s, the construction of additional military facilities at Galena and the nearby Campion Air Force Station provided improvements to the airport and the local infrastructure.

Economic growth for the area followed understandably. The Air Force had built a flood dike around the runway to keep the river from inundating the runway. A road went along the top of it with the main village on the opposite side of the dike.

Residents living in Galena relied on river cargo in the brief summer season for the bulk of their needs, and by air travel to access the outside world. Bev and Max were enterprising. They developed a very successful village store far superior to the other village stores we visited along the river. They were also selling lumber and other building materials. As leaders in the community they were very instrumental in making positive changes.

While Bob and I were there, Bev was cutting smoked salmon up and packaging it. When she got to a curled-up end piece, she tossed it to one of the dachshunds. I was almost ready to get down on the floor and bark as the smoked fish was delicious. Actually, I did get quite a few pieces, and to this day enjoy that special way of cured salmon when I have occasion to find some—it's well named as "Indian Candy." I readily understood why. Bev gave me a nice package filled with dried salmon when we left. I had to lock it up where the dachshunds couldn't get to it.

Not all was fun for our dachshunds. They met the Huhndorf's cat Shu Shu, and very soon learned who was in control. The dachshunds didn't stand a chance. Laughter was shared as we watched Shu Shu prove her superiority by sitting with her back to the dogs.

Fish wheel along bank of Yukon River near Galena

I later worked in Galena staying with Max and Bev a couple of times as well as sometimes staying in a B&B. One of my visits was during the break-up of the river. Flooding water was everywhere and was lapping at the very edge of the property where the school sat. While the school was safe, I was glad to get out of there on that occasion. I readily understood why a dike had been built.

Bob was not feeling well on the morning we were to leave as he had a bad headache. It resulted in our getting a very late start when Max and Bev took us to the airport. It was mid-afternoon when we began packing the plane and ran into Sister Jeanette. She was headed to Nulato 45 miles west of Galena, so we invited her to fly with us. Packing became a challenge as she had two bags although they were small. I climbed in the back seat with the three dogs and held one small suitcase on my lap along with the dogs while she sat up front.

After landing at Nulato we started walking to town and got part way before Eddie, one of the men she knew from the village, picked us up. We went to the nun's house and had a cup of coffee and some soup. Then she took us over to Liz Simpson's house. Liz was one of the teachers in town and had been there for nine years. She did a fantastic job discussing the changes she had seen in Nulato during her time there. She was a black woman who had readily established herself in the community. She promised to ask her high school girls some of the questions I had been asking and to let me know.

We attended Mass while there. An old fellow sat in the back started commenting about drinking during the service. "Look out, priest drinking too much wine." Apparently, it was the first time he had been in church.

Sister Jeanette cornered two women, who came over and were interviewed by me—both had received GEDs the previous April through the Sister's educational program. Both women were also grandmothers. Their insights were very interesting. One told me, "Lots of girls in Nulato are not married but have several children. They don't want to marry the boys because they are shiftless and won't go to work."

That was to the point, I thought. Both women were very proud of their graduation!

CHAPTER 12

Leaving the Yukon then Returning

A yellow harvest moon came up through the clouds and greeted us as we walked back to Nulato's airport shortly after sunset. It was a relatively short flight to McGrath with the moon providing lots of light. McGrath functioned as a transportation, communication, and supply center for Interior Alaska. The Iditarod Trail Sled Dog Race route went through it. (This is an annual long-distance sled dog race run in early March from Settler's Bay (near Anchorage) to Nome, and is about 1,149 miles in length.

Officially it began in 1973 as the Iditarod. While dog mushing as a sport began in the early 1900s, the 1925 serum run to Nome occurred when a large diphtheria epidemic threatened Nome became the most famous event. The only way to get serum to Nome was by sled dog. The serum was actually sent from the southern port of Seward to Nenana by train where it was passed to the first of 20 mushers and over 100 dogs that carried it to Nome. The first race known as the Iditarod was held in 1967.)

We switched rivers as McGrath is adjacent to the Kuskokwim River, and directly south of its confluence with the Takotna River.

The runway was a nice long paved one and easy to find. Once on the ground we headed straight for McGuire's Saloon and Liquor Store after taking the dogs out and feeding them. Aside from alcohol they also served food. While there I ran into one of the women I had met in Fairbanks. She was playing poker. I realized how small Alaska really was at that moment, and in the next few days little did I know but it was about to get smaller in terms of meeting people.

I picked up a conversation with the woman sitting next to me at the bar when she began telling a wild tale. She became more and more upset with her boyfriend by the minute just talking about him. He wasn't there, and it was probably a good thing. She told us that one evening she took out after him with a heavy iron frying pan in order to knock some sense into him. She looked quite capable of being able to do just that! I would not have wanted to be at the other end of her anger. I don't know if the story was true or not as she had had quite a bit to drink, but several days later on the trip surprisingly enough I met the man she had chased. "She was going to kill me!" was all he said.

That night we pitched the tent in the dark right on the airport. We were getting pretty good at this.

The next day I met Ray Collins, the school board president, who was very cooperative and had already contacted a couple of people for me. He took me over to meet Laura Barnard, who was the curriculum specialist. We spent a good hour talking and then she introduced me to Irene Anderson, who was Chief of the village. I was able to interview both women.

I had scheduled another interview with a woman named Ann but didn't find her home. Heading back to the FAA station, however, I caught up with her, so we went back to her house.

Following a supper that consisted of hamburgers, I was able to talk with two high school senior girls. I was feeling good about my interviews, and thought our friend in Galena, Bev, would have been proud of me for the number of Athabascan women I had included.

Between interviews and while we were waiting around on the airport, the dachshunds discovered an afghan puppy who loved the game of chase. The dachshunds would run after him then he would turn around and chase them out-running all three on the first turn. The dachshunds, however, were good at out-maneuvering him. He would fly past them only to put on the brakes when he realized they were behind him. Their game of tag lasted the better part of forty-five minutes.

Another slow start the next morning meant we had lunch rather than breakfast. We left for Nikolai. It was just 46 air miles east of McGrath on the south fork of the Kuskokwim River.

Oline Petruska met us at the airport. She had two daughters—one interested in becoming a pilot and the other doing bead work, at least while we were there. Oline and her husband took us around the village pointing out much of the old town as well as the new section.

I kept seeing signs everywhere that said, "don't litter." It was evident the message had gotten through as it was very clean, unlike so many of the Alaskan villages I have seen over the years.

We visited the fish wheel that "works" 24 hours a day. There were only a couple of fish in it while we were there. The salmon, I understood, were dried and stored for the dogs during the winter months. I was amazed this village also had a saw mill; logs were dragged in by a dog team and then cut into appropriate sizes for houses. All in all it was an impressive community!

The St. Nicholas Russian Orthodox Church was constructed in 1927 there and was a prominent building. The village itself had been relocated at least twice since the 1880s with the present site established in 1918. It had been a trading post and roadhouse during the gold rush days, and was situated on the Rainy Pass Trail, which connected the Ophir gold mining district to Cook Inlet where Anchorage was located. It wasn't until 1963 the local residents made an airstrip creating year-round accessibility to the community. I was not to go back to this community, although I would have liked to have spent more time there.

We left that afternoon for Holy Cross, and managed to get lost, ending up on the Kuskokwim River instead of the Yukon River where we wanted to be. It took us almost an hour of flying around before we found the right river. Since we were low on gas at that point we went to Marshall instead of Bethel as it was much closer.

The runway there was wet, muddy, and had huge mosquitos heading right for our plane when we landed. The village of Marshall was surrounded by tundra and taiga forests high off the river at a place called Fortuna Ledge. It was named for Fortuna Hunter, a child born at a placer mining camp in the early 1900s.

We ended up walking into town and met Exenia Ficka, who teaches the bi-lingual program in school. We discussed the program over a cup of tea, and I went through the interview questions. Some of her grandchildren and one of her daughters came by to visit.

Marshall is unique among the villages in Alaska because until statehood it held Territorial status and served as headquarters for many state and federal agencies, including the Fish and Wildlife Service. It had its own U.S. Marshal and a Territorial elementary school, not a Bureau of Indian Affairs school like most of the villages. It is the only Alaska village that has two official names, Marshall and Fortuna Ledge.

CHAPTER 13

Descendants of the "Smokehouse" People

We were just 80 miles north of Bethel, our next stop, which was less than an hour's flying and had a population of 4,400. This was, by far, the largest community we had visited. Reading about its history I discovered it was an Alaska Commercial Company trading post during the late 19th century, and only had a population of 41 people a hundred years earlier according to the 1880 U.S. Census. That surprised me when I saw how much it had grown. It was located on the Kuskokwim River.

The general area had been the traditional location in Southwestern Alaska of the Yup'ik people and their ancestors for thousands of years. They called their village Mamterillermiut, a name I didn't even try to pronounce. It meant "Smokehouse People" and was named after their nearby fish smokehouse.

In 1885 the Moravian Church established a mission in the area under the leadership of Rev. John Henry Kilbuck, Jr. and his wife Edith. They both learned Yup'ik, which greatly enhanced their effectiveness as missionaries. Rev. Kilbuck made Yup'ik the language of the Moravian Church in the community and the region. He helped translate scripture into the people's language. The missionaries moved Bethel from Mamterillermiut to its present location on the west side of the Kuskokwim River.

Bob and I stopped by the FAA station upon landing. We let the dogs out at which point Schnapsie met a large collie. It was love at first sight! Moose and Otto, however, wanted no part of the collie and went about marking their own territory near the plane.

There was no public transit other than taxi cabs or our own two feet. We opted to spend the $5.00 per person that was standard for a cab ride from the airport to town. It turned out to be quite an experience as one just never knew whom one might be sharing the ride with.

The three dachshunds, Bob, and I climbed into the first one that came along. The driver took us to the town's only hotel—the Kuskokwim Inn. We checked in and found the room definitely needed help. There were holes in the ceiling, fixtures were burned out or missing light bulbs. Cleanliness was obviously not in the vocabulary of its caretakers and, in general, the place was a mess, but it did have a real bed. There was also the sweet smell of pot permeating the halls as we walked to our room. It was illegal. Bethel was also a "dry" village, but I don't think anyone cared. On the subject of "dry" villages, I have never had so much alcohol offered to me as in Bethel and was convinced the water taps ran hot and cold liquor.

I realized later that evening that I had goofed at the airport and forgotten our toothbrushes in the plane. For Bob that was the straw that broke the proverbial "camel's back"! First of all, we had missed eating at the brand new Greek restaurant as it had already closed by the time we had settled into our room. We headed to the pizza parlor just as the lights went out. The cook was inside, curling up in a sleeping bag between two aisles when we arrived. No way was he getting up! We then walked to the hamburger stand, where we were met with locked doors. No supper! Bob swore he was flying straight back to Seattle the next morning. Of course, he was. It was more than 2,000 miles distance. Ha!

Later that evening one of the dogs had an accident in the room, which I cleaned up but not before Bob stepped in it with his cleated boots. Not wanting a repeat performance, I got up early the next morning and took the three of them out on their leashes. I ran into a slightly tipsy Eskimo on the way back to his room. I'm not sure if he was drunk or "stoned" but his eyes bugged out at my appearance in the hallway. He closed them, shook his head, and opened them again. He looked straight down at the dogs, and quickly closed his eyes a second time. I didn't say a word. He didn't say anything either. Opening his eyes, he reached for the wall clinging to it as we passed him. Dachshunds are not something one sees in Bethel let alone three of them at one time! I guess that was more than he could handle.

Bob knew Charlie and Nora Guinn. Charlie was the owner of the building materials store there and was a "character". Their son John managed the business. After breakfast, we made our way to the Guinn's home with all three dogs in tow. I wanted to talk with Nora. She held the double distinction of being the first Native and the first woman to be appointed a District Judge in Alaska. She served as Deputy Magistrate and Magistrate in Bethel from 1960 until 1967 at which time she was appointed District Judge. She retired from the bench in 1976. Her daughter, Susan Murphy, was also there; she was the Assistant Administrator to the Superintendent at that time for the school district.

I asked Nora how she handled the drunks in town when they came before her remembering the incident with the dogs that morning. Her eyes danced with glee as she explained. "It doesn't help anyone to lock them up and fine them. So, when a drunk came into my court, I gave them a little community service project!"

Laughter crossed Nora's face as she went on with her story. "I had them dig up a coffin from the old cemetery and rebury it in the new one."

I guess I must have looked puzzled. She went on, "The river is washing away some of the land on the bluff where the old cemetery is located, so the graves have to be moved to the new cemetery." She added, "Most of the drunks want to stay out of my court room."

I almost felt sorry for some of those drunks who found their way into her court. I told her about the one I had encountered earlier that morning while taking the dogs out to do their business. We had a good laugh.

Both women gave me a few names to help with my interviews. I didn't do any interviews then as we were going to return to Bethel and spend more time there as Bob needed to spend the time working with Charlie, who owned the building materials store, and John, his son who managed it. We left and went to the laundromat after spending an hour and half with the two women. Several adults and kids descended on us when they saw the dogs. We left with clean clothes and happy dachshunds.

We hailed another taxi and went back out to the airport.

Schnapsie was bored, I guess, and ready for action. She disappeared once out of the taxi! Schnapsie didn't take long to discover a few little holes. She already had her nose down one going after some poor critter with the determination that only a dachshund can exhibit. Bob caught her in the act and pulled her up by her tail. Schnapsie fortunately had a good, strong tail.

With our luggage and all three dogs safely onboard, we taxied to the gas pump, filled up, and took off in a low ceiling—maybe 400 feet. With careful navigation through lots of clouds, we followed the Kuskokwim River until it narrowed and headed east. We then headed north continuing at a low altitude relying on the compass and found the Yukon River. From there it was a quick hop to the village of Holy Cross. It was not actually on the main river, but on the west bank of Ghost Creek Slough off the Yukon River. There was something about the name that should have given me a hint about what was coming, although at that moment I was not thinking about ghosts!

CHAPTER 14

A Haunted House Complete with a "Ghost"

I was beginning to feel a special relationship with the Yukon River as we flew back and forth above it a number of times. There were a number of villages along its banks that I wanted to visit. I suppose that was quite natural since it was the main "highway" in this part of the world. It carried boats during the summer months while in the winter its frozen waters sustained all manner of vehicles—cars, snow machines, dog sleds.

We were back in Athabascan country, at least, for one overnight stay. Our intentions were to go on to Mountain Village and Saint Mary's (both Eskimo communities) and then return to Bethel before we headed south. After landing at the airport, Bob and I walked into Holy Cross looking for Martha Demienteiff. Bev, from Galena, had particularly wanted me to meet with her. It was a short walk and a small village of 245 people.

We found her down along the river near a barge helping to unload it from what I could see. She gave us a big welcome when I introduced myself. She and her husband Claude had just returned from the summer's trip going up and down the Yukon as they were transporting supplies to the villages.

I thought it was fortuitous we kept getting lost or running out of gas on our way to Holy Cross. If our visit had not been delayed by a few days, we would have missed Martha as she would have been on the river.

We were invited aboard the barge to have coffee. I became a little nervous when several other men came on board. They had all been drinking. While introductions were being made, one looked Bob squarely in the eye and asked, "Ever see an Indian with only four fingers?" He held up his hand and sure enough there were only four fingers. Bob, not to be intimidated, looked him square in the eye and asked, "Have you ever seen a bald-headed white man?" He took off his hat as he said it with a big grin on his face. That immediately broke the tension hovering in the air when they joined us. I breathed easier until one of the new men asked to buy a bottle of whiskey for $100. I knew that was illegal and I didn't want to be witness to the transaction. I was also surprised by the dollar amount offered.

Martha looked him straight in the eye, and said, "The Demienteiffs don't boot leg. You know that!" Liquor of any kind was not for sale. I also knew Holy Cross was another "dry" community. I had the feeling there was liquor around but it couldn't be bought in the village, and Martha made it clear that it was not for sale on the barge either. Of course, that didn't mean people didn't have any.

We walked over to their house, and ended up having supper with Martha and Claude, his brother Rudy, who was a bit drunk. A couple of other men from the boat were also there. One of the men turned out to be the younger brother of Fred whom we had also met in McGrath at McGuire's Saloon. Small world I thought to myself as I heard a familiar story from a different perspective.

The men confirmed the woman in McGrath chased her boyfriend with a large iron skillet. "When she gets angry, you don't want to be anywhere around her. She was going to kill me!" one of the brothers laughed. "I ran like crazy to get out of her way!"

Martha invited us to stay the night in the house when she learned we planned to camp overnight on the airport. Without batting an eye, she said "The house is haunted, you know!" She also volunteered that her husband along with his brothers Rudy and Fred had been born there. I was curious but never did get an answer as to why it was haunted.

Rudy became a bit belligerent at one point after we finished eating, but Bob's good nature didn't take offense at his comments.

I guess he decided we were all right. Rudy was upset over "whites" coming in and shooting moose for the antlers and leaving the meat to rot. I didn't blame him one bit. Moose meat was precious and a staple in this part of the world. It carried families through the winter months. I remembered one of the conversations about moose we had had with Max in Galena. There had recently been some trouble with a couple of white hunters in the area. The discussion dwindled down after that. Finally, everyone went to bed, that is, except Martha and me.

She was fun to talk with, so much so that I stayed up with her until three the next morning. We shared a bottle of brandy discussing changes in the bush communities, my questionnaire, and I'm not sure why the house was haunted, but by that time I couldn't hold my eyes open any longer let alone concentrate on potential ghosts. I also didn't want to think about the fact we were drinking in a "dry" and very small village.

Later that night one of the men came to the door of the room where I was sleeping and started to open it. Moose nudged my face with his nose giving off some very low growls. He woke Schnapsie and Otto who joined him with their own warnings—no barks just very low but very audible growls. The man turned around and left. Maybe it was a ghost. I gave Moose a big hug, and fell right back to sleep.

CHAPTER 15

Swimming Char in a Chamber Pot

Sourdough waffles were a good incentive to get up that September 1st morning after not getting enough sleep. Once fortified with breakfast the walk to the airport didn't seem that bad. Martha's house was one of the closest houses to it. Holy Cross was the last Athabascan village I visited on that trip.

Our next stop was Mountain Village, an Eskimo-Yup'ik community on the lower Yukon. It was another short flight to a familiar village. We had been there in the spring five years earlier in 1975 just two days after the ice breakup.

The village was fairly large, and, unlike many of the Native villages throughout Alaska, had a cannery. Some of the finest salmon in the world comes from the area as the salmon in the Yukon have a lot more oil in them and the taste is out of this world!

On our 1975 trip we found some of the cannery personnel were already at work getting ready for the rush of salmon. They were putting cans together on one of only seven or eight machines in the world that did that kind of work. Once the cans were put together they were taken downstairs to wait for the fish. We were told there were probably 150 fishermen who supplied the cannery with four or five boats making pickups on the river. The fish were transferred to the cannery, processed, canned, cooked for several hours. Then they were packed, awaiting shipment to one of several large fish distributing outlets in the U.S. I remember that we stayed in the cannery that night, getting up early the next morning and enjoying sourdough pancakes.

It had only been a little over two weeks since Bob and I had left our home on Vashon Island. I had a number of interviews under my belt, so was feeling pretty positive, although I knew there were many more to complete.

With the thought of ghosts and haunted houses behind me, I asked several people where Winnie Bean lived. She was next on my list to interview. As a bonus her daughter, Agnes Kelly from Fort Yukon, was there visiting and agreed to be interviewed, too. They had just finished packing fish in a barrel for the winter months. The barrel was huge, or so it seemed. It wasn't one to be moved around—at least when full of fish. Winnie told me, "There are over 65 salmon packed in each barrel."

My interview questions on change were interspersed with our conversation. I asked the women what they had done to get the salmon ready for the barrel and was told that each fish had been dried and partially smoked. Salt was then put over each layer to preserve the fish. A cover was finally fixed to the top of the barrel to seal it up.

"We used to put a barrel of fish up that was two thirds bigger than this one," Winnie said. "That's a change," she added with a twinkle in her eye.

When the two women explained the process, I realized how different the preparation and preserving of fish was from what I had observed in Ambler and Shungnak. These fish were smoked whereas in the other villages along the Kobuk River they were cut in a certain pattern and hung outside to be air and wind dried. What I didn't know was what they did with the fish once they had dried, or how they stored them for winter's use. I didn't think to ask at the time.

I needed a bathroom break while I was there. I held out as long as I could before I asked where I could go. I wasn't sure what to expect. Both women laughed and pointed me in the direction of the "Honey Bucket". Winnie then told me that she once put a couple of live carp in the bucket when a visitor showed up.

I have to admit I checked the bucket out before I sat down. I wasn't sure if she was joking or serious. Thankfully, no fish leaped out!

Winnie asked us to stay for lunch which included dried fish, soup, and pilot bread. She told me I should spend a week there with them, and do some of the stuff instead of write and maybe I would get a little Eskimo inmy blood by eating Eskimo food. She had a good point and I wished I could have done so. I particularly liked the idea of picking berries and taking lots of pictures. But that wasn't in the cards.

Barrel of Preserved Fish
Mountain Village

Mountain Village is accessible by river boat or barge from mid-June to October. I remembered the barge Bob and I had just visited in Holy Cross. There is a road that connects Mountain

Village to Pitkas Point and Saint Mary's. It's used mainly during the summer months.

The day when Bob and I left in the first snow of the season, we headed for the airport and took off for Saint Mary's just 20 miles east of Mountain Village. Snow touched our windshield but was quickly blown off as we became airborne.

I wasn't to return to this community until several years later when I was working as an itinerant school psychologist. Mountain Village had become the school district headquarters for the Lower Yukon School District. I don't recall ever getting any "Eskimo food" there in the school as local foods are not served by the schools. That's common practice statewide. Usually, it's awful canned vegetables and dried hamburgers, hotdogs, or other frozen meals like pizza that were shipped.

I was curious about the name, Mountain Village. A little research quickly revealed that the original name of the village meant "beginning of the mountains to the north and to the south," The mountain was a reference to the 500-foot Azachorok Mountain. The village sits at its base. This mountain, although nowhere near as massive as anything in the Alaska Range, had been the first mountain encountered by those traveling up the lower part of the Yukon River.

The airport was built on an incline. The mountain itself was hardly what I would consider a mountain. Actually, the cannery was just below the end of the runway!

A Covenant Church missionary school had been built there originally. In 1923, a post office was also built, and since Mountain Village was a fishing village, a salmon saltry company was opened in 1956 and then the cannery eight years later. All three have since been shut down, seemingly ceasing all viable commerce for the community. It was later selected, however, as the headquarters for the Lower Yukon School District, a fixture in the community that helped maintain its population and economy. This village is larger than most of the others we had visited, but it maintained a relatively low profile. It had a population of 625 when I first visited it, with an estimated 35 white residents. In later years the population increased by 50 people.

CHAPTER 16

An Unexpected Swim and a Girls' Dormitory

No problems were incurred taking off from Mountain Village's downhill strip. Our wheels were barely up when Bob set up for landing down by the river in Saint Mary's. The two villages were only 20 miles apart.

There was a much larger commercial airport up on the hill four miles to the west of town, but Bob opted for the tiny strip right in Saint Mary's. It didn't look as if it had been used much at all, and the strip was close to the private Catholic high school. It was a boarding school and that's where I wanted to go next.

I had met an Eskimo Catholic nun earlier and very much wanted to include her in my interviews. She was living in Saint Mary's as part of the high school's staff. She was originally from Chevak.

Almost all of the kids attending the boarding school were from other villages. As I understood it, there were only three Indian students including one of Max and Bev's sons. All the rest were Eskimos. I was later to make many trips to Saint Mary's to work with the school district, but at this time all my contacts were with the boarding school. In 1987 it was closed because of a student suicide, well before I started working for the Saint Mary's School District on a regular basis. I was never to land at that small air strip by the river again but rather up on the hill at the commercial airport several miles out of town.

I met with the high school's staff. Bob and I were invited to stay in the girls' dormitory while we were there, and so were our three dachshunds. The dachshunds proved to be a special treat for the girls and definitely were a "magnet." Having guests there was an additional bonus for the residents. They crowded into our room spending free time playing with the dogs. What an opportunity for me!

I was able to talk with a number of the girls, and was particularly impressed by Esther, a senior from Kotlik. I interviewed her quite late in the evening. She was one very bright, young lady! It was fun talking with her and about her plans for college. As I remember, we talked about Dartmouth in the east; however, I imagine she ended up at University of Alaska Fairbanks.

I also met one of the sophomore boys from Marshall who was at the school. George was not quite four and half feet tall, but he made up for his lack of height in his conversation. Could he talk!

While I interviewed and met with some of the kids, Bob and the dogs had their own little adventure or I should say misadventure that began with an aluminum row boat and one oar. He found the boat overturned down along the Andreafsky River (120-mile tributary of the Yukon River). Bob had his fishing pole with him. His idea was to paddle and fish very slowly in front of the village. I'm sure it was an awkward path they took with only one oar and Bob trying to fish.

He decided to return to shore after no bites and made his way back to his point of departure. He beached the boat, at least the front end of it, got out with Otto and Schnapsie right behind him, jumping down to dry land. Moose, as I understood it, was at the other end of the boat in the stern and that was still in the river. Moose wasn't about to jump into the murky water. Why he didn't follow the other two off the front end remains a mystery. Bob must have become a bit threatening, when he picked up a switch and yelled, "Moose, come!"

Moose leaped out from where he was in the boat and immediately sunk down and disappeared into the muddy river water. He surfaced and frantically started paddling for dear life when Bob reached down and grabbed him pulling him out of the water. In doing so Bob lost his balance on the slippery shore causing him to fall into the water.

Now Bob was just as wet as Moose and probably as upset! Moose wiggled out of his arms onto dry land once Bob fell. He headed straight for the girl's dormitory and all those girls he knew would protect him. Bob called after him again and again. Moose wasn't about to stop nor did he turn back to even acknowledge Bob. He didn't hesitate running the equivalent of a couple of city blocks and totally ignoring Bob's repeated calls.

He got a swat for not obeying Bob, but I guess felt it was worth it to get to the front door of the dorm. That's when I walked up and rescued him. Poor Moose!

Looking up the history of the village I found the community of Andreafsky had been established as a supply depot and winter headquarters for the Northern Commercial Company's riverboat fleet. The village took its name from the Andrea family that had settled on the River and built a Russian Orthodox Church. Then in 1903, Jesuit missionaries set up a mission downriver to educate and care for children orphaned by a flu epidemic in 1900-01. The mission school flourished, and by 1915 there were 70 full-time students. The village, which was on an island in a slough connecting two arms of the Yukon River, "silted-in" severely resulting in the villagers moving to higher ground.

Materials from an abandoned hotel built during the gold rush were used to construct the new mission and several village homes at the present site. In 1949, an unused 15-by-30-foot building and other building materials from Galena Air Force Station were barged to Saint Mary's by Father Spils, a Jesuit priest. These materials, along with a tractor borrowed from Holy Cross, were used to construct a school. In 1967, Saint Mary's incorporated as a city, although the residents of Andreafsky chose to remain a separate community. By 1980, the two communities combined. This was the same year I was doing research for my dissertation. I was sorry to learn a student suicide in 1987 forced the Catholic Church to close the school.

When I returned to Saint Mary's a number of years later, I didn't recognize the village at all. The small airstrip where Bob and I had landed down by the river was no longer there as far as I could see. It seemed where it should have been had been made into a road surrounded by houses.

Old airport in front of Saint Mary's Catholic High School

CHAPTER 17

Return to Bethel and Heading South

We left Saint Mary's and the Yukon River behind us and returned to Bethel. Bob had several days of business there, and I was planning to finish my interviews. Being tired, I managed to read our air chart incorrectly, but eventually we did find Bethel after a little joy ride around in the area. Neither one of us had been paying that much attention to the maps.

In Bethel it was *déjà vu* all over again with another $5.00 taxi ride and checking into the Kuskokwim Hotel. This time we found ourselves next door to a Great Dane that was tied up outside the room. Our dogs hit the ceiling with his first bark, but soon grew accustomed to it as he continued to let them know he was there. His bark followed every noise. I thought, no drunks to worry about that evening!

Bob went over to work with John and Margaret Guinn at the store and warehouse, while I ended up at one of their relative's homes visiting with Stuffer and Cookie who had three Samoyeds. I was told that Kobuk, the biggest of the three, liked to finish off little dogs. I kept all three at a safe distance from him when Bob along with John and Margaret arrived with our dachshunds. The dachshunds were tired as they had been playing in the warehouse all afternoon so paid little attention to the other dogs.

I suppose it was understandable that the past three weeks of travel, irregular meals, little sleep, and weather changes would catch up with me sooner or later. I guess I was lucky to be in Bethel when it happened and not camping under the wing of the airplane on some remote airstrip. I felt very tired and achy and made a couple of calls the next day before I went back to bed with no energy. Things got worse as I had what I determined was the flu—sore muscles, diarrhea, vomiting, and a slight fever. I managed to get up for some lunch but then lost it in the lobby of the hotel. Bob brought me some tea and a cheese sandwich that I shared with the dogs. It was a miserable day all in all.

The next day (the 5th of September) I was back at it and felt much better. I met Betty Huffman and two other women. Betty took me over to the Bi-Lingual Center with its staff of ten. There they wrote, printed, and illustrated books as well as coordinated teaching throughout the area. I decided they must work at least 24 hours a day to get everything done. Bob tracked me down to the center. I guess he wanted to check up on me.

I found getting around in Bethel by taxi beat walking. Private cars were prohibitively expensive and so was gas. It only cost $2.50 a ride regardless of where one went in town. The airport was the only $5.00 ride in town as I mentioned earlier. The drivers knew where people lived so I found it much easier to let them take me than try and find an individual's home on my own. Besides walking along the dusty and muddy streets was not what I wanted to do. Once a taxi was called, the driver came by and honked until someone came out. He would then go pick up several more people dropping individuals off and picking more up as he drove. If the driver didn't know where a person lived, he would ask the passengers. There was a certain element of gambling that I would get to where I wanted in a timely manner but I always did.

We had planned to leave the next day. That didn't materialize. I ended up meeting with Nora again and had lunch with her talking about all sorts of things. She was an interesting and fascinating woman. I also met with two other women that afternoon so was very glad we stayed the extra day. It provided me the opportunity to visit the Moravian museum and gift shop as well, where I picked up a wonderful Eskimo pen and ink drawing that currently hangs in my home.

Back at the hotel the girl at the desk referred to us as the people with the "little family of dogs." Some of the locals were beginning to recognize us. Amused faces greeted Bob and me whenever we went on walks. One morning several men seeing Bob walk the dachshunds were staring at him in disbelief. Bob saw them and thought it funny to point at our dachshunds, and in a loud voice identified them as "Alaskan sled dogs."

We finally left on September 7, 1980, and flew on to Hooper Bay further south. The airport was along Bering Sea's windy shore. I remembered it had been windy and cold the last time we had been there, too. We walked the almost two miles to town.

I had arranged an appointment with Neva Rivers but learned she was visiting her sister. We tracked her down but not before her son who was on the police force showed us a puppy injured by a bigger dog. He drove us out to airport on his three-wheeler where we got some disinfectant to fix the pup up. It was a bad gash, but it only looked skin deep. We dressed the wound as best we could, then went on to the sister's house.

On the subject of three-wheelers, I decided then and there they were dangerous. If one was on the back, there was nowhere to hang on, and it would be extremely easy to get feet caught in the wheels or on the ground! Years later I had occasion to go ice fishing at Shaktoolik (north of Unalakleet) and was driving one of them in the snow. The front wheel caught in a snow rut, and I tipped over. Nothing serious happened, but the potential for disaster was duly noted.

Neva and her sister, Helen, told me there were severe drug and alcohol problems in the village and also mentioned a lot of girls getting pregnant. Others had told me in earlier interviews that the boys were pampered, and what I observed in Hooper Bay substantiated this.

Neva was the health aid for the community as well as for Chevak (17 miles away) and Scammon Bay (25 miles away). I didn't think that was very practical although both communities weren't too distant from Hooper Bay. I had been here before and like the previous time came away with mixed feelings about how boys were raised differently from girls. In retrospect I observed this in other villages as well.

As we returned to the airport, several people were standing by the plane. One girl was rubbing a stick on it. Bob stopped that immediately! Then two boys came up and asked me for some peanuts—uneasiness on my part surfaced, not about the nuts, but memories of kids in Mexico who were not well behaved and wanting things. Why they asked for peanuts didn't make sense. Maybe they were associating us with an airliner. Ha! Nothing came of it. There didn't seem to be any adults around—just kids seemingly bored.

Hooper Bay was a larger village compared to some of the others I had visited. The 1980 census reflected 627 people living there. The village is located on relatively flat land that is surrounded by tundra and ponds. Sand dunes, beach, and the Bering Sea could be found just a couple miles west of town. It was situated on the Yukon Kuskokwim Delta, home to Yup'ik people of Hooper Bay, who had subsisted for thousands of years on the rich natural resources found in the area.

We left this large community and headed for Tuntutuliak with its much smaller population of 225 people. Bob stayed with the dogs and the plane while I met with a woman who had been widowed six years. She told me she gathered berries for subsistence and traded with other villagers for items she needed.

After my interview with her we continued our trip following the coast line and made stops at Togiak, Manokotak, and Dillingham where we spent the night.

Dillingham's hotel made up for some of the not-so-pleasant overnights under the wing of our plane particularly when rain accompanied them. The building was new, belonged to one of Bob's business associates, and was plush with wall-to-wall carpet, a television set, and lots of places for our three dachshunds to hide. Bob Kallstrom and his wife, who was Native Aleut, had known Bob from previous trips. They took us to dinner and drinks at a nearby restaurant. We had a great visit—talking about everything from flying to building materials to my research project, and hopes for a family someday.

Drying Fish in Togiak

Marilyn interviewing woman along Bering Sea—Togiak

I have to admit we didn't get up as early as we intended the next day. Once in the plane we taxied to the end of the small unpaved strip, although Dillingham also had a nice, paved commercial strip. Bob did a run-up of the engine and turned the plane around for takeoff. Ahead of us I could see Kallstrom's wife running towards us and waving something about a foot and half long. She obviously wanted us to stop. Bob did.

I opened the door, got out and jumped to the ground. "I wanted to give you this for good luck," she said. "It's an Oosik." With that she gave me a quick hug and headed off the runway. I might add that I still have the Oosik in my home.

Now rather than say any more I decided to quote a poem that was written by an unknown author.

Ode to an Oosik

Strange things have been done in the Midnight Sun,
    and the story books are full—
But the strangest tale concerns the male,
    magnificent walrus bull!

I know it's rude, quite common and crude,
    Perhaps it is grossly unkind;
But with first glance at least, this bewhiskered beast,
    is as ugly in front as behind.

Look once again, take a second look—then
    you'll see he's not ugly or vile—
There's a hint of a grin, in that blueberry chin—
    and the eyes have a shy secret smile!

How can this be, this clandestine glee
    that exudes from the walrus like music
He knows, there inside, beneath the blubber and hide
    lies a splendid contrivance—the Oosik!

"Oosik!" you say—and quite well you may.
    I'll explain if you keep it between us;
In the simplest truth, thought rather uncouth
    "Oosik" is, in fact, his penis!

Now the size alone of this walrus bone,
    would indeed arouse envious thinking –
It is also a fact, documented and backed,
    There is never a softening or shrinking!

This, then, is why the smile is so shy,
    the walrus is right fully proud.
Though the climate is frigid, the walrus is rigid,
    Pray, man, is not so endowed?

Added to this, is a smile you might miss—
    though the bull is entitled to bow—
The one to out-smile our bull by a mile
    is the satisfied walrus cow!

With that we took off waving goodbye and headed for King Cove, then continued to fly down into the Aleutians visiting False Pass, which was, by far, the smallest village I visited on the trip. It was the only remaining Aleut village on Unimak Island with a population of 60 people. I suspect if one added the bears there would have been a lot more! They came into the village during the summer months and would sit on peoples' front doorsteps sunning themselves!

The Isanak Strait in front of the community connects the Bering Sea with the Gulf of Alaska, although in early times sea captains thought it too shallow to accommodate their ships hence the name False Pass. It is, however, a major thorough way between the North Pacific and the Bering Sea for all but the largest vessels.

Getting out of the plane I noted a few very plain wooden houses that dotted the area to the west of us. Behind them Roundtop Mountain dwarfed the village. The community itself was surrounded by a beautiful and wild landscape. It was a short walk to the small wooden structures where I met with my one interviewee. I glanced outside as the weather began moving in. My heart sank as I left the woman's small house in a hurry; it was not unheard of for people to be stuck there for days at a time because of inclement weather. Fortunately, I had finished the interview although I would have liked to have talked with her a bit more. Instead, Bob and I took off running for the airplane as neither of us wanted to stay there for who knew how long!

Serious and angry clouds were moving in rapidly from the east; we watched them as they sped our way running as fast as we could. We climbed into the plane at the False Pass airstrip in haste and took off. There was no time to even think about giving the dogs a quick walk.

Of the villages visited after leaving Bethel, I was to visit King Cove often in the future and False Pass occasionally. My son ended up working in False Pass one summer to earn money for college. I never had occasion to work in the other villages, although I did make several trips to Dillingham because of Bob's business-related friends there.

Bob was feeling quite sick. We headed for the nearest community with a good airport, namely, Cold Bay. The airport was first built as a United States Army Air Forces airfield during World

War II. It is the fifth largest airport in Alaska, being one of the main airports serving the Alaska Peninsula while Cold Bay is a very small community.

I think Bob must have caught whatever I had had in Bethel. That night was spent in the hotel's Quonset hut that had several rooms for visitors. The hotel's name was the "Weathered Inn" and was where I spent a number of nights in future years when I visited Cold Bay.

Once we were assigned a room Bob went to bed leaving me with the dogs. Needing to get a bit of exercise I went outside with them. There were very few people around. In fact, I didn't see anyone close by. Otto and Moose busied themselves marking the territory when they encountered a very friendly black Lab. A few friendly greetings were made, but he was far more interested in Schnapsie. The two boys continued digging and investigating and ignored the Lab for the most part. They were happy to just be out of the plane when they startled a mouse that dove back into a hole under the Quonset hut. Schnapsie, however, found a particularly rotten salmon head right outside the door. Maybe she wanted that special perfume for her new-found black Lab friend.

I didn't question Schnapsie's motivations but quickly picked her up and called Moose and Otto to come back indoors with me. We headed for the public showers in the building. I chose one towards the back, as I figured anyone suddenly coming in would be startled at some woman showering with a dog that was trying to avoid the water. Schnapsie ended up very wet, and very clean. Her forays after that in Cold Bay were limited to walks on a leash when we were outside. I never did tell Bob about the incident.

We headed north on the Aleutian Peninsula late in the day and landed at King Salmon the next evening. Bob, as a retired military officer, had privileges that included staying in military housing. We rode onto the base in a military vehicle complete with armed guard. The dogs even got a smile from the straight-faced uniformed man. The housing office assigned us a room and gave us some obscure directions for getting to it. The maze of hallways created confusion. There was no one around to ask as it was fairly late in the evening, but we finally found the right room.

When I opened the door, it was like walking into a blast furnace. Bob quickly opened the one window that immediately closed when he let go. He stuffed a garbage can into the opening allowing a small amount of fresh air in but blocking most of the opening. The heating system had been designed for the long, cold winters in the area. I think they kept the system set at the same temperature year around.

I often visited King Salmon in later years mainly because it was a hub and planes flew in and out frequently. It was the next major airport with a long, paved strip north of Cold Bay. The Lake and Peninsula School District had village schools throughout the area with its district headquarters right in King Salmon. The Bristol Bay School District located in the nearby community of Naknek served kids from King Salmon as well as Naknek. I later worked in both of these school districts. On this trip, however, I did not interview any women from either district as I did not have any contacts.

Right next door to the airline terminal was a wonderful but very small museum showing much about the wildlife in the area. I often visited it later when I had the chance. The airport terminal also had a nice little gift shop, in which I managed to buy several tee shirts and other items over the years.

We headed up to Anchorage from King Salmon and then down to the southeastern part of the state. I met with women in Haines, Klukwan, Hoonah, Juneau, and Metlakatla before we returned to Vashon Island.

I was awarded my doctorate degree the following spring from Seattle University. The individual stories and memories from the women I met on the six-week research-gathering trip formed a cornerstone for my Alaskan experience. Bob retired from his position as credit manager for Palmer G. Lewis Company in the fall of 1981 but continued to do some consulting work for several clients in the area. The two of us traveled in our 32-foot motor sailor to Southeastern Alaska following my graduation from Seattle University.

We spent the summers cruising the waters on vacation. I continued to work in Washington State as a school psychologist during the winters until the end of the 1982-83 school year at which time I was hired by South East Regional Resource Center (SERRC) located in Juneau, Alaska, to become one of two itinerant school psychologists. That opened up a career I was to follow until I officially retired in 2007.

Transportation in the Winter
(Photo by Marylu Martin)

Eskimo Girl in Shaktoolik

PART III

1983 to 2006

Work in the Alaskan Bush
and
Times in Between

CHAPTER 18

Beginnings in "Isthmus Town"

I was pestered initially with a sense of dread in making that first on-the-job trip out to one of the villages. But then I always felt that way the first day of any new job. Bob had already left Juneau in the airplane with the dachshunds. It was mid-August 1983 and I was headed to Angoon, a Tlingit village in the Chatham School District. It was approximately 45 minutes from Juneau by air. The name meant "Isthmus Town" in Tlingit and was very descriptive of the village's location at the northern end of Admiralty Island on an isthmus.

I climbed aboard the amphibian plane and fastened my seat belt. It was the first time I had flown in a Grumman Goose. As we took off from Juneau's airport the waterway below gave way to trees, and then I could see more water as we headed out towards the channel. My thoughts swirled around what had led up to this moment. I was excited and a little scared. I very much wanted to do a good job and had no idea what to expect.

Earlier that spring Bob and I had flown up to Juneau where I was interviewed by Twyla Coughlin (Twyla Barnes). I had been offered the position of an itinerant school psychologist for South East Regional Resource Center (SERRC) based in Juneau. The pay wasn't fabulous but it was in Alaska.

Alaska had become the 49th state in 1959. Resource centers like SERRC began as a result of new educational demands following the landmark "Molly Hooch" decision in October 1976. For the first time a generation of village leaders was likely to emerge from among students who were being educated through high schools in traditional villages instead of going away to boarding schools as they had done previously. Before that historic decision kids had to leave families and friends for the school year if they wanted to get a high school education. There were a high number of dropouts as a result. I thought of Lilia Aghook in Anaktuvuk Pass who only had a seventh-grade education and was fired because she didn't have enough education to do bookkeeping for the post office. I also remembered my first visit to Arctic Village compared to when I visited it seven years later with its newly-built school.

The decision was named for the Eskimo girl, Molly Hooch, whose name headed the original list of plaintiffs suing the state in 1972 for failing to provide village high schools. In 1976, the case was settled by entry of a detailed consent decree providing for the establishment of a high school program in every one of the 126 villages covered by the litigation unless people in the village decided against a local program. That led to all kinds of educational services becoming available to the various communities.

Individuals were hired who would travel to the villages and make assessments and whatever else was needed for an appropriate education. It was far more cost effective to send specialists to a village several times a year depending on the needs than hiring several specialists for each community. The villagers also wanted high schools of their own because high schools meant gyms—both the kids and the adults would benefit as basketball was a favorite sport.

SERRC needed a second psychologist to fill the demand and complete the contracts for services. I applied for the position.

Bob and I had spent the previous two summers in Southeastern Alaska with our dogs aboard our boat. We had discussed the job after my interview. Bob knew I wanted to work in Alaska. We were on the boat and tied up for the night at Kingston Harbor heading for Alaska for a third summer up there when he encouraged me to "go for it." I had been working in Washington schools for the past ten years, first in Edmonds and then in Central Kitsap school districts and was getting somewhat discouraged about Washington's Special Educational system.

Bob suggested I stay aboard the *H.M.S. Glenfiddich*, our 32-foot motor sailor, during the winter months and take the job. Then he started to list all the positive supports I would have in Juneau. His oldest son Rob lived in Haines, which was just north of Juneau. Rob could be down in a few hours either flying or on the ferry in an emergency. Janice and Larry Schultz, friends of ours who had been neighbors on Vashon, made a trip with us to Alaska and had ended up moving to Juneau. Larry was an extremely competent furnace repairman and very good at anything requiring mechanical knowhow. And, Bob said he would be up once a month with the dachshunds. It was as if he wanted me to take the job. He had retired in 1981 and I figured that he wanted an excuse to fly north.

That's all I needed. I accepted the position and became one of those traveling specialists going into remote villages and assessing kids for Special Education services. My job was to determine factors that might affect kids' education including cognitive abilities, learning styles, reading, math, and other skills. It would be an adventure. In retrospect, I wondered if Bob thought I'd only last a month or two and quit. He was wrong, of course, but he didn't know it.

My early trips to Alaska starting in 1973 as well as interviewing women for my doctoral dissertation in 1980 had given me a unique background for traveling and working in the Bush. My undergraduate degree in sociology had exposed me to several cultural anthropology classes that I found fascinating. I also had ten years of experience as a school psychologist in Washington's schools.

I took my car up on the ferry before the school year started in order to have transportation in Juneau. The first two years I lived aboard our boat in the Douglas Harbor (across the bridge from Juneau on Douglas Island) in a "hot slip," meaning I might have to move to another slip at a moment's notice but it wasn't likely. I didn't volunteer that bit of information to Twyla, my new boss. My third year was spent in the Harris Harbor in Juneau. I spent most of the weekends at the office writing reports when I wasn't traveling.

Winter months sometimes meant coming home from a village and having to chop my way through the ice on the boat hatch or door in order to get inside. I also became quite adept at shoveling snow off the deck.

One seriously stormy winter day full of bold and aggressive snow I had a call from my office in Juneau while I was traveling. My boat would sink from the heavy snow if someone didn't get down there to shovel it off. I paid one of the young men in the office to do the shoveling. That only happened once in the three years I lived aboard the boat. I later wrote to a friend, "I am once again excited about being a school psychologist, and the flying into villages, logging camps, and other isolated 'Bush' communities is icing on the cake."

Winter months in Juneau were challenging in the Harbor

August 1983 finally arrived and the first work trip was suddenly upon me. My first school was for three days in the Tlingit village of Angoon. I rode in on the mail plane—a Goose—and flew back out the same way. There was no landing strip. Instead we landed in a narrow channel next to the marina. A young man caught the mooring line and quickly tied us up to the dock once the pilot cut the engines. Did I say I was excited and a bit scared as I jumped out? That was probably an understatement. My baggage was pulled out of the nose and placed on the dock. I got a ride to the school district's office about a half mile away.

A cup of coffee in the assistant superintendent's office was followed by a ride to the elementary school where I tested two kids that first day. The weather as I remember was spectacular the entire time I was there, but I didn't get to enjoy it as much as I would have liked as most of the daylight hours were spent testing in a small store room about the size of a closet with a light—the 25-watt variety—high overhead. I was somewhat used to these out-of-the-way testing "rooms" from working in Washington's schools, but usually I didn't have the interruptions I did that day. Teachers and even one parent who was a classroom aid came in for supplies, and, of course, I was testing a distractible child at the time. I began to wonder if they wanted to see what I looked like. I persevered, so did the boy I was testing.

That evening back in the room where I was staying I alternated between looking out the window for a pod of whales that had been reported but never arrived and writing recommendations for the children I had tested in order to meet with the teachers the following day.

Three and a half hours were spent the next day with one angry high school girl who walked out on me at least four times, beat her fist against the chalk board, kicked the wall a couple of times, and slammed down testing equipment for good measure. I didn't think she was emotionally disturbed but rather a very frustrated girl particularly when it came to school. We finally finished the testing. Her English teacher's remarks confirmed my thoughts.

I stayed at the Kootznoowoo Inlet Lodge—no toilet paper and worse yet no old telephone books or Sears catalogues were available. But the food was excellent. The first night we had salmon cooked in a way I have never had before, and I promptly asked about the recipe that consisted of baking the fish in a tomato sauce with onions. The second night it was New York steaks. I could get spoiled with this treatment.

While at the lodge I met two construction workers and one *National Geographic* magazine writer called back from the Far East to "beef up" a story on SE Alaska.

Later trips to Angoon I found the food was not what it had been that first trip although it was adequate. It seemed that when there was just one person staying at the lodge, it wasn't anything special but when several people stayed there, the meals dramatically improved.

Those first few days of testing I noted serious articulation problems with several kids who had very few teeth evident. Their mouths were a disaster to put it mildly. I suspected soft soda drinks were the culprits as the kids consumed them by the gallons. Years later when I visited Brevig Mission, northwest of Nome, almost all of the kids I saw had rotted teeth and I was told it was from chewing tobacco. That surprised me.

Each day after testing I walked back through the village to the lodge. It was about a half mile down a darkened, wooded, and isolated gravel road. I knew Admiralty Island where Angoon was located was famous for its brown bears. The island had long been the home of the Kootznoowoo Tlingit group. The name meant "fortress of brown bears".

Rumors about bears having been recently seen roaming around near the village reached me. I didn't want any part of them nor did I ever encounter any in Angoon, although years later I did get closer than I wanted to a black bear playing in a school yard on another island in Southeastern Alaska. That time the student had come in for testing on a Saturday morning. We were the only ones in the building. A large window in the school's classroom where we were working was the only thing that separated us from the bear in the adjacent playground. I don't think the bear even knew we were there. It was having too much fun playing on the swings.

I also walked within ten feet of a small black bear feeding from a garbage can in downtown Juneau one very early morning years later as I walked to the office from the hotel where I was staying. No one was on the streets except me and the bear. I quickly passed the alley and crossed the street briefly glancing behind me.

On later trips to Angoon I met a very friendly and big furry dog that walked right up to me and smelled my clothes and licked my hands. Oh my, did he stink—had to be rotten fish I guessed, and the odor transferred right to my gloves. But a dog is a dog, and I petted him.

There was also another dog that I became friends with named Fluffy. He was a small collie living with the owner of the lodge. Every morning when I'd leave the lodge and walk to school Fluffy was right there either behind me or running up ahead of me. We were buddies. Once I got to the first house in the village, however, he'd stop and turn back. At night on returning to the lodge I would get a wonderful greeting just as if he'd been waiting all day for my return. He'd roll over on his back and close his eyes as I patted him on his head. Fluffy was also a great watchdog. Oftentimes in the middle of the night I could hear him bark. I thought maybe he was discouraging some of those rumored bears from getting too close.

I returned to Juneau that first trip to my home-away-from-home, our 32-foot motor sailor, the *H.M.S. Glenfiddich*, moored in its slip in Douglas Harbor. I curled up in my sleeping bag and quickly went to sleep but not for long. The rains came that night. So did several quite drunk fishermen who had tied up nearby. Their "party" was within earshot and lasted well into the morning hours.

I later learned that Angoon has a less-rainy climate than most of southeastern Alaska and was valued by the Tlingit for that reason. I realized it was no accident that I had sunshiny days while visiting the village on that first trip.

There was a leak in our boat that kept the floor wet. Bob and I had been looking for it since we bought the boat three years earlier. When the rain started, I could see a couple of drops forming directly overhead and then fall straight down. I thought to myself this was another thing for Bob to check on when he came back up here. The leak had to get fixed and now I discovered exactly where it was coming from.

Twyla, my boss, expressed concern about my living aboard a boat and not lasting the winter. I told her I had a land phone line aboard so could telephone at any point should an emergency arise. During the days when I wasn't traveling I would be in the office. The boat was a place to sleep. Our boat I thought was the least of my concerns although I expected it might get rough at times. My real concern was missing my husband and my dogs.

I returned to Angoon three months after my first trip and met with one of the mothers whose boy I had tested on the earlier trip. She was fun to talk with and told me she had worked in Chatham Cannery as a girl. She told me about all the fun they had there including parties with lots of dancing and fun. She then started telling me about who bought out whom and a resulting bankruptcy resulting from a number of lawsuits that were pending related to discrimination. I remembered the burned-out cannery we had visited four years earlier with the Calvins on the *Morning Mist*.

Just before returning the second time in November to Angoon, I was sent to Tenakee Springs to talk with a 14-year old alleged "sex molester" as well as test a couple of girls. The 14-year old was a scared-to-death kid when I met him. He was vomiting blood and experiencing headaches as well as stomach aches and had been for the past three weeks. The day I was there I understood that a counselor from the State Department as well as the police were also supposed to arrive. The boy told me he lived with his father with whom he couldn't communicate, and during the summers lived with his mother in California whom he was also unable to talk with. Both parents had remarried and neither of their partners acknowledged the boy. I guessed his behavior was a cry for help. Sad situation! I never found out what happened. I could only hope some professional help would be provided for the boy! He seemed like a good kid who made a bad choice.

One of the girls I tested had been molested by another boy no longer in Tenakee. The community had a very strong senior citizens group, a high school teacher who downed straight "shots" of whiskey as soon as school let out, and no toilet in the school—one ran outside to an outhouse. The building itself was paper thin and there was faulty wiring or so I was told. The school was in a mess I decided. I understood that Angoon was the parent school and what that meant I wasn't sure. I suspected it may have something to do with the allocations of money by the district.

I wondered what kind of education the kids were getting. I found some of the teachers in the various villages I visited were very dedicated, while it was no more than a pay check for others. The final child I saw on my visit to Tenekee was in the high school and needed a three-year reevaluation. She came in walking with difficulty. Reportedly she had a progressive disease possibly arthritis. I was surprised that she was classified as a "learning-disabled" child. I wondered why she wasn't receiving additional services under a "health impaired" label. I knew she should be getting more services. Minimally, a physical therapist was needed to evaluate her. It was something I could recommend, I thought, although she was a senior in high school and would only get benefits for a year if she qualified, which I strongly suspected she would.

And with that I caught a float plane for Angoon for my second visit.

In later years, I stayed in an apartment for itinerants when visiting Angoon's school, and sometimes with the English teacher and her husband who was the assistant superintendent of Chatham Schools at the time.

CHAPTER 19

The Aleutians

I left Juneau for Anchorage on Alaska Airlines, and then flew out of Anchorage on Reeve Aleutians Air to Cold Bay, the "gateway to the Aleutians," on one of their four-engine turbo props. It was shortly after my first visit to Angoon. I was traveling every week those first years and writing my reports at night or on the weekends. We landed in a light rain. Both flights had been on time, but I figured my luck was about to change when I walked into Cold Bay's small waiting room and found it full of activity unlike the previous trip when Bob and I had flown there in 1980 and found virtually no one there.

I had another flight to catch and didn't know what to expect as this was my first trip to King Cove (September 19-23, 1983) as an educational psychologist. One of the couples in the waiting room was trying to get to Nelson Lagoon and had been waiting a couple of hours. Another man was planning to go to False Pass. I went up to the counter and learned that the school district had called ahead and set up a charter for me to fly to King Cove. More importantly, it was available as soon as I arrived in Cold Bay. Surprised, I realized I didn't have to wait at all. The couple heading for Nelson Lagoon had to wait still more until the charter dropped me off and returned for them.

I walked out on the tarmac with the pilot to a Cherokee Six that was waiting, fueled, and ready to go. Once in the air I found it much louder than I expected. It was a short flight of only 18 miles but rained the entire time we were in the air. King Cove was southeast of Cold Bay and on the Pacific side of the Alaskan Peninsula. The rain became serious once we landed. I had been told that someone would meet me at the airport, which was no more than a runway. I didn't see any one around. We taxied up to a discarded shipping container, the kind that carries freight aboard cargo ships.

The pilot jumped out and unlocked the padlocked door on the van and unloaded my baggage as I got out of the plane. He took off without saying much at all. He was in a hurry to get back to Cold Bay. I watched as the plane took off and disappeared as I stood there with the rain coming down around me.

A couple of old airplane seats and some wooden pallets on the floor greeted me. Looking around the inside of the container the only other evidence of someone having been there before me was a couple of beer bottles near one of the pallets. They were empty. I hauled my test kit and backpack out of the rain and sat down on the better of the two seats. Outside I could hear dump trucks as they drove past with their loads of sand and dirt—the airport was being widened. I was to learn that road work between town (some three miles away) and the airport was also in progress.

It was cold and eerie as I waited. Rain fell continuously. Each drop hit hard against the thin metal roof without mercy but the inside of the container remained dry. I had no intention of walking to town particularly in bear country and certainly not with all the baggage I carried. At least there were dump truck drivers not far away in the event a bear showed up, but that was highly unlikely as there was far too much human activity I reassured myself for any bears to expose themselves.

Finally, after a considerable wait time, a vehicle pulled up to the entrance of my "waiting room". "Dr. Mosley?" The driver greeted me and apologized for the delay. I nodded to him and breathed a sigh of relief as I climbed into the car. He had been delayed because of a steam roller—in fact the same one that delayed us on the way back to the school.

Once at the school and after several brief introductions I followed Lorelei Justrus (Lorelei Mack) to one of the supply closets with testing kit in hand and a child in tow. She was the Special Education teacher. Talking with her I just didn't see the pressure that I felt in Angoon or later in other districts. Neither she nor anyone else asked me how many kids I could test in a day. That was refreshing.

"Waiting Room" at King Cove Airport

I hardly had time to walk into the school when I had an invitation to the principal's home the following evening for dinner with his wife and their three-year old daughter. The family had a cat that liked to play. I enjoyed the evening and definitely had fun with the kitty.

After I finished testing that first afternoon I walked down to the glass case just outside the school's gym with a stuffed bear known as "Tundra Jack" inside. Standing up on his back two legs he was fierce even behind the glass enclosure and stood well above me. He was the school's mascot. I had been reading *Alaskan Bear Tales* that was full of stories about people being mauled, so was just as glad to see this one stuffed rather than encountering him on the tundra fully alive.

Across from the bear was a marvelous mural. I walked over and started studying it. Individual pictures were done by the kids. A resident artist had cleverly put all of their work together into the mural. Everything was there including wildlife, fishing boats, the tundra, mountains, and, of course, in the middle of it was a Tundra Jack symbolizing the terror of the Aleutian region on the basketball court.

King Cove was an independent school district at that time. Later it was absorbed by the Aleutians East Borough School District for which I also worked. District offices for it were in Sand Point and included Akutan, Cold Bay, False Pass, Nelson Lagoon, and Sand Point. I continued visiting King Cove after it became one of the schools in the larger district in addition to visiting every one of the other schools.

I stayed in the V.I.P. quarters owned and run by Peter Pan Seafoods while in King Cove. The room costs $60 a night and included two meals. The per diem I received more than covered it. On that first visit I shared a bathroom with the visiting doctor. He came around about twice a year scheduling his fall trip in conjunction with goose hunting in nearby Cold Bay, which apparently was the place to go for geese. I was told that both Honkers and Brants came through the area on their annual migration. I couldn't help but think how beautiful the Brant geese were when they arrived in front of our house on Vashon Island heading for Alaska and later after making their way back down the Alaskan and Canadian coastlines. I hoped a lot of the hunters turned out to be lousy shots.

Mural created by King Cove students and assembled by visiting artist

I ate in Peter Pan's mess hall. The food was quite good and

there were lots of choices when going through the food line. One morning, however, on a later visit to King Cove, I goofed making a very bad mistake. I loved fish and certainly King Cove had lots of fish. I enjoyed sardines, herring, and just about anything else that swam. Fish for breakfast didn't bother me. When home, I would sometimes eat left-over fish if available.

I went through the breakfast line as usual and spotted some little fish that were about the size of a small sardine. I added several of them to my plate. I sat down. Interested in those little delicacies from the deep I took a big bite, almost the entire fish as I remember. I thought I was going to die right on the spot. Flashes of fermented seal came to mind. I couldn't get that little fish out of my mouth fast enough. The taste remained with me for the better part of the morning. There were a lot of Asians employed in the cannery so I don't know if the recipe was from the Far East or if it was a choice food of the Aleuts. I didn't ask. I wanted to forget the whole experience.

The Aleut people had lived in this remote area of the Alaska Peninsula for more than 4,000 years. Its economy depended almost completely on the year-round commercial fishing and seafood processing industries. Peter Pan Seafoods was one of the largest operations under one roof in Alaska. Up to 500 non-residents were brought up to work in the processing plant as needed.

The first night after supper I took a spectacular walk up the board walk and right out across the tundra. The wind had kicked up a bit but the rain had stopped. The air was crisp, and I was out of town on a cliff that overlooked the inlet and was away from buildings in no time at all. I looked back and could see the entire village as well as Peter Pan Seafoods and the harbor. A few gulls were playing a game of tag in the air. The water shimmered below. A few of the buildings were reflected in the late afternoon's light. I inhaled the salt air, and felt as if I belonged. Houses were built in later years where I stood and dotted the area, but that first trip I had it all to myself.

When I stepped off the board walk and onto the tundra, the ground gave a little. There were millions of small plants growing and making it very soft. I looked out across the inlet and into the harbor and could see fishing boats. Some were lined up at the plant's dock. I found a sea shell covered with barnacles, and wondered how it got up on the cliff where I was. Now it's in my suitcase, and someday someone else would find it and wonder where it came from.

I almost expected to see a brown bear or Tundra Jack in the living flesh but didn't. It's funny what one's imagination can do. I was coming to the end of my book about bears, and polished it off that evening and then read an Ellery Queen story I found left in the room later that night.

The next day I saw three more kids in the supply room, and got a stiff neck from sitting on elementary school-sized chairs leaning over testing equipment on a small child's desk. I spent the week in the community typing up my reports and recommendations in the evenings, and left those reports on site with the superintendent.

On the last day of testing and with an even stiffer neck, I tested a 14-year old boy who had been in Special Education for years. He earned enough money running one of his father's fishing boats to pay cash for a new Ford truck. He told me fishing was poor that year where they were so they closed the area early. All the fish had apparently gone over to the nearby Bristol Bay area as that community had the second largest harvest in history. I suspected that in a good year this 14-year old made a better salary in a month or two than I did all year and I doubt he got a stiff neck from sitting around. I chided Lorelei about what she was going to write on his IEP (Individual Educational Plan) for work-related goals. Managing his money and the boat would be key.

I later learned that if a fisherman had a son, that son would inherit his commercial fishing license. But if he had two or more sons, there would have been a problem as he only had one fishing license. I wondered if this boy had a brother or not. Somehow, I kind of doubted it.

I was to make many trips to King Cove in the years that followed. I always looked forward to my visits there and anywhere in the Aleutians for that matter. Wind shear was a major factor on King Cove's airport making landings tricky at best. Snow was not unusual. Most of the times I visited that community I found snow everywhere. The superintendent called it "Aleutian sunshine." He had another favorite response to people who asked him how he could stand it without any trees, and that was "trees just get in the way of the scenery".

The superintendent there was very personable and so was his wife. I found it funny, however, but during the time I worked for that district I never saw him after lunch. Before, yes, but not afterwards. I used his office in the afternoons and evenings to type my reports as those first years I didn't have a computer available to me nor did I know how to use one.

King Cove was accessible only by air and sea. Almost all of my trips were by air frequently in a twin Navajo and a few times in the Cherokee Six. There was one occasion, however, that I ended up on a fishing boat going the long way around to Cold Bay. I distinctly remember the boat when I arrived at the dock as being larger than I had imagined from a distance. It was definitely much bigger than our boat in Juneau. To get aboard I had to climb down a vertical ladder onto its deck as the tide was out. The crew was very helpful.

Several of us were headed to Cold Bay's airport and sat tightly packed in the small cabin inside the boat and out of the weather. The sea was rough once we got out of the harbor. Waves pounded the sides of the boat and occasionally crashed over the stern. The air inside the boat was stale. Outside it was cold and way too windy to stand for very long although now and then I stuck my head out the door to get a fresh smell of the salt air.

Once at Cold Bay the vertical ladder was a required feature of getting off the boat and onto the dock well above my head. The water was rough. Swells continuously moved the boat. Scrambling up the ladder was not high on my priority of things I wanted to do. I was relieved when I had both feet firmly planted on the dock. Fortunately, the deck hands transferred my baggage off the boat.

I enjoyed the people I met in King Cove including the teaching staff. Lorelei was the special education teacher almost all of the years I went to that school. We still exchange Christmas cards. She was extremely well organized, an excellent teacher, and had very specific questions for me about the kids I tested.

I had become good friends with Cole Lehmann, one of the young teachers I met initially in False Pass. Cole was one of those outstanding teachers who were naturals at getting kids to learn. There were no behavior problems in his classroom. He was fresh out of college when I first met him. I recognized a truly talented educator when I saw him in the classroom at False Pass. He was a first-year teacher at the time. He later transferred to Nelson

Lagoon, and then King Cove.

Cole was responsible for getting me a box of Japanese glass balls that floated onto the beach near Nelson Lagoon. We had some great discussions on my visits. He talked about his father and step mother and growing up in the Pacific Northwest. On one particularly stunning afternoon we took a four-by-four out beyond the airport as far as we could go. Then we hiked along the upper ridge of a valley. Across the valley on the opposite side was one of those Tundra Jacks I kept hearing about, or I thought it might be as it was a very long distance away from us. It appeared to be eating berries. At least that's what I suspected it was eating. After all, it was the height of the berry season and the bear was no dummy as winter would soon arrive. It was too far away to get a good look and my telephoto camera lens didn't help much. But the outing did wonders for my spirits after being "locked up" in the school for a week.

The years flew by and the community grew as did the airport. The container that had initially served as a waiting room disappeared at some point to be replaced by a real waiting room. The muddy airstrip was also replaced. In my mind's eye though I can still see it as it had been the first time I arrived to go to work that early fall in 1983. I returned there off and on during the next 15 to 20 years seeing those changes. I never lost the excitement I felt when returning to King Cove or anywhere in the Aleutians for that matter.

Akutan was farther south in the Aleutians East Borough School District than any of the other schools I visited. For those trips I flew to Dutch Harbor, stayed all night, and then flew to the village by float plane as there was no airport on Akutan.

There was no room at the hotel in Dutch Harbor one late April 1991 trip. That wasn't too unusual during fishing season but presented a problem for me. I ended up contacting a teacher, Linda Miller, from Unalaska School. She took me in, fed me, and then took me on a tour of Dutch Harbor/Unalaska area. Afterwards, we went to the Unalaska School for another tour. What a school! It was an eighth of a mile long and beautiful. The new high school was complete with a spectacular gym, sauna, swimming pool, and a second smaller gym. I was very much impressed.

The next morning brought terrible weather, but I was finally able to fly in Peninsula Air's Goose to Akutan. I tested the 6-year-11-month old child who turned out to be a year younger and stayed in the "hotel" of sorts in the village then flew back to Dutch Harbor and on to Anchorage the next morning. Flying out of Dutch Harbor at the close of a fishing season could be a challenge as there were often no seats available. The plane was usually full of drunks once one got on it. Made for interesting flights.

Akutan had lots of feral cats. They fed off the fish from Trident Processing Plant. When I initially walked into the school that first time, I saw the teacher had a taxidermy project set up involving three cats that had been found dead under the school—ugh!

One of my last visits to Akutan was after my first hip replacement in December 1996. The teachers invited me to go with them on a little tour of the harbor by boat. I found the area from the water fascinating. The tide was just right, according to one of the teachers, so we headed out of the harbor and around the corner where there was an opening and cave large enough for the boat to enter. Inside was a natural grotto that was beautiful and continued for maybe 50 feet or more to what opened up on the other side of the rock outcrop to a small beach. I found it absolutely spectacular and a wonderful memory of this remote island!

Stored Crab Pots
King Cove

CHAPTER 20

Gone Forever and Ever

"You forget, boy's your grandson," the younger man angrily snapped back. "Boy don't like man's work, no good in school, not good for much of nothing." A lonely place with a rich history, I thought, man against his environment, man against man. Fierce storms scoured the land. Strafed by 100-knot winds, smothered by Bering Sea fog, weather ruled. Henry's family had been hunters in this wind-swept region for as long as anyone could remember. They were Native Americans, Aleuts, or at least their forebears were before the relatively short-lived Russian domination changed the people forever.

I spent a couple of hours testing Henry. I ended by having him draw a self-portrait. His tiny drawing, a mere shell of a person, had no eyes, no nose or mouth, or even ears, just an empty circle for the head. Henry, as he viewed himself, I thought.

Henry complained about his stomach.

"Did you eat breakfast?" I asked.

"No," came the reply.

"Go back to class, have your snack. We'll finish another day."

I followed him, wanting to observe. He entered the multi-graded classroom, and pulled out a bag of corn nuts. I sat by a large celestial globe in the corner.

Nearby "paper-mache" planets hung from the ceiling with a

big yellow sun in the middle while children's clay animals stared unseeing from a desk top. The smell of coffee drifted from behind the teacher's desk. Several plants ringed the room. Stuffed animals, sea monsters, and filmstrips reached for the ceiling atop one of the room's many book shelves. After a quick glance around, I shifted my gaze back to Henry.

The noise from a burst of wind against the window caught his eye. He turned. The girl across the room, the one in the red tee-shirt, coughed. He looked at her. He stuffed another corn nut into his mouth, and chomped it loudly.

A yawn slipped out then Henry stood and grabbed a broken pencil. He sauntered past the cluster of desks where fifth graders sat, stopped, picked up a picture book about ships, and thumbed through it. Several minutes passed before he continued toward the pencil sharpener; it was an electric one. Henry watched the teacher as the pencil ground away.

He turned, made a face at the boy nearest the bookcase, then walked behind the book shelves, going the long way around past the aquarium where two geckos peered at him from inside their glass world. A small sign, "Teacher's Pets," was taped over the crack along one side.

He punched the boy by the bookcase who snarled back at him, "I'll get you, Stupid."

"Henry, sit down," the teacher said automatically, hardly pausing as she read *Aliens for Breakfast* to the third and fourth grade children.

Henry slouched down in his seat.

"Henry, are you paying attention?" It was the teacher's voice again.

Others stared at him.

"Henry, what's the story about?"

Henry looked at the teacher and after a long hesitation, admitted, "I don't know."

There was snickering in the back of the room. The girl next to him whispered so the teacher didn't hear, "Re-tard!"

Twenty minutes passed. I remained in the classroom. A writing assignment was given.

"Henry, you need to get your paper out, everyone else is writing. What's the matter with you?"

He removed a piece of notebook paper from his desk.

"Henry!" The teacher looked directly at him then turned her back to help another child.

Someone kicked an eraser. It hit Henry's chair. I watched closely as Henry pushed it away with his foot. The girl next to him shoved it back. He stretched to get a good swing at it.

The teacher looked up. "Henry what are you doing? Get busy!"

She found fault quickly, I realized, and didn't give him support. Henry's foot slammed the eraser across the room with a loud bang.

"Henry!" The teacher walked over to his desk.

I understood some of Henry's anger as I left the classroom but still had many questions about him. Later that afternoon I returned just before time for Henry to go home.

What will his weekend bring, I wondered, and what about his family, what were they like?

The following Monday afternoon his mother met with me to discuss testing results. She initially didn't say much, just listened.

"How was Henry's weekend? I asked.

"It's time the boy goes out with the men," the mother responded, hesitated then added, *"but he's only nine years old."*

Before I could say anything, the mother talked about the previous weekend.

As I listened, I put myself in Henry's shoes and imagined the details of what happened from the scant descriptions the mother gave. Her voice was hesitant at first but gained strength as she told the following story.

The grandfather was visiting. Henry was old enough to go hunting with the men. His father and grandfather had a trip planned. He wanted to be like boys his age. They go hunting, that's all they want to do, that and fishing.

It was on Saturday morning she began. My mind swirled around her words as I felt what she was saying. I put myself into Henry's shoes, into his feelings, carefully listening to the woman. I envisioned every detail adding what she doesn't say in my mind to her words. I became one with the moment as I relived Henry's weekend.

Day breaks the next morning in the purest of pastel blues, while the air is like something for drinking. The new born sun toasts everything it touches without searing so much as a blade of grass. In spite of its promise for a spectacular day, Henry wakes up reluctantly, turning away from the sunlight streaming through his window.

He shivers while he eats a piece of jerky swallowing part of it whole so it rubs dry against his throat. He chomps a few corn nuts. They don't taste much better. Not much of a breakfast for a hunter but that's the kind Henry eats when he eats at all. His thin, frail body testifies that this isn't the first time he has skipped a meal.

His father has the guns ready. Henry climbs into the back of their four-wheel drive. The smell of gasoline causes him to sneeze.

"It's time the boy goes out with the men," his mother says. His grandfather nods then he opens the door and gets in.

Henry watches his mother as they drive away.

Soon the vehicle bounces to a stop near the lagoon. All three get out. Tiny plants dressed in every shade of green cover the ground. The tundra is spongy and soft, and full of life as Henry steps down. But already the minute leaves have turned to shades of red and orange.

Common cow parsnips, which Henry's family calls "*pootchky*," have long ago lost their whiteness. Instead, their dried stalks are a reminder to Henry how good this abundant weed tastes but it's the wrong time of the year to eat it. The brownish stalks do not look appealing. Henry wishes now that he had eaten something more than the jerky and few corn nuts.

They walk toward the water—the father, the son, the grandfather. Short bog grasses along the shore slap against his legs. Henry sinks down and notices water beneath his feet. It oozes up around his shoes. Wet grass clings to his pant legs. The lagoon smells musty. Many of the tiny orange lichens have already turned yellow and even brownish. Henry looks up into the deep sapphire-blue sky.

It's not long before a large flock of geese fly over. Their continuous honking breaks the earlier silence. All but a few are out of gun-shot range.

There's a burst of shot, the smell of powder and Henry is deafened for a moment. He closes his eyes tightly until the tears come, then opens them.

Quickly slipping past the men he goes to the water's edge. A goose is hit. Henry's eyes grow round as he stares at it.

"It's big!" he calls to the older men.

The bird squawks loudly, and thrashes around. The men walk to where Henry stands, shading their eyes with their hands against the glare of the bright sun and peer down at Henry, then over to the goose.

Its wing hangs loosely and, as they watch, a feather drops away and slowly floats out into the lagoon.

Henry wades through the thick grass and picks the goose up tenderly as if it were a fragile thing. The goose begins to flutter, but its wings are uncoordinated and, amid much flapping and flying feathers, it becomes exhausted and calm as Henry caresses it.

"It's not even frightened of us," Henry says, more to himself than to the older men. The younger man nods, and the two men walk off toward the back side of the lagoon.

Henry walks back to the truck to a spot where lichens and ground cover have woven together to form a soft bed, and folds his legs up under him careful not to disturb the goose. He holds it tight but not too tightly. There are a few drops of blood where the pellet hit the wing. Henry pets the goose, smooths its feathers then runs his fingers lightly over its head, fondling the short feathers at the top.

The goose lightly pecks the edge of his nose and snuggles down deep in the protection of Henry's warm arms. It's young and hasn't developed its full wildness yet.

The sun is high overhead. The father and grandfather shoot now and then but Henry shows no interest in the hunt. He has his goose.

He kisses the goose's bill. "I love you," hesitates then adds "Oh, you're so warm. I'm sorry they hurt your wing."

The goose shakes his head.

"You love me, don't you?"

The goose runs his neck along the boy's arm.

"I really love you."

The goose is soft. Henry hums a little song, something he heard in his childhood, long ago. "Rock a bye baby in the tree top, when the wind blows the cradle will rock."

The goose closes its eyes. Henry feels tingly and happy inside. The sun continues its westward trek across the sky. A breeze rushes around the edges of the boy's jacket. He is only faintly aware of it.

Towering thunderheads build overhead. The white, fluffy clouds change quickly into dark, opaque storm clouds. The air becomes cooler. But Henry has his goose, he's warm all over.

The shooting stops. Soon the father and grandfather return. They are empty-handed, not having hit any more game birds during the hunt.

"Too high," the old man says. "Birds flew too high."

Henry glances up as the two men approach the truck. Both look disgusted. Henry is happy his face glows radiating love. He thinks about the trip home; he can hardly wait to share his new-found friend with his mother. Then he looks into the cold, steel-blue eyes of his father who roughly grabs the goose, tearing it from Henry's arms.

"Noooooooooooo!" screams Henry.

But the man pays no attention. He wrings its neck as the boy stares.

Henry sees a white veil come over the eyes as the beak unhinges. Its body separates from the head, jerks a number of times then straightens out with a final tremor, and the bird lays still. Henry tries to look away but his head won't move. His eyes feel wet, his throat dry. Blood stains the feathers and falls to the ground. The red blends in with the orange and yellow plants that blanket the tundra. The mossy surface quickly blots it.

"Don't be silly, it's nice fat goose for freezer!" the father says as he hands Henry the head.

Henry shakes all over, fighting back the tears that well up around his eyes. "It's dead! You've killed it, you've killed my goose."

All he can think about is that his goose is gone, gone forever and ever. Still clutching the head, Henry turns from the men and climbs slowly onto the truck's bed.

"What kind of son you raise?" the old man asks.

"You forget, boy's your grandson," the younger man angrily snaps back, then adds "Boy don't like man's work, no good in school, not good for much of nothing."

The older man throws the goose into the back of the truck while the younger one starts the engine.

Henry drops his head, wipes the blood off his hands on a dirty canvas cloth and turns away. Tears sting his face as the truck bounces over the road back into town. I awake as if in a trance as the mother finished the story. "It's unfortunate, you know, what happened—he cuddled the goose for hours."

She looked up at me suddenly, then added, "You know, it's time for the boy to be a man; *he's nine years old.*"

Shortly after telling the story she left the classroom.

I closed my eyes, and thought about last Saturday when I had driven on another back road near where Henry had held his goose.

I remembered the tundra, stained with red and yellow and orange, tiny lichens woven everywhere into the colorful ground cover, as I stepped from the land rover. Sleeping shoots of pale green rye hid under the white yellow slender stems and blades of grass. The one-flowered cinquefoils' yellow blooms were long since spent, their old brown leaves crowded at their base. Arctic cotton grass still marked time by the marsh. Long runners and solitary, slender culms reached upwards, while the goose down nest hidden by short bog grasses and sedges, lay abandoned and swayed back and forth like an empty cradle.

The tundra sprung back with each step I took.

So can the boy I thought, *so can Henry.*

CHAPTER 21

Freshwater Bay

There were a number of logging camps in Southeastern Alaska during the years I worked up there. Some of them were family camps and consequently had schools. Each one was handled a little differently as far as the school was concerned, and that depended on the teachers as well as the owner or operator of the camp.

My first logging camp experience was in Freshwater Bay that was part of the Chatham School District. The district had several other logging camps scattered around and near Chatham Strait and I eventually visited them all. Southeast Island Schools had a larger number of logging camps, some of which I visited. They were located in the southern part of Southeastern Alaska mostly on and around Prince of Wales Island. I made a lot of visits to Thorne Bay as well as working in some of the other ones in later years.

The local logging industry had been in trouble because of the pulp mill in Sitka. Low school enrollments resulted in the camps with the threat of school closures ever present. Freshwater Bay's school was one of those schools. It was a family camp and at times had upwards to 150 people, but in the winter the numbers dropped to 20 or less. It was mid-October in 1983 when I flew out there the first time. The population at the time I visited was "25" or at least that was the number written with duct tape on a sign next to the float plane dock so it could be changed at a moment's notice by incoming or outgoing residents.

Freshwater Bay Logging Camp was actually in operation for about ten years before it finally closed and had been operated by a couple of different operators. Margaret and Bob Andrews handled the school. Watching them in the classroom quickly convinced me that they were very competent and experienced teachers. They were innovative and were always trying new things. Their own two sons Josh and Jeremy attended the school there. Both boys were bright and both were being tested for the gifted and talented program that first trip.

I knew I had my work cut out for me when I saw the list. I think I tested or was involved in IEP (Individual Educational Plan) meetings with most of the school-age kids there in one 24-hour period. It was also my first experience having a float plane buzz overhead while I was meeting with a parent. That was my signal that I had only minutes to get down to the dock before it landed to pick me up.

The school was a large trailer divided into two rooms. There were no closets or other hidden away rooms for testing so I did it in the teachers' kitchen right across from the school. One large gray Persian cat named Dusty joined me swishing his tail under my nose and supervising each student I saw. None of the kids minded. As for Dusty, he knew every one of them. He was joined by an old springer spaniel named Mike that smelled to high heaven and also supervised through half-closed eyes curled up under my feet.

Freshwater Bay was located on the eastern side of Chichagof Island, and opened up onto Chatham Strait. It was the next bay north of Tenakee Inlet. The bay itself had all five kinds of salmon, Dolly Varden, cutthroat trout, and halibut. Clamming, shrimping, and crabbing were available. Trapping included mink, marten, and otter. Brown bears and lots of deer completed the list of wild things that lived there. Chichagof along with Baranof and Admiralty were the only three islands in Southeast Alaska that had brown bears.

Living in this natural paradise the Andrews' pretty much lived off the land and sea in and around the bay harvesting what nature provided. One of my favorites was the fiddleheads or young beach fronds that Margaret collected along the beach and canned. She served them with fresh sliced radishes that first evening followed by a great meal. I finally relaxed a bit when Bob pulled out a bottle of peach brandy to polish off the food.

The two of us stayed up rather late drinking a couple of glasses and discussing everything imaginable. While Margaret was actively involved in the conversation, she didn't drink. I learned that initially Bob was a bit hesitant about having a female itinerant psychologist come to the camp. The fact that I was living on a boat I think helped break the ice.

I learned that they were not happy with SERRC. I knew different individuals saw things differently and from their own perspective. They told me several SERRC people had come out to the camp, spent a few minutes looking around and returned to Juneau on the next plane without physically doing anything except look and talk. Margaret and Bob thought that was a waste of resources, and I suspect had good reason to since they were being threatened with a school closure. I listened more than talked when the subject of SERRC came up. After all that was my employer.

That night I understood the difference between teachers who came up to teach for a year or two considering their temporary quarters a physical place to stay, and those teachers who came up and made where they were their home. It was very evident in the Andrews' trailer as it was very homey and welcoming. I learned the couple had been Vista volunteers in the Appalachian Mountains where they met each other, and had also run a house for emotionally disturbed kids. The next day when the plane finally picked me up, they loaded me up with frozen salmon and halibut.

I overnighted in their trailer. I had no problems falling to sleep after all the peach brandy I had but awoke suddenly in the middle of the night to find I could barely breathe. Something very furry and heavy was pushing down on my chest. Dusty had found a warm bed and was not shy about making himself comfortable. The next morning, I was told that he liked people and had spent more than one night curled up on top of some visitor staying in the trailer.

Dogs were a different story as Dusty terrorized every dog that had the misfortune of meeting him. He attacked them and chased them out of the yard yelping. Razor-sharp claws and strong fangs sunk into their hides if there was any hesitation on their part in leaving. All canines avoided the Andrews' trailer with a wide berth as a result of his guarding instincts. Mike was the exception. After all he lived with Dusty and was part of the family. I could see Bob was particularly proud of their guard cat as he told me about the cat's ferocity in dealing with dogs.

We became good friends although I only got to Freshwater Bay a few more times, and would have liked to have spent much more time there. Unfortunately, the school was closed and the Andrews moved into Haines and then to Klukwan, a native village just north of there that was also part of Chatham Schools and where they ended up teaching. I saw them more often. They eventually lived in the apartment above the school.

Life in Freshwater Bay Logging Camp

My husband flew up on one of his trips after the Andrews moved out of the logging camp to Haines and before moving to Klukwan's school apartment. Our two remaining dachshunds were with him when we decided to go visit them in their new home. Dusty had moved with them as had Mike. Margaret expressed considerable concern for the safety of our dachshunds when she knew they were with Bob.

"Not to worry" was my response. "Dachshunds are a little different than most dogs. I doubt your cat will scare either of them especially Otto."

Schnapsie sat on my lap when we pulled into their driveway. Otto remained in the back seat. When Margaret opened the front door to greet us, Otto began to quiver. He had picked up the scent of Dusty. Without thinking Bob opened the car door and stepped out. Otto shot right between his legs and before you could say Otto backwards he was up on the steps and past Margaret who stood there with her mouth open.

Excited yips disappeared inside the house. I was right behind him yelling. Screaming was more like it. I had intended to leash him before we went in, but Bob hadn't seen any reason to do so. Foolish I thought to myself. Not good, not good at all!

Once inside I spotted Otto with eyes glowing and his breath coming in short gasps. He nimbly jumped up on some of the furniture. Ahead of him was Dusty clinging to the curtains trying to get higher and well out of Otto's reach. He was at least twice Otto's size although that did not deter Otto in the least bit. Grey fur was flying through the air. Otto must have connected with the tip of Dusty's tail.

Our demon dachshund was at the base of the curtains barking for all he was worth. Dusty jumped down from the curtain onto a nearby table then tore through the kitchen and onto the top of the refrigerator. Otto was relentless in his chase and close behind him. He started jumping. I guess he was hoping to get up on the counter and leap to the top of the refrigerator. Smoke and fire were almost evident coming from his eyes. He wasn't about to let that cat get away.

All I could do was yell "STOP! Bob was shouting. Margaret stood in shocked disbelief at the behavior of her guard cat and this little innocent-looking dog terrorizer. Bob Andrews came into the house also in shock and complete denial that his cat, the terror of Freshwater Bay and the horror all dogs dreaded, was running for his life and worse from a tiny little dog at that.

Dusty caught a light stand as he flew back into the living room causing a crash and shot right out the front door. Bob grabbed Otto as he headed for the open door fortunately, or we might not have seen him for days.

Dusty disappeared for three days after the incident. It turned out Dusty hated dachshunds! Surprise! I wonder if he had met any before. He seemed to know exactly what to do when he spotted Otto. Escape!

Otto, Jr., Terrorizer of Cats

I am still good friends with the Andrews. One year they took all of the kids in grades four through eight from Klukwan School on a week-long field trip by ferry to Seattle to teach them about traveling. The whole group came over and spent one night with us on Vashon Island. By that time I had probably tested every one of those kids so got to know them fairly well.

When we adopted our two kids from Peru at the end of 1986, Bob and Margaret became their God Parents. The kids also stayed with the Andrews for three weeks going to school in Klukwan and living in their apartment above the school in the spring of 1987 shortly after we arrived back from Peru in January of that year.

CHAPTER 22

The Police are After Us

Metlakatla, the only Tsimshian village in Alaska, is located on Annette Island. It is a short flight from Ketchikan. I had a contract with the Annette Islands School District for 40 days my first year and consequently traveled to Metlakatla on an almost monthly basis. That was the most days I had with any school district that year or most years for that matter.

The main island is across the Revillagigedo Channel from Alaska's mainland on the east and across from Revillagigedo Island on the north. The island's one village was originally laid out in a neat grid pattern and contained a church, a school, a tannery, and a saw mill.

There were a number of red-headed natives in the village, more so than usual for a village this size. Historically a community of Tsimshian people had followed a missionary William Duncan from the Anglican Church of England to their new home in Alaska after leaving their previous home in British Columbia, Canada. The United States Congress granted recognition to the new community in 1891 by creating the Annette Islands Reserve, a federal Indian reservation. History according to several residents told me that William Duncan had red hair.

I stayed at the "Tea House," part of an old cannery that operated during the summer but was used by the school district during the winter months for visitors like me. There were six bedrooms and one very ugly dog named "*Ikyek*". That means "ugly" in Eskimo. She was part husky and part pit bull, and belonged to the special education teacher and his wife who managed the Tea House and who had transferred from Eek in the Lower Kuskokwim School District hence Ikyek's Eskimo name. She was a love. In addition to getting a "dog fix" when I visited, the district provided me with a room as well as breakfast and supper.

There were always interesting distractions for me ranging from meeting artists to making sure I took home a bag of frozen shrimp I had purchased from the cannery when they were available. I met a couple of artists who taught in the school. I purchased a print from Tsimshian artist David Boxley of "the killer whales battle with the devil fish". I also bought two very nice water colors of surrounding islands by Norman Campbell, another teacher, in 1985.

Most of my trips to Metlakatla were in a de Havilland Beaver on floats. It was a single-engine, high-wing, propeller-driven aircraft that I rode to and from Ketchikan's airport, although there were a couple of exceptions that were noteworthy as I will explain later.

The first trip to the community caught me arriving the afternoon before I needed to be there and that meant free time. It allowed me to explore the community with my camera. The couple in the Tea House lent me their pickup, drew me a map, and sent me on my way. I drove past the cemetery to the beach then walked along its shore. A momentary breeze carried the smells of salt and mud and fish. Fall colors blended in with the outgoing tide. The wet sand left behind reflected the sun's rays as they played tag with the retreating waves. There were a few broken clam shells on the beach. The beauty was momentarily spoiled when I looked down and saw a dead duck—shot in the neck. How senseless it was to kill I thought to myself. I felt very badly as I could hear shots in the distance and wondered about other ducks.

I climbed back in the pickup and drove a little further to a large water duct under the road. A few of the salmon were making their last attempts to complete their life cycle—some had already made it through the duct at high tide and were depositing their eggs and sperm. Many more were flopping around as the tide continued on its journey's rush out to sea. Some of the fish had already died.

Blue jays were busily feeding on them. The jays flew off when I arrived, and would not come back as long as I was there. I suspected with good cause. I watched for a while and knew this was the way things were with salmon. Even those who made it to the other side of the road would die once they deposited their eggs and fertilized them guaranteeing future generations of the species.

Flying into Metlakatla's Float-Plane Dock

Driving back to the Tea House I actually got lost and finally had to ask for directions. It was a good-sized village having around 1,300 plus people living there. I got turned around.

That night the special education teacher insisted I go with him to meet the principal. The superintendent was there as well. They seemed glum. I learned one of the 16-year old high school students had almost died from an overdose of Angel Dust the previous Friday evening. He was from an old Tsimshian family. I ended up testing him the next day not because he had overdosed but because his three-year re-evaluation was due. I also spent some time talking with his parents. One wonders how real "almost dying" is for a 16-year old who looks as healthy as a horse—he said he was afraid of dying, but that thought I suspect was quickly buried until the next time if and when he was foolish enough to get into drugs again. I also tested a second 16-year old boy whose father was Aleut and who had just moved from Old Harbor on Kodiak Island.

Metlakatla was a comfortable place to work. I didn't feel the pressures there as I did in other communities. Maybe I got too complacent as that was one of only two schools in which I had something stolen from me. My wallet was taken on the last day of one of my visits complete with a St. Monica medal I carried and all the cash I had necessitating a need to borrow money in order to get home. The other theft occurred years later in Sand Point School in the Aleutians where one of the students stole a stop watch I carried. Fortunately, it was a spare.

Margaret Piggott, a physical therapist, who also worked for SERRC, frequented the district almost as much as I did. One of my more memorable meetings with her was not the time we spent there but in leaving Metlakatla on one of my later trips.

Both Margaret and I found ourselves leaving the community at the same time. This time we would fly out on the same plane together from the land airport rather than going out from the float plane dock right in town. The airport was out of town and not used much at all. I was surprised. Bob and I had landed there once ten or more years earlier just to look around. At least at that time there were people at the airport, only one or two as I remember, but people were working there nevertheless.

We loaded our gear into a shuttle van that the district provided along with a couple of other travelers who were visiting the district and heading back to Ketchikan. I sat directly behind the driver in the second row while Margaret was in the third row and in the middle seat. One of the others sat next to her and the other passenger was in the back row.

The weather was good, the road while not paved was quite passable, and we were all busy talking. The van suddenly lurched forward and came to an abrupt stop after swerving into the ditch at a rather odd angle. We were stuck, although we weren't going fast enough to cause any real damage. Despite all of us being jostled around, the van appeared okay. No one seemed to be hurt, just shook up. I was still clinging to the seat back I had hold of when we hit. It turned out later that Margaret broke a front tooth.

I looked at the driver and wondered if he had fallen asleep at the wheel. He didn't appear impaired, and certainly there was no smell of alcohol on him. The young man radioed for help and got out to make an assessment of the situation.

He returned to his seat. Another vehicle drove up shortly

thereafter. We transferred our baggage into it and continued to the airport. The plane, a PBY, was waiting for us to arrive. Everything was quickly loaded into the baggage compartment and we boarded.

The pilot taxied out onto the runway and did his run up first checking one engine and then the other. He applied full throttle as we roared down the runway for a smooth takeoff. Looking back out the window I could see a police car racing after us with lights flashing trying to get the plane to stop. Sirens could be heard faintly above the engines' roar. We just kept going. The police were after us.

The pilot wasn't about to turn around, land, and wait for each of us to be interviewed to determine what happened. I doubt that any of us would have been able to add much to a police report anyway. We flew on to Ketchikan.

Other times when Margaret and I got together provided mini adventures as well. Both of us found ourselves working in the Pribilof Islands at St. George School in the Pribilof School District at the same time years later. Margaret took off hiking along the cliffs and on the beach below the town after she finished seeing kids while I stayed and wrote reports although I was tempted to go. She told me she found some interesting birds as well as a fox with his snout firmly in a plastic bottle. The bottle covered his face and eyes. She chased him and tried to throw a coat over him so that she could get the plastic bottle off. I understand she seized the plastic bottle but couldn't hold on to it. The fox ran towards the cliffs and disappeared down the sheer slopes. That time I regretted not being with her to provide additional help to catch the fox and pluck the bottle off his nose.

Another meeting with Margaret was in King Salmon when she asked the special education director in a very startled voice, "What is it?" pointing at his wire-haired dachshund named Nicky when the dog followed him into the room. I had already met Nicky.

We became friends, although both of us were usually quite busy and our time together in a school was brief. When Bob passed away in June of 1995, I flew to Scotland and spent two weeks traveling with Margaret all over the country. She was from Scotland and decided to spend that summer with her mom. I confused the date of departure and missed my flight back to the U.S. Her mother from that time on always referred to me as

"Margaret's American friend who missed the flight to America." But that's another story.

Usually flying back and forth to Ketchikan's airport went without a hitch. But one Thanksgiving the weather didn't cooperate. Referred to as "the Thanksgiving Day Storm" flights had been cancelled because the weather was so bad. The only way off the island was by ferry. I had a shot at the one jet going through Ketchikan that day by catching the ferry. After a rough crossing that lasted at least two hours with some of its passengers getting sea sick we landed at the ferry dock in Ketchikan with the airport fully in view but on the other side of Revillagigedo Channel. I remember getting off the ferry and standing on the dock looking across the narrow body of water that separated me from the airport almost in tears as I watched the last and only jet that day take off for Seattle.

CHAPTER 23

Some No-Win Moments

It wasn't very long into the first year when Bob made it quite clear he was not happy with my new job. In fact, he was very unhappy with my working in Alaska. I wasn't expecting that. His comments about coming up every month petered out before the end of the first month, although he did make occasional trips. Once in Juneau he was fine. But back on Vashon he was angry and let me know it.

I had made a commitment and I wasn't going to let my new boss down. When Twyla indicated she was concerned about my "not lasting the winter" I wondered if she had had a conversation with Bob that I didn't know about. Possibly, I thought, but I made up my mind that I was not going to quit.

During those first few months I telephoned Bob almost daily when in Juneau and frequently ended up in tears. His comments were designed to lay a guilt trip on me. He became overly demanding about the money I was making and what I was doing with it. He was an accountant and I was careful to send him receipts, list telephone calls I made, and let him know about every dime I made in detail. I wanted to keep him involved. I was beginning to have a hard time meeting his demands and maintaining my job.

There was no doubt in my mind that I missed Bob and the dogs. Most of my waking moments were spent thinking of reasons for him to come up with the dachshunds and be with me. There had been no hint of Bob's being upset with me before I accepted the job, or if there was I missed it. He encouraged me to take it. But now! Our phone conversations were a surprise as I wasn't expecting his negativism. We had just never discussed that he was at the end of his career while I was at the beginning of my career. I tried to include him when I could.

Added to Bob's negative attitude, not all of the places I visited were easy. Occasionally it was like fighting a no-win situation in working with the kids. Maybe reality was setting in. "The honeymoon was over," so to speak, as far as my having the perfect job, but then I knew it would be a challenge, and that's part of what I enjoyed about it. Hydaburg was one of those districts in which it was an uphill battle trying to turn a negative situation around.

Hydaburg, a Haida village on Prince of Wales Island in Southeastern Alaska, had a new school superintendent and a new special education director when I first visited it. The director was from the Lower 48 and panicked over the phone when I indicated I had a full schedule in the fall. He was facing some serious problems and wanted me to come right away. I sensed he was almost in shock. I agreed to visit the district at the end of the month—that was back in September when I had talked with him.

False Pass

It was the first of October in 1983 when I initially visited the community.

Flying there the previous day from Ketchikan I thought seriously of getting off the plane when we made a stopover at Klawock to let some passengers off. The fog and bad weather moving in made for very poor flying conditions. The pilot wasn't very old in spite of his balding spot, and he was "cock sure" of himself—those were the types that bothered me. I felt they took chances, unnecessary ones. I didn't want to be flying on their planes. Bob's comment that "there are no old, bold pilots" came to mind.

One of the agents mentioned a problem before I got on the plane. That set the tone for the flight as far as my thoughts went. The unknown "problem" and heading for Hydaburg unnerved me bit. I wondered about the pilot, and if whatever it was affected his flying. The noise factor from the Beaver's engine on the morning flight also added to my discomfort. It was just as bad with the Otter's loud engine on the return flight. It wouldn't take very many flights I thought before I would end up with a significant hearing loss. I needed ear plugs.

Despite my concerns the plane I was on made it just fine to Hydaburg without incident, landed in the water once there and taxied over to the dock. Everything looked normal as I climbed out of the plane and headed to the school. The agent helped me with my belongings.

I was fascinated by the totem poles in front of the school building. They were weathered and had not been kept up as had the totems in Klawock, another community located on Prince of Wales Island and one I also visited.

Added to the weather and loud engine, negative comments about the district had surfaced. I knew it was the lowest paying district in the State and that teachers usually left after one year of service if they lasted that long. I wondered at the time if it was only due to salary. One of the fathers later complained to me that "when you pay bottom salary to your teachers, you draw inexperience or 'bottom of the barrel'."

I had also been told by someone from SERRC that on one visit they made to Hydaburg, they had to hide in someone's home to wait for the plane because they were afraid some of the locals who were after them and hinted potential violence. I was curious as to what that was all about and when it had happened. I was never to learn the specifics nor did I ever feel threatened when visiting the district.

If that wasn't enough, a state CPS (Child Protective Services) worker I had met told me that well over 50 percent of the sex abuse cases were in Hydaburg. She added that upwards to 90 percent of the child abuse cases were also from that village. The teachers didn't dare report abuse if they wanted to keep their jobs even though they were required by law to report suspicions. They were afraid of the local residents.

What did the village elders think, and what did they imagine tomorrow's generation would be like? The answers didn't come. Perhaps the ancient legend of the Killer Whale with two dorsal fins was indeed returning but not to overturn a boat with some boys aboard, but to overturn a people because they did not heed their own traditions.

I met an Eskimo woman while there who was the daughter of one of the women I had interviewed three years earlier in Marshall on the Yukon River. She was one of the mothers, and had a three-year old son she was concerned about raising in the community. She also told me that in order to make it she had to take in visitors to cover expenses. I was staying with her at the time. I couldn't help but wonder why and how she ever left Marshall and moved to Hydaburg. I didn't ask. Sometimes it was better not to know.

When I later heard about one of the locals taking a chain saw to another individual, it really didn't surprise me. It almost seemed the norm based on some of the situations I heard about while in the community. Violence was the norm as well as abuse both physical and sexual. Much if not all was related to alcohol. I wasn't sure about drugs, as they had not been mentioned unlike other communities I had visited. I suspected they were there. I just didn't hear about it.

On that initial trip I saw my first FAS or Fetal Alcohol Syndrome child. She was six and a half years old. She had been deformed prior to birth although her facial features were not nearly as bad as kids I later saw in other communities. Apparently, certain foods, like sugar, caused violent reactions in the girl—chemical reactions similar to being drunk I was told. She was quite small for her age, and had been identified as a communication disordered child, but appeared okay in most language areas at the time I saw her. There were suggestions on the intelligence scale that she had some bright spots, but there was a lot that could not be retrieved because of prenatal damage.

A plane took off while I was testing her. She heard it and told me her mom was on the plane. Later, her teacher told me that meant the mother would be gone for several weeks if not months to Ketchikan and would be drinking the entire time. I was told that the mother had been drunk much of the first trimester of her pregnancy with the girl. I felt very badly when I heard that. Fetal Alcohol Syndrome was very preventable. I knew there were lots of other kids out there like her. The father, in this instance, was reported to be a very caring man and took good care of the little girl. She had been identified early so she was able to get needed services including speech therapy. But I knew there were a lot more learning problems than speech therapy could solve.

Waiting for the plane to leave Hydaburg I saw one large dog "humping" another one. I couldn't help but think of the pups that would probably result and wondered about their future. I had heard about "dog-shooting" when I was in Metlakatla. Any dog caught off leash was taken out to the dump and shot! It was something that happened in the villages. There's some finality in that, but I know I couldn't save all the dogs in Alaska or any other place. An aside, I did save two pups many years later in the Aleutians. Tosca and Lucia lived with me until they passed away at fourteen plus years old. Their daddy was a village dog, while their mom was a purebred griffon pointer that some teacher foolishly let run with the locals while she was in heat.

On the flight back to Ketchikan I did a lot of reflecting.

Bob finally decided to fly up to Juneau and bring the dachshunds with him at the end of October. It turned out to be a big mistake that would leave me devastated but neither of us knew it at the time, that is, until Halloween night when we lost our dachshund Moose. The bush plane dropped me off at Ketchikan Airport's floatplane dock. I made my way up the long ramp making a couple of trips in order to carry all my baggage as well as test equipment to the top of the ramp. The tide was out so it was steeper than usual. My shoulders wanted to scream when I came up the second time. I ignored them.

Once in the airport terminal I found I was the only passenger.

It was a funny feeling to be the only person sitting there. People didn't come to this airport until the last minute. I watched as a patrol car drove the length of the runway, checking, I supposed, for foreign objects before the jet landed. That was comforting. The tiny ferry from Ketchikan should arrive shortly and would have people aboard who were meeting the jet as well as passengers catching the outgoing flight.

There was a cat in the terminal, and he had been there a long time. He stayed downstairs and did not go up to the passenger lounge or at least I don't think he did as I had never seen him up there. He was long-haired, and often curled up on one of the chairs. Sometimes he strolled to the baggage-check area. He looked very well fed and happy, and would roll over for a scratch on his belly or stop for a few scratches on his head. I know. We had met.

CHAPTER 24

Where the North Wind Doesn't Blow

Hoonah brings back a mixture of emotions. I had visited the community twice before I ever worked in Alaska when I made my first trip to the village as their official school psychologist on October 4, 1983, and right after I left Hydaburg! I associated it with ravens, possibly because they were always there when I arrived and there were so many of them.

Previous to that October visit I had been there three years earlier in late summer with Bob and the dachshunds in the Bonanza. When I first flew into this community, there was nothing at the airport except the runway and the ravens. The moment I opened the door of the plane I could hear them calling. A hundred yards from us I saw four of them in flight. The dachshunds saw them as well and wanted to chase.

Getting out of the plane in 1980 we headed towards town on the nearby road that led to the village. A dark and very damp forest soon closed in around us as we walked along the dirt and gravel roadway. No people were around. A few steps into the trees the largest raven I have ever seen stood on a moss-covered log that was rotting. He blended in perfectly with the trees' shadows. His piercing eyes were directed towards me as he quietly sized me up. A most uncanny feeling settled over me. It was as if the ancestors of many previous generations were staring at me and asking me "what are you doing here?" His shining eyes continued to follow me until I came to a bend in the road.

Later as we walked back I looked for the unusually large raven as I passed by the decaying log. He wasn't there.

The marina had been expanded by the time Bob and I made our second visit to the community. This time we were on our boat during the summer months. The dogs were with us as well. The marina had a new rock barrier built up around it. By then the airport had a partially-built terminal I learned.

Hoonah (*Xunaa* in Tlingit) is a largely Tlingit community on Chichagof Island located on Alaska's panhandle in the southeastern part of the state. It is thirty miles west of Juneau. I reminded myself that Chichagof was one of those three islands in Southeastern Alaska that has brown bears.

A group known as the Huna Tlingit had lived in the general area for many hundreds of years, originally occupying what is now known as Glacier Bay as well as Icy Strait, Cross Sound, and the outer coast north to Sea Otter Creek. Historically, two catastrophic events forced them from their homeland: first there was the rapid glacial advance in Glacier Bay, and the second was a landslide-induced tsunami that made landfall in Lituya Bay along the outer coast. Tlingit oral tradition recounted these events as well as the clan's ultimate resettlement in the 1750s.

The clan chose to permanently move twenty miles to the south where they had subsistence-harvested each summer. The new settlement was referred to as *Gaawt'ak.aan*, or "village by the cliff." Later its name was changed to *Xunaa* or "where the north wind doesn't blow" in the Tlingit language. Hoonah became the official spelling in 1901. It had a population of 1,089 in 1980 when I visited there to interview women for my dissertation. The population fluctuated and dramatically increased during the summer months with fishing and later tourism.

Upon further research, I learned that on June 14, 1944 a disastrous fire destroyed much of the town. Sadly, homes filled with ancient and priceless objects of the Tlingit culture were lost. The federal government helped to rebuild the town by diverting World War II housing that was in route to Hawaii to Hoonah. These houses, located in the downtown area, were called the "war houses." The Hoonah Packing Company built in 1912 and shut down in 1953 became a tourist attraction. There is still a cold storage operating there which freezes and ships salmon, crab, cod, black cod, and halibut.

This was one of those villages I visited fairly often when I started working for SERRC. Bad vibes hit me when I walked into the school the first few times. Maybe it started with anticipation of the kids I was scheduled to see as there were some difficult situations although I always faced challenges head on. Or, possibly, it was the staff and the disagreements they were having with each other. I continued to have negative feelings for some time as there were a number of problems.

I soon discovered there were a variety of places to stay including a small down town hotel, a lodge on the road to the airport, and in later years a Bed and Breakfast. Usually the chefs were good as they cooked for the tourists as well as other visitors, so I ate well in the evenings. At least one of those chefs, however, had a drinking problem and didn't last very long—too bad, I thought, because he was an excellent cook. School lunches were okay as I recall. I visited the preschool several times and on one occasion had morning snacks with the kids. I mostly observed while they ate.

I slowly began to feel more positive as I visited the district more and more. Part of it, I suppose, was that I met some of the teachers and staff and felt I was welcome in the community. I knew that in some schools it just took longer for me to establish myself, and this was one of them. Getting to know the superintendent and his wife who was the preschool teacher also helped. Tom and Susan Brown were wonderful people and fun to know. I still hear from them at Christmas time.

I thought about the art class I had seen. The teacher was focusing on Tlingit art. I really liked the paddles that some of the students had done and was able to purchase one that had been painted by a native high school girl. I look at it hanging on my office wall from time to time and think of my long-ago visits to this village that I remember as being almost magical. It was the ravens, I thought, and their almost mystical presence every time I visited.

One visit I made the discovery of two small kittens, possibly abandoned, living under the lodge. They had survived the winter months so all couldn't have been that bad. Both seemed fearful of humans. Neither one was about to have anything to do with me, but I reasoned they must be getting fed as they did not look skinny. Both of them were gray, one with long hair while the other had short hair.

I had often been asked if there were different problems among school children in Alaska than in the Lower 48. My response was "Kids can't read in Alaska just like they can't read anywhere else." One particularly reflective evening in early May of 1985 at the end of my second year working in Alaskan schools, I thought about that comment as I sat and began writing that evening in the lodge that was located on the road to the airport. There were many problems particularly when I considered the village only had roughly a 1,000 people in it. The population and the frequency in which problems occurred was overwhelming when compared to each other. I thought about situations that were evident on my current trip.

The one girl I evaluated earlier that day was a victim of abuse. Older alcoholic brothers still in the home and an alcoholic father were suggested as her abusers. Those were the stories I heard from others. Her emotional response to policemen was guarded, but then another one of her brothers had been the police chief at one time, couldn't stand all the problems and blew his brains out or so the story goes!

Or, I thought to myself about one of the boys I was supposed to see. He didn't return from halibut fishing the day before so was unavailable. He had just moved from New York to live with his dad, and he couldn't read very well. The local villagers began looking and found the camp where the boy, his dad, and his dad's friend had been. The fire was out and cold. Dead halibut were floating around nearby in the water. Later the "kicker" or boat motor was found as well as life preservers. They were last seen alive on the previous Saturday. It was four days later.

The night before I was told about an old drunk woman who fell on the road. Later she was run over by an inebriated logger. Rumors ranged from a "broken arm" to "she's dying!"

These stories all happened around one trip. I thought about the previous summer when Bob and I had our boat in the harbor. One of the engine repairmen came down to the dock to help Bob with some repairs. He told us about a mother chopping her husband to death the night before and in front of their four-year old son. I later saw the newspaper clipping. I realized I had just seen that child on this trip when I went through his records.

A flashing blue light passed the lodge where I was staying on its way to the airport. Some emergency I thought to myself. Was it an accident or what? I was never to find out what happened.

Monday, an airplane in route from Hoonah to Juneau hit a mountain in the Funter Pass terrain. Both the passenger and a very young pilot were lucky as a helicopter picked them up three hours after it happened. Both were unhurt. I often flew over that pass as it was a shortcut to Juneau.

I continued writing. When I looked up again, I noted the emergency vehicle was going back towards town.

The field next to me conjured up all sorts of images in my mind, including bears, deer, and especially the ravens. But what did I see, nothing more than a large black cat running along, attacking some unsuspecting bug mid-air then continuing her return home. It was almost black outside, although there was a bit of light that added character to the cat that had long since lost her shadow due to the on-coming night.

CHAPTER 25

"Closest to the Fish"

Flying to Pelican from Juneau I spotted a brown bear near Hoonah running along a salmon stream. I suspected the bear was running as a result of the noise from the plane going over head. We weren't very high. At the time I was in the Goose, one of the amphibian planes flown by Channel Flying Service. It was my first visit to this community that had been founded as a fish processing site in 1938.

Pelican is one of those interesting Southeastern Alaskan fishing communities located on the northwest coast of Chichagof Island on Lisianski Inlet. It is roughly 100 miles west of Juneau and 90 miles north of Sitka. Much of the town was built on pilings over the tidelands and connected by a broad boardwalk. "Closest to the Fish" is the community's motto as it boasts both freshwater and salt water fish availability. It was no surprise to me that there were lots of fishermen in town when I arrived.

Commercial fishermen loved to drink and party when they were on shore. I had heard that Rose's Bar and Grill was their hangout and the place to be as it was a fairly notorious establishment on the boardwalk between the marina and the school. By day it appeared to be a quaint little place to relax and enjoy. At night, however, when the boats were in, there was a dramatic transformation as things livened up.

Not only did I eat an occasional meal there in the evening, I also stayed in the "hotel" that was right next door and also run by Rose. It was separate but adjacent to the bar. I distinctly remember noise drifting into the room as I tried to sleep on one of my later trips to Pelican. I had heard rumors that Rose tried to "pants" or partially undress the men once they were drunk amid yelling and raucous laughter. Whether this happened or not, I don't know as I never observed. I guess she left the women alone although I suspect there were very few women there. When I did eat there, few people in the bar either male or female were evident.

After testing all day that first day on October 17, 1983, I found my way to a 53-foot motor sailor, the *Demijohn*, which had been set up as one of the hotels in town. I had jumped at the opportunity to stay aboard the "yacht". The marina was fairly good sized but the *Demijohn* with its mast was easy to find among the other boats tied up at one of the docks. The air smelled of damp and salt, and in the back ground there was always the constant murmur of the tide. I made my way to the *Demijohn*. I always felt good on a boat snug in a harbor.

Quite a bit of weather had moved in by the time I had finished in the school that first day there. It was raining, really raining, when I boarded the boat. It was fortuitous that I had brought my serious rain gear including bib overalls and boots, although I didn't bring the right kind of jacket. Gail Corbin, owner of the boat, loaned me one so I was set for the next two days.

I felt very comfortable aboard even though the boat was moving around on its mooring lines. The wind caused the rigging to hit against the mast in the middle of the night and that put me right to sleep. It was a familiar sound.

Looking around the boat the first night I discovered that there was a three-year old Dickinson heater aboard and no problems with carbonization. I was thinking of our boat and why we had problems. The top of the heater, however, was not good according to Gail's comments as it was aluminum. As we talked a bit, she learned I was from Vashon. It turned out her husband's grandfather built up Corbin Beach on Vashon Island maybe a mile north of where Bob and I lived. Small world I thought to myself.

I ate supper that first night at Amelie's home. She was the main teacher I worked with at the school and seemed quite knowledgeable about the community. They had an overfed dog named Nicki and a very playful cat named Cricket, although he would have been better named Bandit because of his black mask similar to that of a raccoon.

While at Pelican's school on that trip, I only had three gifted kids to test plus a reading inventory and test for another child. It turned into an easy schedule for me particularly after having just visited the two communities of Hydaburg and Hoonah earlier in the month with all the problems they had and a difficult schedule of testing. I left in the middle of the afternoon on Wednesday for Juneau and didn't even go to our boat as I had a 6 pm flight on Skagway Air heading for Haines, so I just stayed at the airport.

The Demijohn—in Pelican

I have to admit in retrospect that if I had had the choice when visiting Pelican, I much preferred staying aboard the *Demijohn* in the marina than at Rose's even though the latter had lots of "color" and was closer to the school. I only stayed the one time on the boat as it wasn't available on later trips much to my regret.

On another visit to Pelican after testing at the school I managed to get some freshly caught black cod to take back to my boat. I distinctly remember arriving in Juneau with the fish, going to the boat harbor in Douglas where our boat was, and having to cut the fish up and pack them into usable packages. There was an icy wind that evening. With bent head against it I could feel its sting against my face as I hovered over my bag of fish on the end of the dock with a hose and fresh water as I cut up each fish. I was cold and tried to stay relatively dry as it started raining in earnest. My fingers felt frozen as I didn't have any proper gloves for working with fish. It was a bad decision to bring the fish home but later the fish tasted delicious when I shared them with Bob. Before I had finished processing them, I vowed I would never bring home any more unpackaged fish. Obviously, I changed my mind when I tasted them.

Bob had flown up for a few days right after this trip and loved fresh fish almost as much as I did. He was still unhappy, however, with my working in Alaska and once he returned home his negative remarks on the phone continued. Some of the time on Vashon, I think, he was bored and resented my having adventures without him. During the summers, of course, the two of us spent together cruising in Alaskan waters.

CHAPTER 26

A Lost Moose

Finally, October 1983 was almost over and Bob flew up with the dachshunds to spend time with me and work on the boat, making a few repairs including the ceiling leak I had discovered and getting it ready for winter. I think he wanted a break from the accounting he was doing on Vashon for one of his clients. It was really good to have him as well as the dachshunds back with me even though it was only for a few days. Little did either one of us know that our few days would end in a tragedy.

Once in Juneau Bob seemed happy about being back in Alaska. He almost seemed to have fun making some of the repairs needed, and visiting with our friends, Larry and Janice. The dachshunds immediately recognized their home away from home on the boat and ran around inside and all over the deck with excitement having a wonderful time chasing their tails and playing. As for me I couldn't hug them enough. While I was at work they spent the days with Bob. I had lots of reports to write from the busy month I had just put in and was trying to finish them up as I was scheduled to go to Skagway on the first of November.

The afternoon of the day before Bob was to leave he called me with the dreaded news that Moose was gone. He had disappeared and was lost. He had searched all over but he couldn't find him. It was Halloween. Panic hit me square in the stomach. It wasn't just an uneasy feeling. I was afraid, really scared. An empty feeling settled inside me.

I immediately left the office; my reports could wait. Bob met me with the car and we headed out towards the airport where he had been with the dogs.

Bob had stopped by a repair shop near the airport to pay a bill, and had tied the dachshunds up to the bumper of the car. He got to talking with one of the men inside and took longer than he intended. Along came some kids in Halloween costumes and scared Moose who bolted and backed out of his collar then ran to get away from them. The kids tried to catch him without letting Bob know that he was gone. Bob kept talking and talking to people in the shop and didn't come out until Moose had completely disappeared. By then Bob realized the kids had scared him.

Why he had tied the dogs up to the bumper of the car and not put them inside the car where they would have been safe remains a mystery to me to this day. Bob tried to find Moose in the immediate area before he called me. This was the same little Moose who had accompanied us 13,000 miles all over Alaska while I was doing research on my dissertation. He was my very special little dog. He had been my Moose since the middle of the night when I heard whimpering and found him outside under the cedar tree where his mother had just given birth to him. I carried him inside along with his mom where she then had his five other siblings. He became the story teller in my first book.

"Moose!" There was no sign of him. "Moose! Come, Moose!" I called and called his name again and again. We didn't hear any familiar barks nor did we find anyone who had seen him. We kept hunting for him, driving up and down all the nearby roads and calling his name until well after dark and very late in the evening. During that time the two of us drove up and down every road we could find near the airport and then we drove back over them again and again. I called and called and prayed that we would find him. The main highway wasn't far away but we didn't go out on it, because surely Moose would have stayed away from the highway. He didn't. We were to find that out later.

The next morning the local radio station announced that a dachshund had been hit on the highway and taken to the local veterinarian and left. I called the vet, and it very much sounded like my "Moosie". We drove out to his office, which was between the airport and town. I knew it was Moose. After all Juneau wasn't known for having dachshunds. I was sick when we walked in and there he laid cold and stiff. He had died after being dropped off.

Bob left that day for Vashon with our other two dachshunds. Needing to make a trip to Skagway I took Moose's body with me to bury him in the Lingle's backyard. His father, Otto Senior, had been tragically killed and buried there almost three years earlier on the Fourth of July so I wanted to bury Moose next to his daddy. Otto's death had happened just a month before the remaining three dachshunds, Bob, and I had left on my research trip flying all over Alaska in 1980.

Bea dug a grave next to Otto's and we buried Moose once I arrived.

Then she poured me a drink, and kept pouring them. Bob told me I was drunk on the phone when I called him as by that time he was back on Vashon. I guess if he says so, I was, but I didn't feel that I was.

I wrote a "thank you" note to the radio station for letting its listeners know that Moose's family had been found. Larry Schultz, the neighbor from Vashon who had moved to Juneau, said he heard "Uncle Fats" say here's a letter, and started to read it. He was the local radio announcer. He choked up, played a record then came back on the air and read the letter in its entirety saying it was good to know someone really appreciated little dogs. Larry went on to tell me the announcer had two little Pomeranians himself.

I doubt I ever got completely over missing Moos—every time I thought about him I started to choke up. Testing the next day in Skagway I almost lost it and teared up.

We don't know how very lucky we are until we lose something, and Bob and I both lost something very special when we lost Moose.

I returned to Juneau on November 5th and went directly to the office. There were some flowers and a note signed from Rob and Mikke (his golden retriever and Kodi's sister). Rob was Bob's oldest son who was working in Haines at the time.

CHAPTER 27

Shades of the Wild West

It finally happened—a parent greeted me at the front door with a revolver strapped to his waist. At least, I thought to myself, it wasn't drawn so I could only assume it wasn't for my benefit.

Towards the end of my first year, March 8, 1984 to be exact, I drove up to Mosquito Lake Elementary School. It is 27 miles north of Haines and near the Canadian border. Bob and I had flown over the area a number of times in earlier years when we went over the pass north of Haines and into Canadian airspace but it wasn't until that day in March that I realized how beautiful the valley was. There was quite a bit of snow on the ground. The nearby river still had some ice remaining in it. Most of the trees were bare of foliage and offered a stark contrast to the snow and glistening ice. Against the blue sky the area appeared as if it had been part of an artist's painting.

The school was part of the Haines Borough School District, but was located north of Klukwan, which was a small Tlingit village in the Chatham School District. The other schools in the Haines district were located in Haines proper and included an elementary school, as well as a junior high and high school. Kids graduating from Mosquito Lake's elementary school were bused in to Haines for high school as were the kids from Klukwan despite it being in a separate district. I served both districts over the years.

I didn't even know there was a school in Mosquito Lake until

I was asked to go there and do a three-year re-evaluation on a boy who had been diagnosed with autism. I doubted I would have much to add to the recommendations already made, but it was required by law.

Bob's oldest son Rob lived in Haines, and among other things drove a school bus for the school district. He lived in the apartment in the building that housed Haines Home Building Supply, and did some work for Bruce, a one-time customer of Bob's. That included shoveling snow off the roof of the building. When I worked in Haines, I sometimes stayed with Rob in the apartment.

Rob loaned me his Volkswagen beetle to get around, and on this occasion for the drive north to Mosquito Lake. I always enjoyed any kind of a road trip. Three or four thousand eagles congregated in mass mainly in November to feed on the salmon just south of Klukwan. The river didn't freeze up as early as other rivers and salmon were still crowding its waters providing a much sought-after food source for the eagles. It being early spring, however, meant I didn't see very many eagles although there were always a few hopefuls hanging around. They were used to cars stopping and people getting out to take pictures. I was one of those people stopping with a camera in hand on several occasions.

I had never been on the road north of Klukwan, although I visited Klukwan fairly often. I think I saw almost all of the kids in the school there at one time or another and before they went to high school in Haines.

A spectacular blue sky greeted me that March morning. The road had been plowed. It was warm and sunny, while Juneau had been socked in with drizzle and fog. It always amazed me to find Haines and Skagway beautiful and sunny while Juneau was experiencing nasty weather as they were only about a half hour flying time apart.

I arrived at the school and tested the boy. I reviewed some of the materials the teacher had for him including a handmade picture dictionary with pictures showing his schedule hour by hour allowing him to follow his school day. That was his "clock", his daily guide to follow. I also reviewed his records.

His parents had asked to meet with me after the testing was completed so I drove out to see them. Their house was easy to find and off the road maybe thirty feet with a driveway leading right to the front door.

I pulled into the driveway and immediately recognized my mistake as I became stuck in the snow. I walked up to the front door, knocked and when the door opened I found myself facing the dad complete with a six-shooter strapped to his hip. I was invited into the home.

We talked about the testing results, about recommendations, and about the boy's school program. I have to admit I was very careful in what I said. The community of Mosquito Lake I had understood at that time was made up of a number of free thinkers who wanted to stay apart from the towns and communities that were more populated. They wanted to do their own thing. They were part of the last frontier and lived off the land. I very much respected that.

No mention of the gun was made. I found it interesting, however, that he wore a revolver around inside his house and yard. He left shortly thereafter and his wife, a big woman, came out with me to the car when I told her I was stuck. She single-handedly pushed the Volkswagen right out of the snowbank with what appeared to be a minimum of effort on her part. She looked as if she could handle most situations. I was very appreciative to get back into the vehicle and be able to drive back to Haines.

As for the boy, he was getting the kind of educational program that he needed in this remote community at least at the time I saw him. His teacher was skilled in working with this autistic child and had his program well under control.

*One of many eagles along the highway between Haines
and Klukwan*

CHAPTER 28

A Dark Place

Described as beautiful, quaint, and out-of-the-way, Elfin Cove lies half hidden on the northwestern corner of Chichagof Island, 85 miles west of Juneau. Glacier Bay National Park was only a short boat ride away but could have been a million miles as far as I was concerned. Elfin Cove was part of Chatham's school district although there wasn't a school. My assignment—should I choose to accept it although I really didn't have a choice—was to test every school-age child there. The community was too small for a school, at least, an official school with certified teachers, but there were a few kids living there and an aid from the correspondence program.

I climbed aboard the Goose along with a fellow worker. She was headed for Pelican, a community that I also visited that was not far from Elfin Cove but a separate school district. The weather wasn't bad, but it was far from being good. Typical for Southeastern Alaska I thought as I sat in the plane. We made it to Pelican okay, and Linda got off. Oh, I wanted to get off with her, but, of course, couldn't. I was scheduled to go on to an unknown situation. The whole trip had come up rather suddenly for me, something the superintendent wanted done quickly. I only knew what he told me and that was very little.

The Goose shot across the water, took off, and in a few minutes made a landing in the middle of a large bay called Port

Althorp. We landed at an imaginary point in the middle of the bay. An open skiff complete with two outboard engines approached the plane. It had been idling in the water waiting until we stopped then moved into position for "easy" access, and I use the word loosely, to the plane. I climbed into it while two men jumped from the boat to the Goose as they were headed back to Juneau. My testing equipment and other belongings followed me with the help of the pilot.

The plane's door closed behind me. We slowly backed away from it. I turned around to take another look as the plane started to taxi across the water. I still recall the isolation and loneliness I felt as the Goose took off. My eyes followed its path through the water until it was airborne. I continued to watch until it disappeared from sight. I took in a deep breath then exhaled.

The school district's superintendent had told me to be prepared as he had experienced salt water coming into the boat on his trip to the community and had taken refuge behind a framed window—part of the freight. I didn't have a framed window to hide behind, but I did have my float coat and rain gear for boating, fortunately.

We started off, and kept going and going. The waves became higher and higher, and we just kept going. I had no idea where we were headed exactly. Oh, I had found it on a map, but that was different.

I sat holding a bunch of bananas for the teacher that I was meeting feeling a bit ridiculous. All the time I was fully aware that some stranger was keeping the outboard engine going. The second engine was a backup engine, I guess, in the event the first one stopped. I was the only passenger on board. It was a fairly small boat. The skipper seemed to know what he was doing. Salt spray hit me in the face. Even with my heavy float jacket on I was cold. My muscles ached. An hour later, or so it seemed, we suddenly turned directly into shore, ducked behind an outcrop of rock, and there was Elfin Cove.

I was greeted by the "new teacher" at the dock. She was one of the aids for the correspondence study program in bush Alaska. Her start date for this community was the following week.

She offered me a cup of tea—I readily accepted. Just then a parent came in followed by a second one. They had concerns. My heart dropped like an anchor in deep water. I felt as if I were the subject of the Inquisition listening to them. Parents naturally wondered why I was there. Secretly, so did I. I couldn't share everything because it was confidential.

I had two goals. The first was to test all of the school-age kids living there, and the second, while it included the first, was to assess two possibly handicapped kids who had just recently moved there. The superintendent didn't want me to focus on these two kids because of the smallness of the community; he didn't want to draw attention to them so he said "test them all". The local townspeople probably knew more about the second reason, I suspected, than I did. "The potential handicaps" had not been identified.

The minutes ticked away, and I realized time was crucial. I had to go to work. I downed my tea and followed the teacher to where I would be testing. Boardwalks connected the buildings and homes of about 20 year-round residents.

My office was a small cabin in among the trees where I would also be spending the night. Test equipment was dragged over to the building and one by one the kids came in to see me. By 10 pm that evening I was just about finished with the last girl for the day, when the lights went out. Katie, one of the oldest students I was testing at that point, volunteered, "It's the generator."

We lit a couple of candles readily available and continued with testing. I wondered about the validity of the testing in the semi-darkness, but Katie had good eyesight and was bright, very bright as a matter of fact, and handled it well. We did the Coding subtest and then one more verbal test and she left. I was sorry to see her go.

The cabin was lonely and away from the rest of the houses. In fact, there were no other buildings near me. My imagination started churning when I reviewed peoples' responses to me earlier in the day. The adventure of visiting this isolated community bothered me. People had seemed to be talking behind my back and would suddenly hush up when I came within hearing distance.

I conjured up all sorts of images as I pulled out my sleeping bag and laid it on the cot. My thoughts went wild, so much so I decided to block the door with my backpack and testing equipment. At least, I would have a little warning. Warning of what I thought to myself? Once I blew out the candles, blackness greeted me, and that night it was very dark as there was no moon or stars. I could barely see the trees outside as there was no reflective light from anywhere, although I knew they were there because I had seen them earlier in the day.

My mind began playing tricks on me. I wondered if something happened to me how long it would take before they found my body. "Stop this thinking!" I whispered to myself. "You're being ridiculous!" I had been reading too many murder mysteries I decided. I was safe. Just because the parents were asking lots of questions earlier was no reason to jump to the dark place my mind had taken me.

The next morning, I was awakened by sunlight, lots of it. The area's stunning scenery was spectacular. I realized my momentary lapse into the dark side last night was all in my imagination. I saw some more kids right after breakfast including the two "handicapped" ones. There were emotional problems but did not appear serious from what I could see. That afternoon Katie, the last girl I had tested the night before, invited me over to supper with her and her father.

The meal was excellent and fun. I felt relaxed. Both were friendly, interesting, and explained that the people in the community were on edge the previous day because of on-going problems with the generator. After all, it was their life line. They didn't want to worry me with the difficulties they were having so hushed up when I walked near anyone.

The following morning, I finished testing students fairly early. This time a (DHC-2) de Havilland Beaver on floats came up to the dock on the other side of the community from where I was when I arrived, so no boat ride or climbing into the Goose. Instead I had only a rather short walk over a small rise and just beyond the cabin on one of the boardwalks to the dock. I hadn't realized there was a dock there or that it was so close to where I was staying. The rise was just enough to block out what was beyond when I had entered the cabin. The superintendent hadn't mentioned it either, or if he had I wiped it completely out of my mind. It wasn't the first time I had flown in with one carrier, and out with another as the small air carriers serving these communities didn't go in every day. The mail, for example, might come in once a week and with whichever air carrier had the contract.

The pilot loaded my gear and me into the float plane and we headed for Juneau. I was the only passenger.

CHAPTER 29

Leaving a Logging Camp

Some of my trips were less stressful than others. In fact, some were sheer joy particularly when the weather was good and the testing went well. I remember one such perfect flight in Southeastern Alaska, but then that was the only part of the state where I flew in float planes. It was the right kind of day to fly and was what made my job extra special.

Float planes were always a fun way to travel around in the area. In some ways they were also safer when there was low visibility as one could theoretically land almost anywhere because of so much water in the area.

I smiled remembering one teacher telling me that she was in one when they were forced to land in a back bay to sit and wait for the weather to lift. She said she finally couldn't wait any longer and had to get out of the plane and crawl out on one of the pontoons in order to pee. She was on her way to one of the logging camps as a first-year teacher. When I heard that story, I thought to myself what an introduction that must have been to flying in southeastern Alaska.

As for me I was never on a float plane that had to land in an emergency and wait it out, and for that I am thankful. There were a few scary flights over the years when we took a short cut away from the water with a low overcast but they all ended well. I loved to fly in amphibians and always looked forward to it when I could.

That bright sunny day when there wasn't a cloud in the sky was memorable. I had been at Corner Bay, one of several logging camps I visited in the Chatham School District. I had a nice charter flight that cost $420 both ways; I was glad I was not paying. There were just seven kids enrolled. I had spent a day and a half there and had seen a couple of kids, including one girl who was deaf. I was quick to find out after meeting her that she read lips quite well, so I was feeling good about my testing. I also had a table with me that allowed for standardized scores to be interpreted for deaf kids. There was nothing wrong with her other faculties. She was fun to meet.

The girl had already been qualified as needing Special Education services because of her hearing impairment, and had recently transferred in to Corner Bay's tiny school. I understood the teacher wanted additional information in order to give her the best possible program. Besides it was the law that kids be assessed every three years. Her three-year evaluation was due. Some of the teachers in these small schools worked very hard at providing a quality education for the kids living there. This girl was lucky as her teacher was one of those dedicated individuals.

Once the testing was finished, I packed up my testing equipment and headed for the door. The maintenance man was already waiting to pick me up along with my baggage. He drove me to the dock and once there carried my testing kit and baggage down the ramp. After letting me out and saying goodbye he jumped back into his pickup and left. The plane was already waiting for me. I breathed in deeply as I walked down to join my luggage.

It was coming up on high tide so there wasn't much of an angle to where the plane was tied up. A smile surfaced. I had been known to set my testing kit at the top of a ramp during low tides and let it slide to the bottom praying the kit wouldn't burst open. It was heavy and took a toll on my shoulders every time I hauled it around.

The big "slide" occurred mainly at the Ketchikan Airport float dock. No problem here I thought as the pilot loaded my baggage quickly aboard the plane. Being the only passenger leaving the logging camp I jumped into the front seat next to the pilot's seat. We were headed for Juneau where there was always some air carrier employee available to handle baggage and get it to the main terminal unlike Ketchikan.

The bay was mirror calm. Once aboard the pilot closed my door, released the mooring lines and hopped onto the pontoon closest to the dock. He was quick to crawl under the plane's belly to the other pontoon where he stepped up into the plane. I snapped my seat belt into place. I was glad to be the only passenger. I definitely enjoyed riding in the "co-pilot" seat and didn't have to arm wrestle some other passenger for it although many individuals preferred to ride in the back seat. They didn't know what they were missing as the better view was in the front.

He started the engine. The propeller caught on the first try as we drifted out and away from the dock. The wash from a small motor boat passing in front of us reached us. It created tiny waves that were just big enough to gently rock the plane.

Excitement surged through me, the kind I always felt when I was flying especially in small planes. The pilot pushed the throttle full forward demanding we move straight ahead. The forward thrust pushed me back into my seat at the same time the plane sank down into the water just a bit. The water offered resistance at first keeping us earth bound. As the plane increased its speed, we rapidly picked up momentum. Abruptly the water released its hold on us as we became airborne gaining more altitude each moment. We shot out and over the water. I breathed deeply.

Directly ahead of us I could see two ducks dive deeply. Several more flew off to the sides of the plane's path. We couldn't have hit one if we had wanted to as they knew what they were doing, I thought as I watched them. They weren't about to become someone's duck dinner.

The pilot headed out towards Chatham Strait. Content I was at peace. I felt good all over as I watched the shoreline for deer or possibly even a bear. There was a lot of wildlife in the area and sometimes a deer or two could be seen down by the water but not this time.

The pilot eased back on the throttle, trimmed the tabs then adjusted the mixture control. We were only a few hundred feet above the water as we flew along the shore. I never tired of looking out the window. The hum of the plane's engine was soothing.

I looked around and could see Tenakee Springs across the bay to the north. Then, I glanced back to see the logging camp I had just left. Logs were piled high on its dock. They looked as if they were almost tinker toys getting smaller and smaller as we continued away from the camp. I wondered if they were to become a log raft and where they were headed. I knew this camp was owned by the same individual who owned Eight Fathom Bight, another logging camp I sometimes visited. We headed to Juneau. I sat back fully relaxed; after all I had the rest of the afternoon off.

On an earlier trip to Corner Bay I had actually taken a small motor boat from the logging camp directly across the bay to Tenakee Springs, but on this trip I wasn't scheduled to go there. I was thankful to be going back to Juneau, although the flight was way too short as far as I was concerned

Charter Flight Waiting—Corner Bay

CHAPTER 30

Blueberries for the Asking

Another day, another logging camp. This time it was Eight Fathom Bight also in the Chatham School District. It was an unusual name for a logging camp, I thought, but that's where I found myself that afternoon one early fall day probably in the mid-1980s. Schools in Alaska often started in August, and overlapped with the ripening of wild blueberries. That was a plus because the beginning of a school year was always busy, and teachers liked to get assessments done so they could work on goals for the entire year.

I ended up testing kids for two days. Testing was broken up between math and reading tests and general testing including intelligence and other indicators of possible learning problems. I was also testing for the Gifted and Talented Program. Students referred to this program were usually fun for me to see as they were interesting and delightful to meet. Those who qualified for the program would get advanced projects and help in developing their special abilities, or, at least, that was supposed to happen. Unfortunately, it depended on the teacher and the district.

Each district had its own criteria although there were some state guidelines. School districts wanted to qualify as many kids as they could because of money coming from state and federal sources.

A few of the logging camps in Alaska including Eight Fathom Bight were part of Chatham Schools as I mentioned in an earlier chapter with district headquarters being in Angoon. The communities of Elfin Cove, Klukwan, Gustavus, and Tenakee Springs were also part of Chatham. Freshwater Bay where I visited when I first started working in 1983 had been closed due to the low number of school-aged kids living there.

Eight Fathom Bight was on Chichagof Island. It could be accessed from Port Fredrick on the north end of the island about 15 miles from Hoonah. The logging camp itself was situated on a hill overlooking the tidal estuary flats at the head of Port Frederick. Float planes or boats came in at the dock. I always flew there with one of the local air services. Getting off the plane at the small dock was not a problem, but getting from the dock to the shore was a challenge as balancing on a log was required although it was a very short log so shouldn't cause much of an obstacle for me. A couple of individuals greeted me and carried my gear and testing materials to shore, while I prayed that I would make it with the same ease they had.

Excellent opportunities for viewing scenery and wildlife, which included whales, brown bear, deer, shorebirds, and a variety of small mammals were available. I didn't see any of these, however, on that first visit except for the many birds readily flying overhead, waiting, I guessed, for the big splash if I fell into the water. Much to my relief I disappointed them.

The school was a large trailer at the bottom of a small hill. It had two main sections—one was a classroom, and the other was used for storage, files, and while I was there for testing. The houses were also trailers that had been located higher up on the same hill. I stayed in one of those trailers with the Special Education teacher when I visited this particular site. The kids liked her. She appeared to be very competent in the classroom.

The camp was a privately-owned camp and somewhat permanent. The owner lived in it although he also owned several other camps in the area. His trailer was at the top of the hill overlooking the area and next to the main office. He had a small church built there. It was the only camp I knew of that had a church. He was very much in control of who came into the camp. There had been a nagging question of confidentiality of records in the school as he had keys to all of the buildings. I didn't want to think about that.

It was late in the afternoon when I finished the last two ten-year old boys. They were fun to meet, and excited about blueberries and a "visitor" staying there meaning me, namely, someone who was actually interested in blueberries. I still had one more girl to see. She agreed to stay after school so we could finish.

The two boys told me blueberries were everywhere. "What about bears?" I asked as I knew they liked eating berries as well as fish to store up for their winter's hibernation. And, after all, we were in brown bear country.

"Oh, we're careful," the shorter of the two boys said smiling at his friend. "We go to the same spot all the time. The bears have never bothered us."

I wondered about the bears. Looking at the excitement in the two boys' eyes, I said, hoping I wasn't making a mistake, "Yes! But I have to finish one more test."

I knew it would take me at least another hour to finish with the girl. The thought of fresh blueberries, however, spurred me on, and I think motivated her as well. She was laughing and almost as excited about the possibilities of blueberries as I was. My plane wouldn't be there until the following morning so tonight I could relax.

The girl rapidly completed the items. Her reading skills were excellent. No learning problems with this girl I thought to myself, at least not in reading. She was interesting, enjoyed reading and was just slightly older than the two boys. All three of the kids I thought should be eligible for advanced work in Chatham's Gifted Program. All too soon we were finished. The two of us sat there and talked for a few minutes when we heard a commotion outside.

Upon opening the door I found the two small bright-eyed boys both smiling as they made their way into the room. Their faces were covered in a sticky, blue juice, and they were carrying several large bushes—full of ripe blueberries.

It was too late to go picking they said so they brought the blueberries to me still on the bushes.

The four of us including the girl sat there laughing and picking berries eating as fast as we could. It wasn't long at all before my hands were as sticky and my face as blue as all three kids. And that, I thought, ended a perfect day of testing.

I was wrong. That night the Special Education teacher had chunks of fresh halibut for dinner. I thought I had died and gone to heaven. One of her neighbors came over and joined the feast.

CHAPTER 31

Plumber...I am not!

Prior to the 1920s, Port Alexander was the salmon fishing capital of the world according to what I read. That claim to fame surprised me when I first laid my eyes on the area. It was on the southeastern corner of Baranof Island. Much of the area was water. I suspected it boasted a fishing lodge or two that I wasn't likely to see.

I was only in Port Alexander the one time arriving in the afternoon and leaving the next morning. There was a school, a teacher and several kids who needed testing. The visiting special education teacher was also there. It was part of Southeast Island School District. I estimated that the population was somewhat less than 100 individuals including the dogs and cats.

Board walks connected the community as they did in many of the southeastern communities. They wound in and among the trees while one branch went to the marina and another to who knows where. Walking on the left one led to the school. They were placed a couple of feet above the ground. Below them were fallen trees, ferns, and all manner of green things growing out of the wet soil. Moss was clinging to rotting limbs. The earthy smell of dampness was all around me.

I arrived in the late afternoon after having flown in a float plane from Sitka, which is also located on Baranof Island. The kids who had been referred would take me well into the evening hours.

I could finish that day and be ready to leave the next morning. There was always a push in that district. I guess they wanted to get their money's worth while I was there. I never disagreed as long as it was okay with the kids.

It wasn't long before everyone went home and the school was empty except for the one remaining student to be tested and me. The building was quiet. Inside it was warm enough and fairly comfortable. The room we were in was a nice testing room with a door to the outside. I was sorry there were no windows but then it was black outside anyways. The boy was bright and being considered for the Gifted and Talented Program. He had lived in the community for several years.

About half way through the testing I heard a commotion at the door. I looked up to see it suddenly open and a man, not young but not old either, walk right into the room. His clothes were rough, and he probably hadn't shaved for several weeks. His hair can only be described as "grizzled."

"We're testing in here!" I volunteered expecting him to leave.

I wasn't used to having strangers walk in, and even less coming in at night. The boy in front of me sat between me and the door. I doubt he would be much help should a situation arise. He didn't seem to be concerned, however, when he turned around and saw the man.

The newcomer directed his comments to me. "There's a problem with the sewage system. It's bad. I told them about it but it's taken long enough to send someone." His words were slightly slurred.

"Sewage?" I questioned aloud. I was somewhat startled by his remark. "I have nothing to do with the sewer. I'm with the school district and testing kids." My words didn't seem to register with him.

"It's bad. Needs fixing!" He persisted. "Someone needs to get here and fix it."

The boy looked at me, and whispered so I could hear. "He's the town drunk."

I guess I felt sort of relieved, but knew I had to get rid of him in order to finish the testing. He wasn't very steady on his feet, and a potential drunk was not what I had bargained for. He seemed harmless enough. He just wanted the sewage system fixed.

"You need to get someone here." He continued. "Why

haven't they sent someone earlier?"

"I'm the school psychologist and don't have anything to do with the sewage system. I'm here testing kids for the school," I explained again.

"Ma'am, it needs to get fixed."

Looking at the clock and knowing I still had a good half hour of testing, I decided to take a different tack. That's when I told him that I would let them know that it needed to be done very soon. "Go home, and I'll tell them."

Of course, I had no idea who "them" was. "You need to leave while I finish the testing."

He stood there a few more minutes. "It needs fixing badly."

"I promise, I will tell them."

I was relieved when he opened the door and started to leave. I got up and locked the door behind him once he was out of the building.

The boy was smiling and said "Everyone knows him. He's harmless."

That night good on my word I relayed the message to the teacher with whom I was staying. She didn't appear too concerned.

CHAPTER 32

More Logging Camps

Prince of Wales is the fourth largest island in the United States followed by Hawaii, Kodiak, and Puerto Rico. Located in Southeastern Alaska, it has a number of logging camps tucked away in its various bays, hidden coves, and inlets. Some of those logging camps float from one place to another while others are stationary and considered permanent with having a second-class city status. There were also three city school districts including Klawock, Craig, and Hydaburg located on Prince of Wales Island. Southeast Island School District served these logging camps with Thorne Bay being the largest one. This school district was the only one with its own plane that flew out from the office in Ketchikan each morning to various sites. Sometimes I rode on it and sometimes I flew commercially.

I spent very little time at most of the logging camps, although I sometimes spent the night at one of them. I enjoyed those times, but found them exhausting. One long week began in Rowan Bay where I had spent the night. Flying across the island from Sitka the previous day I had seen several mountain goats, and then a large black bear upon landing. The kids there started throwing rocks into the water, and the bear left area disappearing behind a tree and into the forest.

I flew to Lab Bay on the 17th of September, stayed the night there after testing one girl and stayed with the teacher, her three

Siamese cats, and had a fabulous dinner of venison, Shaggy Mane mushrooms, salad, and a couple of beers. The next day I flew to Port Alice where I tested two kids and again stayed all night. From there it was Coffman Cove and testing three more kids (two being from Naukati) and then went on to Thorne Bay. I spent the night with Mary Dahle and her winter dog Bo. I tested one girl there who I had previously tested several years earlier, and the next day four kids including one repeat, a boy from a year earlier. I had suggested his parents look into glasses based on difficulties he was having. The glasses made a big difference from earlier scores. He was being considered for the Talented and Gifted (TAG) Program.

I was up at 5:30 AM the next morning and drove over to Hollis School (one hour and twenty minutes travel time), tested another girl also for the TAG Program and then sat waiting for 7-year old who was coming from Cabin Creek. I had wanted to pick some rose hips in Klawock on the way back to Thorne Bay and catch an earlier flight south out of Ketchikan. That didn't happen. I finally left Hollis at noon, only to learn there were no commercial flights scheduled out of Thorne Bay, so I had to wait for the school plane to pick me up. Driving out of Thorne Bay that morning and before first light I saw two deer standing right in the middle of the road.

I was one tired individual at the end of that trip, and only had a few days at home before I ended up in Anchorage (September 29, 1990), meeting a speech therapist, and catching a plane for Dutch Harbor then transferring to a float plane for Akutan where the two of us worked together.

Originally, I understood that Thorne Bay began in 1960 as a floating logging camp and was located in Hollis. It became a second-class city in 1982 in its present location. In 2001 the logging camp pulled out having been a victim of a breach of contract from the U.S. Forest Service. I'm biased when I say that thanks to the Forest Service there are still some trees left in the area.

During the 1970s and 80s it was considered the world's biggest logging camp, and one I visited several times a year in the 80s and 90s. Most of the time I flew directly to the community by float plane. There were times, however, when I flew into Klawock, Craig, or Hydaburg on the west side of the island and then rode by car to Thorne Bay. These three communities as I indicated above were independent city school districts. Roads had been cut all over the island for logging trucks. At best they were graveled.

Going along the main road from one of the three city schools where I also worked to the east side where Thorne Bay is located there was a visible line where clear cutting had occurred; there was nothing but dead stumps where loggers had cut every tree down that was in sight while the other side was before the chain saws and men had arrived. I was saddened by what I saw. It was like someone had drawn a line with a ruler, and all the trees on the right were gone. I followed the line straight up the hill to the top with my eyes. It was readily evident as to what the forests on the island must have looked like before the loggers descended on it. The trees were tall and proud, abundant and very healthy. I'm sure wildlife lived in their protection and thrived making it a very special and beautiful place.

Upon my initial visit to Thorne Bay the old school stood on one side of the road with the gym across on the other side. I can remember meeting Barb Kline, the Special Education teacher, for the first time. She was coming out of the gym to greet me. Several kids surrounded her and were all talking at once. We walked across the roadway to the main building.

I looked around that first year and was amazed as to where the kids came from as there were lots of them going to school although Thorne Bay itself didn't seem very big as there weren't many houses in the "downtown" section certainly not enough to house all the kids. As we drove around I remember seeing one house with a confederate flag in the window. Independent thinkers, I thought. I knew some of its residents had been there for years and others had just recently moved in with their families.

I learned through one of the students that most of the homes were hidden away among the trees and in the tiny inlets. Mary, a ninth-grade girl, told me she had been in Alaska eleven years. She said she lived out of Thorne Bay about a mile and a half. The only way to get to her house was by boat.

The mystery was solved. Mary had entered an essay for the book, *Alaskan Ferry Tales,* that two friends and I had put together and solicited articles and art work from kids all over Alaska. Mary's short essay was one of those chosen to be in the book. Her comments gave me insight as I realized many of the kids' homes were not located in the downtown part of the town at all. A school boat picked them up instead of a school bus. After all the community was 30.4 square miles with 25.5 square miles of land and 4.8 square miles of water. Flying into the harbor at Thorne Bay their homes were mostly invisible and well hidden by the trees.

Prince of Wales Island was also served by the ferry system with a dock at Hollis, the original site of what was to become Thorne Bay when it floated to its present location and was established. I found the teachers there were innovative, talented, and imaginative. Dee Walker particularly encouraged her students to write.

When I mentioned the book that I was doing on Alaska's ferries, Scott, an eighth-grade student, submitted his essay and was a first-place winner in writing for his age-group. He humanized the ferry Columbia, which was the flagship of the Alaska Marine Highway fleet. He wrote the following as part of his essay, "When the people stroll about me, I feel a new sensation, a feeling of being tickled. I start to laugh. The engine sputters, then it returns to normal."

I still smile when I read those lines from Scott's writing.

Then one year I arrived and found the old building and gym were gone and down the road a new school had been built over the summer months. It was the kind of school one finds in many towns and cities serving kids from kindergarten through high school. It was permanent unlike the portable buildings and trailers where kids were taught in many of the logging camps.

Most of the time I stayed in a small house for itinerants near the school. I distinctly remember several of us there on one trip huddled around the stove with a pot of water on the top boiling and wondering how long it needed to boil in order to be safe enough to drink. It was not unusual for many of the small communities and villages that I visited to have unsafe water in the taps. I think that's part of the reason I ended up drinking as much coffee as I did as I knew the water was heated up to boiling long enough to be safe, at least, I hoped it had been.

I stayed with Barb and her husband, Ken, on occasion in later years. They lived across the bay and that meant a boat ride to their dock. Feeling the salt spray on my face during the crossings made for a very pleasant and relaxing trip and definitely removed me from work. I could only imagine what it might be like on stormy days and didn't want to think about those times. Barb, however, always seemed to show up even on the worst of days. I realized years later that there was a roadway of sorts behind their house that in an emergency, one could take a four-wheeler to the only road that led into Thorne Bay.

Bob visited Thorne Bay with me for three days in early May of 1989 in one of my attempts to share some of my adventures with him. We stayed with the Kline's. He and Ken had a fun time playing all over the area while I was in school working. Ken was on "heart disability" at the time so was free to show Bob around but was limited in what he could do. The two men got along well and Bob seemed to enjoy himself immensely. I couldn't imagine anyone, however, not getting along with Ken. He was an experienced fisherman, owned a charter fishing boat and during the summer months took visitors in and around nearby waterways. He always was laughing and had a big friendly smile on his face. I'm sure Bob saw more of Thorne Bay on that short visit than I did the entire time I worked there.

Harbor in Thorne Bay

Barb was the special education teacher all the years I worked in the community. She knew the kids, knew the parents and also wore a big smile including the time she brought in one very cute little kindergarten girl named Sara who had been recommended for the gifted program and was reported to eat her nose buggers when she was displeased with someone or some activity. I was forewarned, and sure enough Sara lived up to her reputation on one of the more boring sections of the test. I might add that she's now married and works for NOAA (National Oceanic and Atmospheric Administration) from what I understand.

Barb knew how to get the most out of the kids in the classroom, work with the other teachers in developing positive programs for individual students, and talk with parents. She had had several very handicapped kids over the years in her special education classroom and was readily able to coordinate their development with other teachers. One child had "Cat Cry" Syndrome leaving him developmentally delayed. She worked successfully with him and his parents. Barb was a tremendous support to me when I visited the school from that very first visit with an after-school get together featuring clam spaghetti to the final trip I made to the school. Her interactions with other educators showed me that the school had a dedicated group of individual teachers and that's what made it a special and memorable place to visit.

CHAPTER 33

O Christmas Tree, O Christmas Tree!

The child before me was sitting on the floor. He was five years old. It did not make sense to have him move to the table. Instead I sat down beside him under the Christmas tree in his family's home. He was in kindergarten but wasn't doing very well in school at all. "Assess his abilities!" But more importantly I knew the school wanted to see if he met the criteria for Special Education and have it legally documented.

I opted to use the Stanford Binet Intelligence Scale because I knew I could get more information from it for this age child than from the Wechsler Scale that I usually used. The teacher needed help in how to work with him even if he didn't qualify. She was hoping, however, that he would be eligible for special education services. After listening to her I would have been surprised if he had not been eligible, and when I started working with him I knew he would qualify. Being eligible would give her an additional source of help from the visiting Special Education teacher. The community was very small, and the school had limited resources. My report was needed to meet the State's guidelines.

I had been told that the boy had ridden his tricycle off the edge of the dock when he was maybe two or three years old. He had been under water for a few minutes before he was rescued. And then more recently he had fallen into the water again and was under the water for a little while before he was pulled out—how long no one seemed to know. Rumor had it that his father had been wanted by the law and had re-located to this isolated community in Southeastern Alaska. I don't know what he did; it did not concern me except I concluded they would not be moving to a larger community. I was here to assess the child's abilities and look for clues that might be helpful for him in school. An Individual Educational Program (IEP) would need to be developed.

Christmas was just around the corner. Once I finished I would board a bush plane, fly to Ketchikan's airport and then fly on the jet to Seattle so I could be home for the holidays. I was looking forward to decorating my own Christmas tree that I knew would come close to touching our twenty-foot ceiling. But first I needed to complete testing.

I glanced up at the tree above us. It stood tall and straight. I inhaled deeply. The fresh scent of fir reached out to everyone coming into the home including me. Handmade ornaments hung from its branches; there were angels, round balls, toy cars, and felt animals hanging on it. Several popcorn strings went around and around leading upward. A gold star had been hung at the very top. I could see a few candy canes tucked here and there almost out of sight.

The child's mother was in the nearby kitchen. I could see her out of the corner of my eye as I pulled out the small green blocks. The child laughed as he started to play with them. I gently took them from him and showed him what I wanted as I stacked them up in a tiny tower. He smashed the tower down. I tried again then quickly handed him the four blocks. Two blocks went up easily but when he added the third one, his tower fell. I gathered up the blocks and tried again. He watched with interest. I handed him the blocks after setting one down and motioning him to put the next one on top. "Look, you did it just right!" I encouraged him, smiling as he took a third block, and finally the fourth one. "Oh, look at your tower!"

He was laughing at his success, and wanted to play some more.

Now I wondered if he could build a bridge with three of the blocks. I set up an example. He watched but then wanted to get up and do something else. I waited until he settled down. My eyes took in the room as he played. It was small, neat, and clean. His mom was busy fixing snacks in the kitchen area. I looked up at the Christmas tree again. It had been freshly cut and put up with care. There were a few store-bought items here and there, but most of them had been hand-made. The tree reached up towards the ceiling but didn't quite touch. I looked at the gold star as it shined down on the child.

He came back over to where I sat. I motioned for him to sit down beside me. He tried to make the bridge but he just couldn't get the blocks to stay still. Not wanting him to get frustrated, I pulled out a cardboard doll and asked him where the ears were. He pointed correctly then I asked about the mouth. He readily showed me. He was able to point to other body parts. Some he didn't know. The elbows presented a problem for him but he readily pointed to the eyes. I asked him to show me first his eyes, then his ears and finally point to his mouth. He wanted to look at the doll again. "No, point to your eyes!" I said and pointed to him. He was able to do this after resisting a bit. We tried some of the other subtests as well. He did well on some of the pictures, but didn't know others.

Finally, I gave him a pencil and had him draw a picture of himself. There was a circle and a line of sorts suggesting a smiling face. I asked him to sign the picture. He scribbled a few marks on the page.

We spent a little over 45 minutes working before he just stopped. It was time to quit I realized. I gathered up the testing materials and packed them away in my case. His mom gave him a snack as I was leaving.

Once back at Ketchikan's airport I checked in and went upstairs to the waiting room. Emotionally I felt drained and this time went into the bar and had a drink. I wondered what was going to happen to this child in the isolated community. He needed so much more than what he could get there. His teacher, I knew, was a very caring person. She was patient and knew what she was doing but didn't have that much experience with special needs kids. The visiting Special Education teacher was outstanding with a vast amount of experience and would be a good resource to the boy's regular teacher. But she wasn't in the classroom on a daily basis and I doubted she visited even weekly as she worked with many other students throughout the district.

My goal was to show what he was able to do and what he

needed to work on. With the other testing the teacher had completed he was certainly eligible for Special Education programming. I just wished he were in a larger school with more resources available but knew his family would not be going to a bigger community.

I ordered a second drink, finished it, and then went out into the waiting room. It was beginning to fill up with travelers as the jet was on its final approach.

Over a year later I learned that the boy had a brain tumor; he had been hospitalized and was not doing well. When I heard this, I thought about the gold star at the top of the Christmas tree.

CHAPTER 34

Can't Count on Communications

All around me as far as I could see there were pock-marked lakes. They dotted the snow-covered tundra. Snow was on them but also outlined the shores. Pockets of water had accumulated in depressions during the summer months. The water was then trapped on the surface because of the permafrost underneath. Once the deep cold of winter arrived those pockets were quick to freeze over. One could walk across them, drive a snowmobile across, or take a dog team on them following the winter trails from one village to another. Some of these trails were visible as I stared out the window of the single-engine plane. The immensity of the area was overwhelming.

I was back in Western Alaska and it was in the early part of 1985. The landscape below reminded me of a moon scape or what I imagined it would look like. Inside the small plane I was toasty warm, almost too warm as a matter of fact with my heavy down jacket. I was working in the Lower Yukon School District and headed to one of its eleven schools, namely Sheldon Point. It was my first visit to this remote site near the Bering Sea, and I would only be there for a few hours. The entire district had less than 1,900 students and Sheldon Point was one of its smallest if not the smallest school.

This district had my services for two weeks during which time I had been given a list of several sites to visit. The students I was scheduled to see included some new referrals as well as kids who were receiving services and were up for a three-year re-evaluation. Unlike other districts where I had to spend time on the telephone or at ticket airport offices, the Special Education director made up my schedule and coordinated my travel arrangements. That saved me considerable time as I just had to show up at the appointed day.

An emergency occurred with a girl in Hooper Bay losing it and tearing apart the girls' bathroom. That meant an unexpected trip to Hooper Bay had to be fit into my travels at the last minute. I was scheduled to be picked up on a charter flight after I left Sheldon Point. The director wanted an assessment done with recommendations of what the school's staff could do. She told me to telephone the school when I was ready to leave Sheldon Point. The Hooper Bay community was almost two miles from the airport and I would need a ride to get to it. I had been to the community during the summer months on two earlier occasions and before I started working in Alaska so was familiar with the distance between the airport and the village.

Sheldon Point is on the south fork of the Yukon River where the Bering Sea flows into this almost 2,000-mile river that has its beginnings in Canada. Historically it had been a fish camp for many generations. A man named Sheldon opened a fish saltry there in the 1930s, and in 1974 the community was incorporated and named after him. It is known by its Yup'ik name of *Nunam Iqua*, meaning "the end of the tundra." As far as I was concerned it was the end of the world or at least one could see the end from the village. I was to visit there several times during the mid-1980s.

This particular trip, however, was my first visit to this remote school. I didn't know what to expect. I looked down at the tiny airport as we made an approach. A snow machine skimmed along a well-worn trail to the end of the runway and that would be my ride I guessed. The weather was not particularly good when we landed but I had seen much worse. I was to test one six-year old boy and then the charter plane from Emmonak Air would pick me up and fly me to Hooper Bay also on the Bering Sea but further south.

Once in the small building I met with the teacher and then met the child. He was a delight. He was highly motivated, and after having been exposed to one year of school had made excellent gains despite his overall IQ score being a little low. I suspected it was more of a lack of exposure than actual ability. There was no evidence of learning problems. His teacher and I talked about his performance and agreed that he was not eligible for Special Education. I had no doubt that he would be getting all the help he needed and would make good progress because of his positive attitude as well as that of the teacher.

A plane buzzed overhead while I was still talking with the teacher. Time to leave but first I had to make that telephone call to the principal in Hooper Bay. Except, that is, for one little problem—the telephone was out. Whoops! Now what? Neither the district's director nor I had counted on that, and I doubted she even knew about the telephone not working. She had been very good at arranging my schedule and all the flights needed so I dismissed the little concern that found its way to the pit of my stomach. The plane landed but there was no way for me to let school personnel in Hooper Bay know when I would arrive. They knew I was coming at least that's what the director had told me, so I would go as planned. I had not talked with anyone in Hooper Bay so was dependent on her communication with the school.

The plane, a Beechcraft Bonanza, landed but not at the airport. Instead there was a make-shift strip behind the school that was probably part of what I would think of as a very large, frozen pot hole or in the summer a small lake. Emmonak Air had the one Bonanza that was occasionally used for charter flights. When I saw the plane, a big smile erupted. I loved Bonanzas. After all, my husband and I had a Bonanza so I was more than familiar with the plane. This one, however, was a much newer model than the one we had.

Bonanzas were not commonly used by air services in Alaska. This one was one of two I had run into during my years in the Bush. I suspected it belonged to the owner or manager of the air service and was occasionally flown to keep it in good flying condition. I followed the pilot climbing aboard after he secured my luggage and testing equipment in the baggage compartment. I was the only passenger so sat in the co-pilot's seat. I was truly at ease and definitely looking forward to the flight despite a little nagging concern in the back of my head due to not being able to get hold of anyone in Hooper Bay.

End of the World Almost—Sheldon Point from the Air

Once in the air I chatted away with the pilot and had a most enjoyable flight along the coastline for roughly an hour. The weather had definitely deteriorated but despite this we made good time. Hooper Bay was about 20 miles south of Cape Romanzof.

The actual village of Hooper Bay more than a mile inland from the airport, which was right along the sea and large enough for small jets to land on it. Bob and I had flown into it, the last time some years ago while I was researching my dissertation and before I had started working in Alaska but that was during the summer months. There was no question in my mind; it was definitely winter time as we followed the coastline to the airport.

We landed with no trouble at all despite a cross wind coming off the water. Unlike my landing at Sheldon Point I did not see any snow machines coming out to the airport to pick me up. The previous concerning thoughts translated into a fear that touched at the edges of my consciousness as we landed. I knew the pilot could not stay on the ground long at all—just long enough to unload me and my baggage. Any further delays and he would run the risk of the engine freezing up. I climbed out on the wing and down the steps. He quickly pulled my testing gear, sleeping bag, .backpack and other belongings out of the baggage compartment. I had a heavy parka on, warm mittens, outer mittens, and good boots. I was dressed for the situation. It was freezing cold.

We stood there talking for a few moments. No one came. Nor was there any sign of anyone coming from the village. Well, now what? We briefly discussed the situation. "I don't want to leave you here by yourself alone but I can't stay."

"I know."

After sizing up the situation, I told him, "Go in as low as you can and buzz the school for all it's worth. They know I'm coming from Sheldon Point just not exactly when as the phones were out." I sounded confident when I told him to go, but inside apprehension surfaced.

My husband and I had walked into town from the airport when I had been doing research for my doctoral dissertation. That was in the summer months. This was a large Eskimo village of 800 or more people at the time. Now, however, I didn't even dare to take my mittens off as the wind and chill factor would have had my fingers frozen in seconds. The cold was sharp as knives and intensified by wind coming off the ocean.

Okay, I decided, I would walk into town but not carry the gear I had with me. I decided it was better for me to walk rather than wait until someone came out for me. There was a small out building near the runway. I walked over to it and put my testing equipment and other stuff down in a snow bank next to the side away from the water, all, that is, except for my down sleeping bag. I wasn't about to part with it. I could see the town in the distance and would stay in the plowed-out track that led to it. That's where the road was. After all, I had been on it before, but not with all the snow on it or the chilling wind.

The Bonanza took off and headed directly over the village. The pilot was good on his word and flew over really low not once but several times. Someone was bound to hear him. Finally, the plane headed off, banked and headed north where we had come from. Alone! At that moment I was wishing I was on plane. Dusk robbed some of the color from the setting sun. Darkness would soon cover the land.

I knew it wasn't going to help to stand around. I had to climb over a small snow berm in order to get onto the road. No problem, I thought, but was careful not to fall. By now an uneasy feeling had swept over me as I started to head towards the village. Fortunately, the wind was coming from the west off the Bering Sea, so I had it at my back rather than in my face. I was still cold but not freezing. It was late in the day when we landed. I didn't want to be caught out after dark. I didn't know where the school was located or where the teachers' living quarters were but figured once in the village I could find someone to ask.

I wrapped my face scarf up around my neck, put my hood up and started walking. Wind whipped around me. Flying snow tugged at my jacket. I held on to my sleeping bag for all I was worth. There was nothing wrong with my legs. I had walked a lot further before. After all I had hiked the Chilkoot Trail in Southeastern Alaska (all 32 miles of it). But this was definitely different, as I was not used to hiking alone in freezing weather surrounded by blowing snow. The cold found the weak part of my heavy outer mittens, but it was alright as the liner mittens inside were doing what they were supposed to do and protecting my hands. The sun was going down rapidly and much faster than I would have liked. I took a deep breath and started out for the village.

I walked maybe ten or fifteen minutes when off in the distance I could hear the rough chatter of snow machines racing across the surface of the land. Turning in the direction from where the noise was coming, I saw several of them literally playing in the snow. Rooster tails of flying snow were evident as they made a few sharp turns chasing each other. None of them were headed towards the airport or me, just playing tag in the snow. Kids, I thought. I wondered if they even saw me and doubted it.

I set my sleeping bag down and began waving my arms as high as I could; I mean really waving for everything I was worth. One of the machines turned in my direction. The loud, rough-sounding engine was music to my ears. Headlight shattered the on-coming darkness. A couple of minutes later a battered and smoking machine pulled up alongside me. I was right as a young student was driving it. Maybe he was in high school. I told him where I was going and he said "get on" and motioned me to climb on behind him.

Unlike some of the heavier snowmobiles or snow goes as they were sometimes called his machine was small and there was no place to hang on. It had also seen many winters I thought. Fear hit me again. What if I fell! The snow wasn't that soft. I had heard stories of natives having fun trying to dump visitors off. It beat walking, however, I thought as I climbed up behind the young man. I sat down on the seat firmly and with a fierce determination not to fall. I held on to that young Eskimo student for dear life as we shot out across the white, snow-covered landscape and headed directly to the village. If I fell, he'd probably go with me I thought. I said a few "Hail Mary's" along the way. I kept my eyes closed initially but felt exhilarated at the same time. When I opened them, I found we had covered a considerable distance.

The village was fast approaching, so was darkness. By this time the sun had all but disappeared. We roared up to a building almost completely encased in snow and stopped. He told me to wait there as we were at the back door of where the teachers' housing was but it was completely blocked by snow. He went around and then came back after several minutes. We would go to the front entrance on the machine. Oh, my God, I thought. I really didn't want to continue on the snowmobile but then I didn't have a choice. It wasn't as if one could just walk around the building—it was almost buried in snow. Fortunately, it was only a short distance, although we had to navigate around a couple of other houses to get to it.

My chauffer sprinted off the machine and pounded on the door. Once I got off, I headed for the entrance as well. When the outer door opened, a couple of teachers peered out at me then invited me in. I breathed a huge sigh of relief as I shed my parka and outer gear once inside the building. I explained about the rest of my gear being out at the airport in a snow drift. The principal came over and volunteered to go out on his snow machine and pick up my belongings. They had heard the plane fly over the school and thought it was coming through the roof but didn't realize it was to signal them. They were expecting me to fly in the next day. By now it was quite dark. A hot cup of tea really hit the spot as I talked with a couple of teachers. When the principal arrived back with my belongings, he looked like a huge icicle complete with frozen beard. Once the sun disappeared all promises of any warmth had evaporated with it.

Inside it was warm and felt so good. Tomorrow was another day. It turned out the girl I was to see had left Hooper Bay and gone to Chevak before I got there so I couldn't see her. Going to Chevak at that point was not in the cards as it was an entirely different school district although only a few miles away. The Lower Yukon's district office was the last to find out that she was out of the district or they would have cancelled this little side trip.

The next day I did what I could to document several teachers' observations of the incident as well as their overall comments about her, the girl's performance in the classroom and wrote a report but it did no more than establish information for some future time, that is, if the girl returned to Hooper Bay. Or if she remained in Chevak, it would accompany her records. Years later I was to work in Chevak but that was in the distant future.

CHAPTER 35

The Fall Marathon

There were times when I pushed myself more than I should have. I was caught between Bob's criticism of my working, wanting to please him, and doing a good job for SERRC and for the kids I saw. One such occasion occurred in the Fall of 1985 when I tried to fit too much into a very short period of time to ease some of the strained moments we had about my working.

The end of the summer was fast approaching, although we still had several weeks so we took the canoe and headed for Whitehorse in the Yukon Territory and specifically the Yukon River. It was August 13, 1985. Our two golden retrievers plus our two dachshunds were with us. Obtaining a wilderness permit and a fire permit from the RCMP was high on our list. Last minute supplies including topographical maps were purchased. With the last purchase we made our way to Rotary Park and parked next to the retired steamship Klondike on the Yukon.

Crowding everything in before I went back to work and Bob returned to Vashon was a goal. I was about to begin my third year working in Alaska. Bob wasn't happy about my working.

Our 17-foot canoe was lifted off the top of the car in a flurry of activity with dogs going in four different directions. We quickly loaded everything aboard, parked the car in the lot, rounded up the dogs, and left Whitehorse as we pushed out into the water.

The river's gentle current pulled us down stream. Rain

caught us that first night but we had already set up the tent. Several days passed before we finally reached the government camp on Lake Laberge. We had gone all of 38 miles on the almost 2,000-mile Yukon River when Bob complained of not feeling well so we pulled out. He hitchhiked back to Whitehorse, picked up the car and returned for me, the canoe, and the dogs. We drove back to Skagway where we left the canoe and caught the ferry to Juneau. The following year we returned to Skagway and picking up the canoe we continued down the Yukon to Carmack. We left the golden retrievers home and took our seven dachshunds (five were puppies) putting in at Lake Laberge and continuing to Carmack.

Following the first river trip I went to Angoon for two days of work while Bob stayed on the boat in Juneau with the dogs.

On August 27-28, 1985, Schnapsie gave birth to five dachshund puppies—all boys—aboard our boat in Juneau's harbor. Four were born on the 27th and the fifth arrived the next morning. I later named him Moose II after my original Moose, although he was smaller than his brothers. All five of the pups become part of our family.

That afternoon we left for Vashon with the new pups, Schnapsie, Otto Junior, MacDuff, Kodi, Bob, and me. The two big dogs and Otto sat in the back seat while mom and pups sat on my lap. Nasty weather was reported in Ketchikan, so we landed in Wrangell. Once the weather cleared a little we took off for Vashon sometime around five in the afternoon and flew VFR (visual flight plan) all the way home arriving on Vashon shortly before midnight. Bob seemed to be feeling much better.

As if that wasn't enough the weekend meant a quick trip over to Westport on Washington's coast. We took all the dachshunds including the five new puppies where we managed to sneak the whole bunch into the hotel while we attended an Elk's lodge reunion from Bob's home town in north Idaho. What he didn't know was that his brother and sister-in-law were there. Bob was not speaking to the brother as the two had a disagreement over money years earlier. Since I had never met the brother I went up and introduced myself. I liked him instantly as well as his wife.

I went back to Alaska a day later this time on the jet, and fit in a trip to Corner Bay, a logging camp, via Wings Air Service, tested one high school boy and returned to Juneau this time on Channel Air. The school year had definitely started.

On September 10th I woke up to a 6:50 am alarm accompanied by the sound of pounding rain outside the boat. I made a quick stop at my office in Juneau to add a recommendation for the one report written the previous night, dropped off one of my books at the local vet's office as he had seen Schnapsie before she had delivered, and went to the airport where I boarded a Cessna Stationair for Hoonah for another very quick trip.

By the evening of September 12, I was in Reno, Nevada, for the air races, something Bob wanted to do so we flew down in the Bonanza to watch them earlier that day after I returned from Alaska. The weekend slipped by all too quickly. Faced with three reports to write from Hoonah, one from Corner Bay, and a bad cold, I had scheduled myself for a two-week plus trip to the Lower Yukon. I was very much wishing I hadn't planned the "marathon" I had. I honestly think Bob was enjoying my discomfort.

The first week started out in Mountain Village with me testing there and then making a little side trip to Pitkas Point. Driving by car it was only about 20 miles between the two communities. Mountain Village and Saint Mary's were connected and there was an access road near Saint Mary's that went to Pitkas Point. I was somewhat mystified as to why I was sent as there were no evaluations that needed to be done.

Once I arrived the principal was very cordial and began talking about dolls. I didn't say anything and listened very carefully but was still a bit confused. He told me that he had let the girls bring their dolls to school, and that made the villagers mad because it meant there would be continued bad weather. They expected him to ban the dolls. He added that the girls played with dolls most of the year, but if they brought them out at certain times, it would mean more bad weather. I decided in my mind that it was similar to Ground Hog's Day except the Eskimos there took it very seriously. After he finished the story, he thanked me for coming and I returned to Mountain Village and saw some more kids.

It was a particularly cold night when the Special Education Director and I walked back from the school district's office to her house where I was staying. We had remained at the district office talking later than intended. She had wanted to "pick" my brain. Total darkness greeted us when we locked the building's doors and headed for her house. I led the way praying I wouldn't step into a mud hole as they were everywhere. She was right behind me hanging onto my jacket and sort of giving directions. Ahead were several abandoned tires which I carefully avoided—all by Braille. It was close to midnight, and I suspected that the next day there would be a work order for a couple of overhead lights but that wouldn't help me. I really needed a flashlight but didn't have one. There were no other people out, just the two of us. We made it safely to the house without incident. I wondered if she stayed in the office after hours often and suspected she didn't..

The director had me travel with her the next day to Kotlik because of her concern about the special education teacher in that community. While there I tested a couple of kids. Working with that teacher I realized the director was right on target with her concerns as the individual appeared to be inadequate for the challenges. I'm sure she was qualified "on paper" but just didn't have the training or the basic skills needed for the kids in the community.

We spent the night there. I was just finishing up my meeting the next day with the parents of one of the children I had tested for the Gifted Program when the plane flew over and buzzed the school. The director came into the room saying the plane was landing and that we had to go. That was my signal to leave immediately. The remainder of the conference was held basically on the back of a snow machine with my giving a brief summary to the parents who also went to the airport with me on another snow machine. Sure enough, the plane was there waiting for us. We finished the conference as my baggage was loaded into the plane.

The plane took me from there to Emmonak after we dropped the director off at Mountain Village. I stayed in Emmonak Friday through Monday and tested one child before I was off for Alakanuk for the remainder of the week. While in Emmonak I stayed with the Michel's, who were both teachers, and their two little girls. The Michel's proved to be wonderful hosts. I had taken them some fresh apples from Vashon but that was poor payment for their great hospitality. While there I learned how to compose reports on the MacIntosh computer. Up until that point I had been typing all of my reports on a typewriter.

Over the weekend I took my camera out to walk around the village, and met a little girl, maybe three or four years old, playing with her dog. We talked for a few minutes and I asked her if I could take a picture of her along with her husky. She stood smiling and was dressed in a very colorful blue parka with fur ruff and mittens that matched. The dog's breadth stood out because of the ice crystals around his nose and mouth. Fresh snow was everywhere. I took the picture, and later took a copy of it to one of the school principals I had worked with in Washington as his wife was a portrait artist. I commissioned her to do an oil painting of the little girl. The resulting painting captured what I had seen. It now hangs at the top of my stairwell at home. Every time I look at it I think of Emmonak.

On Monday I did more testing, then left for the airport and went to Alakanuk. We were barely airborne when we landed as the villages were very close to each other. On a later trip in the winter months when I went back to Alakanuk, several of us rode on snow machines between the two villages to get a sandwich at the café in Emmonak something Alakanuk didn't have.

By the 27th of September I'd finished the Lower Yukon School District, or else it was finished with me. I had a lot of reports to write, and at that point wasn't even sure how many. I thought about the kids I had seen. It was somewhat depressing when I realized that almost every child I had tested the past week was delayed—all of them were in Alakanuk.

Historically, I knew the village started with five families. It was isolated and quite naturally there were a number of intermarriages. There was also evidence of Fetal Alcohol Syndrome being a problem with some of the kids. Later I was happy about seeing several bright kids from that village.

On the last night in Alakanuk, one of teachers and I walked to the village a mile away from school. Walking back to the school we stopped at an elderly couple's home. Johnson made fish traps. I bought two of them. The smaller one was tied in the old way with strips of I'm not sure what but guess maybe it was seal gut. The larger of the two was tied with rope. Johnson described how they held fish and kept ice away from the opening with an ice net. Mink and muskrats would enter into the trap for the fish and be trapped themselves. He made his traps from willow saplings so they wouldn't eat the willow and allow the fish to escape. The saplings kept the little river critters out as they didn't like the taste. Thia ensured the fish not escaping once they were trapped. The small fish traps were used to catch minnows.

The small trap was no problem getting home on Alaska

Airlines in Anchorage, however, the big four-foot one caused a bit of a stir but the stewardesses were good and put it somewhere safe until I landed in Seattle. Both sit on the floor in my office.

Bob and I had visited Alakanuk in years past during the summer months. He knew the store manager there. When we landed, the airstrip had been wet and full of ruts. It was a miracle we didn't crash. I found everything was frozen on my visit this time. On an even later visit to this particular school, I was staying with the special education teacher who told me that the gym teacher arrived at her door late one evening, drunk and completely nude. She added that he was no longer working in the village.

And I thought to myself, it's only the 27th of September. That fall continued almost at the same pace it started. I was in Barrow by the sixth of October.

Later when I was working in the Yukon Flats District, the superintendent asked me if I had known their new gym teacher as they thought he was a bit strange and knew I had been out to western Alaska. I remembered the story from the special education teacher about the drunken gym teacher. I had seen the new gym teacher in the hallway at Fort Yukon School and noted his sweat shirt had "Alakanuk" printed on it. That's when I put two and two together and remembered what I had been told. Fortunately, I had a very good rapport with the superintendent and told her what I had heard but didn't know if it was the same person.

CHAPTER 36

Saint Lawrence Island

I only saw the Island from the air the first time in 1980 while on my research-gathering trip. Bob and I didn't land because of weather. Instead we headed back to the mainland and on to White Mountain on the Yukon River.

My next trip made before I started working for SERRC was successful. This time Bob and I had a passenger, namely, Ken, one of the building materials salesmen from Bob's company. It was his first trip to Nome. Ken told us he had met Woodrow, one of the local villagers from the Island who had been in a plane crash on top a mountain near the village of Gambell in August of 1975. Woodrow had been on his way home to Saint Lawrence Island from the hospital when they met in the Anchorage airport. Ken wanted to see if he was still there. Bob was intrigued.

The distance between Nome and the Island is 164 miles. The Bering Sea is in between the two. Russia is so close to the Island that on a clear day one can look across and see it from the village of Gambell. Villagers visit back and forth between the two countries. They go by boat as well as on the ice during the winter months with no one the wiser. Some of the old timers don't speak English just Siberian Yu'pik.

Gambell—Frames are covered with skin

Nome's weather was clear and good visibility was reported out on the Island when we decided to go. There are only two villages on the Island—Gambell and Savoonga. I remember hoping this time we could actually land in the Bonanza and walk around to see the village. We did just that on a very clear and sunny day. Ken filled us in on what he knew of Woodrow's story.

Woodrow had been flying on Wein Airlines on the way back to the Island from Nome on a very foggy day. When trying to land the plane, the pilot must have mistaken the lake for the shore line until it was too late. He must have thought he was landing on the runway to the left of the Bering Sea waters, when in fact he was landing to the left of a small lake on the Island that was backed by the 600-foot Mt. Sivuqaq. When he discovered his error, he must have added full power to get over the top. He failed. The tail of the plane hit the top and the plane was flipped on its back as it crashed into the mountain. There had been 31 passengers and a four-person crew on the plane. One passenger regained consciousness and saved others as he pulled them from the wreck. Another passenger amazingly walked away from the wreck and down the mountain uninjured.

Ten passengers were killed. Woodrow was lucky. He along with 18 others ended up in the hospital after being flown to

Anchorage in a Coast Guard C-130 that had gotten word of the accident, striped itself of cargo, and flew directly to Gambell where its crew picked up 19 persons on stretchers.

We landed with no problem at all. It was easy to find Ken's friend, Woodrow. We walked to his home where we met his wife. I listened as the men talked about building materials, Gambell, flying, and the plane crash.

Towards the end of our visit, Woodrow got up and climbed into a storage area or attic above the living room returning with a large piece of baleen. (Baleen is part of a filter-feeding system found inside the mouths of baleen whales and works by a whale opening its mouth underwater and taking in water. The whale then pushes the water out and animals such as krill are filtered by the baleen and remain as a food source for the whale.) Woodrow gave this to Ken as a gift. I guess my mouth must have dropped when I saw it. He went back up into the attic and returned with a small piece of baleen about 36 inches in length and handed it to me as a present. He had etched a couple of fish and three walruses peering out of the water as well as a couple of other figures on the piece. Woodrow was apologetic as he handed it to me and said he wasn't a very good artist but was trying to develop artistic skills since the accident. He had signed the piece of baleen he gave me.

Shortly afterwards, we left and walked back to the airport, flew over to the other village, and landed at Savoonga's airport where we were able to find a ride into town on a three-wheeler. I had heard there were some very fine ivory carvers in Savoonga. While there we met one artist named Floyd Kingeekuk, Sr. I purchased a very nice little piece about ten inches in length with two seals and several ice holes where they were perched ready to dive into the water. The adult seal was spotted, while the baby was spotless. Floyd definitely had an 'excellent eye' for his artwork. The holes in the "ice" were very natural and part of the original piece of ivory. With our purchase we headed back to the airport and flew to Nome as it was getting late in the afternoon.

I was to visit Saint Lawrence Island and the Bering Strait School District several times in later years. I remember testing kids in the basement of the elementary school in Gambell on one of those occasions. I also remember one high school student who needed a three-year re-evaluation. There was some question about how cooperative he was going to be for me to test. One of the special education staff members told me to let her know when I wanted the student and she would go up to the high school and get him. She did just that. She was a good-sized Eskimo woman who looked as if she wasn't someone to mess around with. She took off on her snow machine and returned shortly thereafter with the student in tow, introduced him to me, and promptly sat down on the chair right outside the room for the duration of the testing. He was very cooperative. When we were finished, she took him back to the high school.

On that trip I was surprised to find a two-by-four board used as a door stop in the house where I was staying. At night the teacher slipped the board into a couple of brackets one on each side of the door preventing anyone from breaking through and entering the small house. All sorts of thoughts raced through my head.

I tried to find Woodrow in the village but realized it had been a long time since Bob, Ken, and I had visited. I was unsuccessful. People moved back and forth to Nome from the Island so I wasn't surprised. I stayed with teachers when in Gambell. When in Savoonga, I stayed in the school.

I returned to Savoonga several times. One of my visits out there was for the better part of two weeks. I had flown from White Mountain on the Yukon River direct to Savoonga. The previous night I had spent in White Mountain in the school's basement on a cot near the kitchen and next to the furnace. I didn't want to stay up in the classroom as I understood they kept a snake there and while well-contained, I chose to go downstairs. By the next morning I was well roasted from the heat!

I finished my work and flew directly to Savoonga, where I was assigned a small room in the school that was absolutely freezing cold. At some point in the night I discovered the window was open and I immediately closed it. While I had my down sleeping bag, the outside cold had seeped in enough to thoroughly chill the room. To make matters worse I was running out of cash so couldn't purchase any cough drops, Vitamin C, orange juice, or other comfort food when coming down with a cold so was dependent on the school lunches. I don't know that anything I could have bought would have helped, but at the time I thought it would.

As a result, I did come down with a cold by the end of the

week, and by the following Wednesday when I was testing my last child for the day, I had lost my voice. Fortunately, I was able to finish in a whisper. I went to the principal first thing the next morning and being barely audible told him I couldn't talk. Obviously, I couldn't test any more. Fortunately, the kids needing testing were already completed, and the rest could wait for my return visit. That afternoon I caught the flight back to Nome and continued on to Seattle complete with sore throat. That was about the only time in all the years I worked in Alaska that I actually became sick enough on the job to have to leave a day early. I did get sick on three other occasions but pushed through finishing the work before I left the community.

Over the years I picked up several nice ivory carvings from the Island—mainly Savoonga, including, of course, the one I mentioned from when Bob and I were there. Most of the better ivory carvers were from Savoonga. Dog teams seemed to be a favorite theme for several of them. I visited a man and his wife who specialized in these. The wife painted the tongues of her dogs red while her husband left his dogs' tongues a natural color. I preferred the natural look.

I met other carvers as well and made a couple of purchases. One I remember in particular was from a fellow with a bandage on his head who came over to the local pastor's house while I was visiting. The pastor introduced us and told me he had a small ivory piece to sell as he needed money. He wanted me to buy the carving because he "fell off snow machine and rolled down hill on head." He was touching his head as he told the story. He admitted he had been drinking. Turns out he was going into Nome to see a doctor and needed some cash. I bought the piece, a small dog sled, and wondered how the money was going to be used—probably for more booze. I didn't ask.

CHAPTER 37

Barrow

More than four years had passed since completing my dissertation and I returned to Barrow. It was October, 1985. I was sent there for the better part of two weeks. Excitement stirred through my veins as I checked into a very nice room complete with cooking facilities at the Airport Inn. I would have time to see Barrow especially with spending a weekend there. My previous trip in 1980 had lasted less than a couple of hours. Warm temperatures and rain greeted me. That was not what I expected.

The school district had excellent resources and plenty of money to operate. The high school facility was a work of art. Its wood interior was finished with beautiful tiles found in the bathrooms, on the floors and elsewhere. I was really surprised by the lunch menu that even included a salad bar. One day we had corn beef and cabbage, fresh carrots, rolls, and a lettuce salad with fresh radishes, celery, and tomatoes. There was also a potato salad, olives, pickles, pears, and I think I forgot a couple of the other choices. Such options, especially fresh vegetables and fruits, were unheard of in other schools where I visited. The elementary school didn't have the buffet that the high school did but was still very good.

Not surprisingly the kids were a lot more sophisticated than I had found in the small villages. They had a lot more contact with what was happening in the outside world.

There were some down sides, however, including an elementary principal who seemed a little different (although strange was probably a better word). He kept staring at me to the point I actively avoided him. I felt ill at ease working at the elementary school during the evening hours, so I didn't. Any after hours working were spent in the district office in the Special Education coordinator's office. Sometimes I stayed as late as 9:30 in the evening but never in the elementary school unlike other districts.

Later I met up with Debra, who traveled there regularly and was the main visiting school psychologist. She told me the principal had been charged with sexual harassment of female teachers the previous year. She said the superintendent backed him all the way and helped him get the charges dismissed. Debra also indicated she had been approached by him and was very uncomfortable. Apparently, he had been snapping the bra straps of more than one teacher. Wow! I thought to myself; just what this community needed. I knew then I had made a good decision to stay out of the school once the school day was over.

Over the weekend I went with one of the teachers to see Barrow and the surrounding areas. Our bus tour included seeing the original trading post established by Charlie Brower, who arrived in 1886 as a whaling crew member. Charlie became its first white man. Eventually, he learned Inupiaq and married two Native women. He sired 14 children.

We passed one of the Distance Early Warning sites (also known as the DEW Line that is a system of radar stations in the far northern arctic region of Canada with additional stations along the North Coast and the Aleutian Islands). We also visited Browersville.

That day I saw Point Barrow or Nuvuk, a headland on the Arctic coast nine miles northeast of Barrow, and that I was told "is the northernmost point of all the territory in the United States". Archaeological evidence, according to our tour guide, indicated that Point Barrow was occupied by the ancestors of the Inupiaq almost 1,000 years prior to the arrival of the first Europeans. The headland is an important archaeological site as there are burials and artifacts associated with the Thule culture.

The waters off Point Barrow were on the migration route for bowhead whales. The speculation was the site had been chosen to make hunting easier. Burial mounds in the area were associated with the Birnirk culture, a prehistoric culture of the Inuit of Northern Alaska, and preceding the later Thule culture that pushed eastward across Canada reaching Greenland by the 12th century. "Lots of history," I thought to myself.

I spent some money on two prints in Browersville after meeting one of the artists. One of the prints, now hanging in my office, depicts four Eskimo women dancing. The artist told me one of the women in the painting had filed a lawsuit because she felt he didn't pay her enough for "modeling." I've often looked at the print and wondered which one of the four women had filed.

One of the local teachers told me it was unsafe for a "white person" to walk outside after dark. She had been teaching in Barrow for a number of years so I took her at her word and over the weekend stayed in my hotel room once daylight disappeared.

That particular Saturday night was special: a combination of being payday for the local residents and the weather was warm. It was almost like a perfect storm and I wasn't really surprised when sometime around four in the morning there was pounding on the outside door of the building where I was staying. It was followed by screaming, "Help! My God! Help me!"

Fully awake, I got up and cautiously peeked out the window. Two Native men were fist fighting in the middle of the street. One went down but quickly got right back up swinging. A taxi with the driver standing next to it, and several all-terrain vehicles with people on them surrounded the two men. I decided not to get involved and figured it was in my best interest to keep a very low profile.

That same weekend two kids, ages 18 and 21 years, had been killed. Booze and a three-wheeler were blamed for this tragedy. Later I heard there had been several murders and suicides during the previous month as well.

The next day I attended the Presbyterian Church where the minister was the husband of one of teachers. After the service I spent the afternoon visiting with them in their apartment that was part of the designated teachers' housing. It was in a low building that held several apartments in it. I was surprised when they told me that Natives actually went through the individual apartments uninvited on occasion and looked through personal belongings. I decided right then and there that Barrow could be very rough for outsiders.

Getting to Barrow could be complicated. One of my later trips took me fourteen and half hours on airplanes and in airports from the time I left Vashon. My husband, Bob, sometimes flew me over to Sea-Tac (Seattle-Tacoma) Airport in the early morning hours. It saved time and was kind of fun. He also picked me up at the airport on occasion with his plane—it was an excuse for him to fly into Sea-Tac Airport. On the fourteen and half hour trip, Vashon was completely covered in fog so it meant I took the ferry rather than Bob flying me directly to the airport and that resulted in my missing the 7:00 am Alaska Airlines flight to Fairbanks. Instead I ended up catching a 10:05 flight for Anchorage. Headwinds had been advertised at 60 mph and turned into 100 mph!

Upon landing in Anchorage that day I literally ran through the airport to catch a Mark Air flight only to find it had been delayed. I had a full hour and a half to catch my breath before we boarded and took off only to have an announcement fifteen minutes into the flight that the left flap wasn't working. We returned to Anchorage. On the approach the pilot announced that we'd be landing faster and braking more than normal. I wasn't sure what to expect.

No need to worry as the landing was okay. Passengers were switched to another flight originally scheduled for Prudhoe Bay and Deadhorse and then going on to Barrow. At 4:25 pm we left with stops in Fairbanks, Prudhoe Bay, and finally Barrow at around 8:25 pm. That was my only visit to Prudhoe Bay and I really didn't see it; I stood at the door of the plane and looked out then went back to my seat and sat down. The worse thing that happened that day was that I missed supper at the Special Education coordinator's house!

It was about 15 degrees with freezing winds on that trip when I left Barrow. The weather was changing rapidly. I felt tired but then I always did during the second week and it was only Tuesday. I had three days scheduled in Galena before I could go home but first I had to fly back to Fairbanks, then to Galena as there were no direct flights between Barrow and most of the other Alaskan communities. Making these connections on a long trip especially between two school districts was stressful both from possibly missing a connection or worse my arriving without my luggage and testing equipment.

Two years later in the early spring of 1987 I was to go back to

Barrow. That happened following my return from Peru after adopting our two children. I spent a week working in the schools on that trip and unwinding from two months in Peru; it was their summer months so the weather change from summer to winter was a shock to my inner core. The kids I saw were fun to work with. Once again, I stayed at the small hotel out between the airport and the elementary school near the teachers' housing unit.

One morning the wind was blowing pushing me along as I walked to the big tourist hotel in the main part of the village for breakfast. Having breakfast at the hotel was something I usually did while visiting there. The snow was extremely fine almost like glistening sand. My boots carved deep footprints in the white stuff. After finishing my meal, which took all of thirty minutes, I walked outside. Looking down, my earlier footsteps were almost completely gone! I had never experienced that kind of snow before but had a better understanding of the fact that Eskimos have many different words for "snow" depending on what kind it was. Up until that point in my life snow had always been white and either wet or dry powder.

I made a couple more trips after that in the next few years to this most northerly community. I rarely saw daylight. One trip on January 21st around eleven in the morning I remember looking out a window and seeing a faint glow of light in the sky and in less than an hour it was gone leaving only darkness behind.

CHAPTER 38

Sheldon Point, a Point of Departure

I was back at the "end of the world"—Sheldon Point, and finished with testing for the day. Another charter flight was picking me up. This time it was coming from Alakanuk, six miles to the north on the north fork of the Yukon River. I all too clearly remembered my last little adventure after leaving Sheldon Point's school and wondered what I was in for this time. I was heading inland to Russian Mission on the Yukon River. The weather appeared much better when I looked out the window than it had on my Hooper Bay excursion. But Russian Mission was roughly two hours away by plane, and I knew weather could change rapidly, but I was optimistic.

I didn't hear the plane fly over the village. The first I knew it had landed was when the pilot and two men who turned out to be maintenance men came in through the door looking for me. They were headed for Russian Mission and the district had set up a charter for all three of us. They were visiting various schools in the district in order to check Xerox machines. All three of the men had walked to the school as they wanted to see it. I wondered if the two passengers were hoping to promote a Xerox sale or something. One of them briefly talked with the teacher. I had not met this pilot before, although we were flying with the same Emmonak Air Service that I had been with when going to Hooper Bay.

We piled into the school vehicle and headed for the airport. A Cessna 172—not the luxurious Bonanza that I had flown in before—stood waiting for us. It was a good day to fly I thought to myself although it was getting late in the afternoon. Alaska covered five time zones geographically, but the clock didn't change as Alaska was on the same time throughout the State with a couple of exceptions, one being the end of the Aleutian Chain and the other surprisingly enough was Metlakatla in Southeastern Alaska. The latter community was on a reservation and the people didn't want to change their clocks for Daylight Savings Time so part of the year they were on Alaska's time and the rest of the year on Pacific Standard time.

Since we were in the furthest western part of Alaska geographically except for the Aleutians, sun light would keep us company for at least another hour. I figured we would arrive about the time the sun went down, although we were flying in an easterly direction and would be losing light.

Once back at the airport the two men crawled into the back seat and I sat up by the pilot in the co-pilot's seat. Oh, how I loved that sound as the engine roared to life. We taxied to the end of the air strip, turned and headed into the wind with full power and lifted off with plenty of room to spare.

Once airborne the pilot cut inland to follow the Yukon River as it made its way south to Mountain Village where I had been earlier in the week. I had flown over this area a number of times both with Bob in past years and while doing contract work for the Lower Yukon School District. The times with my husband were during the summer months. Now snow blanketed the ground as I only worked during the cold time of the year when schools were in session.

The Yukon River changed directions at Mountain Village and headed east. We changed directions as well, following its course from the air. I watched the instrument panel, kept track of where we were, and was enjoying every moment of the flight. "I've got a private pilot's license, you know," I said to the pilot. "I always enjoy it when I can be up front." The two guys in the back seat were busy talking with each other. Neither seemed very interested in the flight.

Saint Mary's came up on our left side and below us was Pitkas Point. I had been to both of these places, and smiled when I saw the Andreafsky River flowing into the Yukon from the north remembering Bob's "dunking" in its cold waters. I thought of Moose. I was reminded of Bob's and my stay with our three dachshunds in the girls' dormitory at the Catholic High School there while I was working on my doctorate dissertation in 1980.

Later I was to work for Saint Mary's City School District and always enjoyed my visits to the community. Unfortunately, I never went back to the Catholic High School as it was closed by the time I began making regular visits to the village.

Below I could see Pilot Station also on the north side of the Yukon. I realized all of the villages along the river were on the north and west sides of the river and wondered about the reason for this. We continued to Marshall where the river headed south again and followed it until it made an abrupt turn and headed north.

We were on the last lap of the trip when it began snowing, just a little at first, then getting serious. Daylight was rapidly disappearing. The closer to Russian Mission we came, the heavier the snow fell. Below, fog hung along the river and obscured it at times. Both fog and falling snow robbed us of the little visibility we had. I stared out the window hoping to catch a glimpse of the river below. Yes, I reassured myself, the river's still there as I saw its watery shoreline through the mist.

I continued to track our path on the instrument panel that showed the plane in relation to the ground, so I would know when we were over Russian Mission. The sun had disappeared and it was dark outside. I was beginning to feel a ticklish sensation on the back of my neck. My stomach muscles tightened up. I inhaled deeply. Visibility was downright poor. The village was on the west bank of the Yukon River. There were probably close to 300 people living there.

Historically, the first Russian American Company fur trading post on the Yukon River was established there in 1837. It was another twenty years in 1857 when the first Russian Orthodox mission in Interior Alaska was built. The mission was called Pokrovskaya Mission. The village changed its name to Russian Mission in 1900.

I said a little prayer as the pilot set up his approach. I couldn't see much of anything ahead except white. Snow continued to hit the windshield as we descended down. He suddenly pulled up. I looked straight down and could see the runway lights blinking through the snow. But we couldn't just drop like a helicopter and land. We needed a glide path. The hairs on my arms stood up. I took a deep breath and let it out slowly.

The pilot banked the plane to the left and made another try going a bit lower this time. Somewhere on the right I knew there was a mountain. It wasn't a very big mountain, but it was definitely higher than the surrounding land. The two men in the back seat continued to talk. I don't think they understood the danger in landing in these conditions and were totally absorbed in their conversation.

Another quick pull upward and I knew we weren't going to land this time either. I could see the airport lights again directly below us. The pilot knew I was well aware of what he was doing. I was also aware that he didn't want to fly all the way back to Emmonak without delivering his passengers—particularly on a charter flight and then have to fly it again tomorrow. Nor did I know the weather forecast or how clear Russian Mission would be the next day. He banked again and lined himself up with where the runway should be. The altimeter showed we were going down again, closer and closer to the ground. This time we were closer than we had been on either of the other two attempts. I momentarily stopped breathing.

No way. He pulled back on the stick and up we went making another left turn out over the river. I swallowed hard. There was no forward visibility at all. We were flying blind except for the instruments he had in the cockpit. "I'm going to try it one more time," he said to me. I nodded.

In my mind the mountain on the right grew taller by the minute. I could feel my heart pounding just a bit. I had a sour taste in my mouth. Down we went through the fog and blinding snow. We kept going down and passed the point we had been on the last attempt. Then I saw runway lights ahead of us just about the time the wheels touched the ground.

We rolled to a stop. I let out a big breath of air as I opened the door on the passenger's side. Several people greeted us including a couple of the teachers. "What happened, why didn't you land?" one of them asked. He continued, "We could see the plane but then it pulled up and didn't land. Then you went around again and again but didn't land."

"I know. We could see lights directly below us as we passed over the runway but could not see far enough ahead to land." I said as I was pulling my sleeping bag, test kit, and other belongings out from the baggage compartment.

To this day I don't think the two men in the back seat of the plane knew what happened.

Russian Mission—Winter Solstice

CHAPTER 39

Muskox and Ghosts

I was back in the Bering Strait School District about 75 miles northwest of Nome and across a large inlet with Teller just five miles away. I found this hard to believe. It was late October (10/25/85) and the wind was blowing fiercely. When we had circled the small runway the previous day, I could see construction work below me. Brevig Mission's tiny airport was being expanded.

People crossed the five miles in the winter months between the two villages by snow machines, while in the summer they used boats. I mention this because there was actually a road between Nome and Teller. I was to drive it on one of my later trips but only out of Nome for a few miles to a small river on the way to Teller. Once there I picked up several rocks from the river bed that had a few red specks of commercial grade garnet in them. I hauled a couple of the smaller rocks home.

Tiredness took over as I faced the remainder of what was a very long trip. I had flown from Hoonah to Juneau and on to Anchorage and Nome, and finally catching a bush plane for Brevig Mission—close to 1,500 miles and four separate flights. We landed and I made my way to the school. I had already been in Galena on the Yukon River and before that in Hoonah in Southeastern Alaska. Reports from both of these school districts were yet to be completed. My goal was to get them in the mail this weekend from Unalakleet, the district's headquarters.

The next twenty-four hours, however, had gone by quickly since my arrival much to my surprise. Curiosity about the community peeked my interest. My inner self told me the reports were manageable and the work load in Brevig Mission was light. With three and a fourth more kids to test I would be finished. I smiled thinking about a "fourth of a child." Translated that meant I had one more little reading test to do on the last student I had seen.

The kids were interested in strangers so most of them came by to "look" at me. They were shy. One small boy was badly deformed. I took a quick look and noted he had one eye sunk into the middle of his head with half his face looking as if it had been smashed and torn away. Questions surfaced on my face. The teacher told me "Birth defects". I would guess from the mother drinking during pregnancy. I wanted to look again, but not too hard.

A little girl named Theresa came into the testing area and sat down, smiling and chewing snuff just like an adult. I was taken aback as I wasn't expecting chewing tobacco and in the school none the less. She was small and in the second grade. She carried her own snuff box into the room with her. The teacher later told me that it went everywhere with her. There were only rotted stubs where teeth should have been, at least, as far as I could tell.

I carefully looked at some of the other children during the break. I only saw one child with all of her teeth. Most of the kids were like Theresa. Very few teeth were present, and the ones that were there were so rotted that I wondered how the kids could eat! Almost all of the kids I noted were also chewing snuff. I figured a dentist would have a field day in the community.

Three-wheelers and snow machines were the mode of transportation in this part of the world. The kids, however, came to school on cross country skis, and probably a good thing as there were snow banks surrounding the school and snow as far as I could see. It was also blowing around in the air. "Blows away and goes over to Teller in another month," I was told by one of the teachers.

Embarrassed when I first arrived I realized I had goofed by not bringing any food for the evening meal to share with the teachers. In all fairness to myself there was no place for me to pick up fresh fruit or vegetables before I boarded the plane. I felt badly enough about being so careless, I ended up doing the dishes. My thoughtlessness colored my perceptions. During the evening a teacher from Teller arrived with a bottle of whiskey. When he first walked in, I had the sense of a walking snowman as he was covered with so much of it. The white soon melted and the real person emerged. He was a fun addition to the group and obviously good friends with the teachers here.

The following morning I woke up feeling much better despite snow flying outside with a howling wind accompanying it, but there was a promise of improvement. The sun's appearance brought a smile to me. Yes, I thought, we were going muskoxen hunting with my camera later in the day. The early morning storm wore itself out and the day turned out to be a spectacular Tuesday.

Dave, the Special Education teacher, and I left the school on snow machines that afternoon. I was bundled up in at least three layers and drove the school's snowmobile while he had his own. It was a rare treat for me to have the opportunity to drive one. I usually ended up on the back of one instead of being in the driver's seat. Dave knew exactly where he was going as we headed west to a place he called "California." Driving a vehicle with ski-like runners in front and tank treads in the back was fun. It only took us about 20 minutes from the school to get to the designated spot.

My eyes searched the horizon. Ahead I could see a small herd of ten or fifteen muskox. We climbed off the machines and approached them quietly and very slowly. I didn't want to spook them. More importantly I didn't want them to charge. Dave seemed to know just how close to go and stopped a little less than about 100 feet from them. I hardly dared to breathe. I wanted to get closer but I took Dave's lead and stayed put.

They were aware of our presence, as they slowly formed the beginnings of a circle facing us and protecting a partially grown calf on the inside. None of them seemed too alarmed. They continued eating. I suspected they had seen humans before and weren't terribly concerned but were not taking any chances.

The sun was off to my left and slightly behind me. I could see my shadow in the snow as I raised my camera. The Continental Mountain Range stood out in the background. Its distant peaks rose well above the landscape. It was as if an artist had painted the scene. There was a slight pinkish tinge that graced the land as I snapped away until my fingers felt as if they were going to fall off. After a dozen or more shots, my fingers were screaming for protection. I knew the cold threatened frostbite if I kept my hands out much longer.

Now, I thought, if the film and camera don't fall apart, I'll have some pictures. I regretted not having my more powerful telephoto lens with me. We stood there for a few minutes just watching. The muskox continued to eat, pawing at the snow to get at whatever they ate beneath it—I figured it must be some kind of lichen. There were small scrub bushes all around the area. Maybe they ate some of these as well.

Reluctantly we headed back to the snow machines. I couldn't help but marvel at the almost desert-like environment we were walking through. The snow was fine like sand, but cold. Ice crystals and blowing snow greeted us. We had been lucky when approaching the herd as the snow was at our backs. I suspected our scent was carried to them and is what probably gave our presence away to the animals. I climbed back on the vehicle and fired it up.

This time the wind was right in my face. I was glad for the face mask I had but was still cold. Dave took a different trail going back to the school. I followed him. We crossed an area with some back water on the surface. "Punch it!" He suddenly yelled. I didn't ask why but pushed down hard on the throttle and kept up a good speed quickly going past the area with water on it.

In the back of my mind I thought about the danger of falling through the ice. I wasn't sure for a couple of moments if we were on land or over water. Later, once back at the school, I learned we had gone over a lagoon with a depth of about six to eight feet of water. Dave had already gone through the ice the previous year but I didn't know that at the time. I was glad to find out that little bit of information after we returned to the school!

Exhilarated, I was still relieved to see the village and the school ahead. I felt "home free" until I saw the final 15 feet up a steep incline. I swallowed hard, took a deep breath, hit the throttle and shot up the last few feet then stopped right where I needed to be—the top. I was only too glad to get off the machine in one piece! Given another chance, however, I knew I would do it all over again!

The next day before lunch Dave took me over to meet John Kakoona, who had found artifacts at the old village site near where we had seen the muskox. He produced a five-inch kayak carving from a walrus tusk that very nicely done and obviously quite old. I offered him $200 and he sold it to me on the spot! About a hundred years ago the old village was abandoned after almost everyone died—why? I wondered. No one seemed to know except some disease had killed them. The local natives had been digging up bones, and other artifacts and then selling to ivory buyers, teachers, and anyone else including me. None of the teachers had seen as nice a piece as what I had bought. I felt good about my purchase but also thought it really belonged in a museum. The toy kayak I got that day holds a special place in my Alaskan ivory collection.

During the days I spent in the school when I wasn't testing kids I spent a considerable time talking with the airport construction crew cook, Helen Pope. She was in the school kitchen, liked to talk, and kept me supplied with coffee and stories. She told me the elementary school had been built on an old grave yard site, and funny things happened in the building from time to time particularly at night. "Funny things." I asked, "What sort of things?" and immediately perked up. "Tell me more," I encouraged.

She poured me another cup of coffee then related the story of three bowls and three plates that had suddenly moved and come crashing down off the counter top. No earthquake or other explanation for their movement was offered. "All of them broke when hitting the floor, but instead of spreading out like dishes do when they are dropped the bowls and plates arranged themselves in exactly the same pattern as when they were on top of the table."

No, she didn't see them actually fall, but she was the first person to come into the kitchen the following morning. She found them in exactly the position they had fallen. She insisted she had left them on the counter top the night before. Either she was putting me on, or what? I wondered.

I was a willing listener as she continued. "The custodian on several occasions has seen furniture move around in the classrooms when he was cleaning up the elementary school—chairs moved, tables moved. One chair tipped over right in the room he was standing in one night. He saw it fall. No one else was in the building. It just fell over and he was on the other side of the room." Helen was very serious as she told me this story.

Interesting, I thought, and my imagination ran wild!

"You know, the school is currently built on an old cemetery! The population here has been wiped out several times." She continued, "They moved the village site when the people died." I was getting more curious by the minute. "There was some kind of an epidemic about a hundred years ago that killed almost everyone in the village near here."

Unfortunately, I had to finish testing as the child I was seeing had come in from recess, so I reluctantly went back to the testing area. When I finished, Helen had already ended her work and gone home so wasn't available for further stories.

I left Brevig Mission on the back of a three-wheeler around 4:30 that afternoon. I was supposed to fly to Wales and catch the helicopter to Little Diomede Island, but went to Shishmaref instead, as the plane couldn't get into the small airport at Wales due to weather. A Bering Sea Air Service twin engine Piper picked me up. I didn't want to admit it but I was hesitant as I climbed aboard. It was a very low overcast sky when we took off, but the fact that he had landed safely was a good sign, I thought.

We climbed up through the overcast to 5,500 feet where blue sky and sunshine greeted us. I felt much better as we headed due north on a point zero five-degree heading. I watched the Loran (long-distance navigation instrument) as well as the radar screen so knew right where we were.

Six minutes out of Shishmaref we descended down through the muck and between 1,500 and 2,000 feet the ground came into view. What a welcome sight! After circling the airport once, we landed. We were met by the village agent and a snow machine who took me to the village about two miles away.

The wind was blowing, and snow was flying all around us. As the evening wore on I noted almost complete white-out conditions. I was glad not to be flying and could not see more than a quarter of a block from where I stood!

Later, much later, I learned that in 1918 the Spanish Flu was by far the most devastating single disease outbreak in modern history, killing between 50 and 100 million people worldwide during an 18-month period. In Brevig Mission alone, the 1918 influenza had killed 72 out of the 80 residents living there at the time during a five-day period.

My tiny ivory kayak had probably belonged to a child from

that period of time having been carved by a grandfather, an uncle or maybe a father for his son now so long gone. I wondered if the child had survived, or if any of his family had.

My imagination took hold as I thought about the ghosts or spirits or whatever assembled the fallen dishes back into their original pattern or knocked down furniture in the school for the benefit of the maintenance man cleaning up the classroom. It would have been fun talking with him. Or, was it the cook's way of entertaining gullible visitors like me to pass the time away in this remote village? She had told me that her husband who had some medical problem and couldn't work was living in Anchorage while she went out on jobs in order to support the two of them.

CHAPTER 40

Finally, Little Diomede Island!

I reminded myself I was in Shishmaref instead of on Little Diomede Island as I stood at the window looking outside at the weather. The plan for the first trip was to have me catch the weekly scheduled mail helicopter on Wednesday from Wales to Little Diomede Island. Once there, I was to test kids and return on Saturday since the principal was returning from Nome on a charter and it made sense for me to ride on the backhaul of his charter. Mother Nature had a different plan that meant a detour to Shishmaref, an old village having been in existence some 400 years but was now in its final days. The village sat on permafrost that was quickly eroding and melting away. It was located on Sarichef Island in the Chukchi Sea just north of the Bering Strait on a three-mile long barrier island. Many years in the past there was an inlet on the south side that separated it from the mainland.

Thinking back, my first visit to Shishmaref was made in the late 1970s before I worked in Alaska. Bob and I had flown up there on one of his business trips. His two sons Rob and Mark were with us on that particular trip. We had walked through the village and met the business associate Bob wanted to see. He invited us into his house. He was impressed that Bob had brought his family with him on the trip.

Main Street in the Winter—Shishmaref

After Bob's brief meeting, we walked back to our plane. I remember wondering if we might meet Herbie Nayokpuk, who was a well-known Iditarod musher from this particular community. No other musher in Iditarod history had been more respected or better liked than him. No such luck! We didn't see him, but we did stop in front of the old church while I took a picture of Rob, Mark and Bob. This old church had since burned down. I suspected it was a Lutheran church as Lutherans had settled in Shishmaref.

Now I was back in Shishmaref. One of the teachers went over the list of kids I was to see, and then went over in detail one boy's reason for being referred. He was a very disturbed kid who had cut up his mother's kitten and strewn its innards all around the house. Ugh! I just didn't want to hear about it.

While in Shishmaref I was reminded of some of the physical deformities I had just seen in Brevig Mission. One child particularly stood out to me that afternoon as he had half his face caved in and had horribly burnt hands. I knew the burnt hands were not from a birth defect and wondered what had happened. I wasn't to find out. That night I went over to the two teachers' house for supper. Both women were in their mid-50s with the special education teacher being from eastern Washington and the other one from Montana. We had a good visit inside while the weather seemed to get worse outside. There were whiteout conditions.

The weather cleared on Friday so I was back on track and planned to leave for Little Diomede via Wales, which is the westernmost community on mainland North America. That evening when I called home, I learned my big golden retriever, MacDuff, was going to be put down. He had cancer and essentially had crawled out by the fence to die. We had known for some time that sooner or later he would come to this point. He was only ten years old and I was sorry I was away in the Arctic when it happened. He had been a wonderful dog. I was glad we had his son, Kodiak, although I was a bit concerned that Kodi would grieve for his dad as the two had been together since he was a pup. My night in Wales was spent crying as I slept on the school floor in one of the classrooms inside my sleeping bag on a mattress. I felt badly over being away from my dogs at this time.

Bob was getting more and more negative about my working in Alaska. I almost believed he deliberately tried to make me feel badly when I talked with him about MacDuff. Bob liked the benefits, for example, his medical coverage plus my salary that I was getting, but when I called him, I often ended up in tears because of his comments.

The next morning it was Little Diomede and my first helicopter ride.

During my years in Alaska I made only two trips to Little Diomede Island—the first of which was November 3, 1985. That date in itself sticks out as 25-plus years previous to the day I almost lost my life in a car wreck in November of 1959 in which I fell asleep at the wheel on the Pacific Coast Highway north of Malibu, California. The second visit to Diomede was some years after that in early spring. Both of the Diomede trips were memorable.

The helicopter made two trips from Wales to Little Diomede; I was on the second trip. The pilot pulled out survival suits. We were zipped up in them. I was encased so much so I seriously doubted whether I could have undone a seat belt, opened the door, or even finish zipping the suit up with its hood had the helicopter crashed into the ocean although it was somewhat frozen at the moment.

I was excited. At first glance from the air Diomede appeared to be a wind-swept pile of rocks going straight up. There was nothing flat about it. The geography of the island consisted of almost vertical cliffs going right down into the sea. There was no visible village anywhere. We flew around the island at its north side, and landed on a helicopter pad right next to the school. The village was located directly behind from where we landed on a little rise that appeared to be clinging to the side of the mountain on the only level surface available. Big Diomede loomed directly across from us two miles away although it seemed closer. That, I thought to myself, was Russia!

The door was opened once we set down and I immediately became aware of an over-whelming stench coming from the "meat hole" with its fermenting carcasses. It was located between the heliport and the school and just a few feet from where we landed. I made a quick exit and headed for the school's entrance once I was able to shed my survival suit. Along with the smell was a strange roar that was almost deafening. It was from the generator that went on continuously and sounded almost unearthly. I had entered another world.

Little Diomede Island is the smaller of the two Diomede islands located in the middle of the Bering Strait between the Alaska mainland and Siberia. Between the two islands is where the Bering Sea meets the Chukchi Sea, and where the International

Date Line is. Little Diomede is consequently 24 hours behind the Russian Diomede—one could walk right into tomorrow on the ice. Only 2.4 miles separate the two. One of the teachers later told me there was only about a half mile between the two at the north end. Little Diomede is located 135 miles from Nome. The location of the village was believed to have been used for at least 3,000 years as a hunting campsite. In the late 19th century, travelers reported people living in huts made out of rocks and with skins for a roof. It was on the west side and the only relatively flat area on the island.

The school and the helicopter pad were located right next to the town, although the school had stairs from the elementary school up to the high school which was built at the base of one of the cliffs. The school from the air looked like a giant three-step stairway. The population at both times I was there was around 150 people.

I was curious about what people ate as the environment appeared quite inhospitable for hunting and gathering. The village store didn't give me any clues. Its shelves were virtually empty of anything that was edible.

I stayed with the principal and his wife who was the Special Education teacher. I had a good and as well as informative supper with them the first night. The principal told me that recently, "There are more Russian bombers than private planes visible overhead. They're checking out the new RCA tower that is being built here."

Bonnie, the principal's wife, answered my initial question when she told me that they ate "crabs during the winter once the ice freezes over, birds and eggs, as well as tom cod that individuals catch with their hands." To literally catch fish by hand was amazing to me. Then she added, "They also shoot seals and walruses, which they dump into a meat hole to rot. They like the meat fermented." She wrinkled her nose and went on to say, "About two weeks ago they emptied the large meat hole, and the smell was unbearable even in the open air. Oh yes, they hunt polar bears and traditionally find greens in the springtime."

Full of questions, I asked about the kids, and was told that pot was a major problem. "The 17-18-year-old ones come in and say they want to stop smoking, but can't get away from it; their parents smoke and encourage them to smoke; their friends smoke;

and their siblings smoke."

The other problem, which surprised me, was the high rate of males compared to a low number of girls resulting in the girls being molested. She added that many of the kids suffered from Fetal Alcohol Syndrome. "The parents don't get booze here (or anything to drink for that matter) because of the high cost of freight, but they go to Nome and stay for a month or two and drink." Binge drinking, in other words, was the worst thing a woman could do if she was pregnant although any alcohol was bad!

The first full day I was there, a Sunday, I typed reports all day. This was pre- computer, or at least, before I traveled with a computer. That afternoon I went into the village, just a few steps from the school. Food was scarce and I ended up buying a bracelet out of old ivory which had colors in it from blue to green resulting from mineral content where the ivory had been buried for generations. I also purchased a sweatshirt with a picture of a walrus on it that said, "Little Diomede." I guess I was a tourist at heart!

Monday started off well, or at least the first half did. A plane had actually flown over Diomede but couldn't land because of thick fog. We could hear it but could not see it as it flew away from the area. Then I heard from the principal who had met with the EMT (emergency medical technician). He reported the plane bound for the island loaded with passengers had crashed on the sea ice. "Once word gets out among the villagers, it will be panic." Then he added, "It's unknown if anyone was killed or what injuries might have happened, and almost everyone flying here has relatives living in the village. There's also a newborn baby on the flight."

Bit by bit information sifted into the school. The visiting EMT received information as it came in since he was the only medical person available, and he shared that information with the principal and me. When the plane didn't arrive, rumors began to make their rounds.

The passenger plane had crashed on the sea ice on the east side of the island between Wales and Diomede. It had been heading for the newly carved "runway" in front of the village. Snow had blown into the carburetor and engine overnight while it was parked at the Wales Airport. Part way across to the island the engine had just quit causing the pilot to crash land on the ice.

Fear and panic took hold once villagers heard about the

crash! What happened? Was anyone killed? What about the baby? More and more questions were directed to the EMT and to the principal because they usually could answer them. Word finally came that no one was seriously hurt, just shook up, and the baby was fine.

As I listened to the EMT, I thought those Eskimos out on the ice knew exactly what they were doing when they tore off the rudder and part of a wing to build a shelter of sorts to protect passengers from the freezing wind.

The National Guard started taking survival gear out to the crash site by helicopter from Nome. Then on the return flight they transported passengers back to Nome. In the end all the supplies were on the ice, and all the people were in Nome. What a fiasco! I kept that thought to myself.

The maintenance man, a village woman, and I climbed aboard the helicopter for our return to Wales around noon on the day I left. I ended up waiting at the school until three in the afternoon when a Twin Otter came in and picked me up. We headed to Nome.

Helicopter pad in front of school with Big Diomede in background

My second trip to Diomede began and ended in Nome. It was in the early spring in 1991. I looked forward to the trip with anticipation. I just didn't know how much excitement was in store for me. We left Nome and flew along the coast to Wales where we headed out over the water now frozen. It was foggy. The island suddenly loomed up ahead of us. We went around it and landed right next to the school on the helipad just as I had done on the earlier trip.

Village on Little Diomede with "skin boats" upside down

Once the door was opened I was quickly reminded of my earlier trip when the sickly, pungent smell of fermented seal blubber hit me. I tried not to inhale too much. It came from the large ice enclosed "refrigerator" between the heliport and the school's entrance where locals tossed harvested seals in to ferment. I have never tried this Eskimo delicacy, and had no desire to do so, but the Natives loved it. The generator that powered the school and the town was still running. It was as overpowering as it had been the first time I heard it. I knew it meant life for the inhabitants. Feelings of loneliness and isolation pulled at me. Thoughts of being on the moon crossed my mind.

I jumped down to the ground, took off the survival suit, and quickly made my way into the building away from the smell. The cafeteria was a welcome relief once the door shut behind me. One of the teachers greeted me as I walked in. I was staying upstairs in the library above the cafeteria.

The principal handed me my testing schedule. It was a different man from the first time I had visited. Most of the students to be seen by me were in the upper grades. I had five days to do the work. Easy schedule I thought to myself. I tested kids the next two days and had been invited for supper by a couple of young teachers living part way up the mountain above the school. We were just getting into a great discussion about books when their telephone rang. The call was for me? Surprised, I found the person on the other end was an EMT who was also visiting the site. He was a different one from the one I had met on my first trip.

Was I the school psychologist and could I come down to the clinic? He had a girl down there. I had tested her earlier in the week. She had attempted suicide by overdosing Tylenol. She had taken the whole bottle (or what was left of it). Her mother had been lost in the snow earlier. I wasn't sure if it was recent or how much time had passed. The woman had never been found.

The teachers' house was at the top of the three-terraced stairwell of buildings and was the top rung so to speak of steps above the high school on the cliff along with several other tiny houses. To say I flew down the steps would be an exaggeration, but I didn't waste time as I hurried down, entered the high school and continued down some more steps to where the clinic was located just outside the school. The building was tiny with one room for seeing patients with probably sleeping quarters in the back for visiting EMTs, nurses, and others visiting the clinic.

Sure enough, it was one of the girls I had tested earlier in the week. She was half sitting/half laying on a gurney of sorts. She was fully conscious. The EMT was trying to pour some medication down her throat to counteract the effects of the Tylenol. Could I help? At this point she was cooperative. He had a very limited supply, and, of course, the closest pharmacy was in Nome. Worse, weather had deteriorated considerably making it impossible for any flights to come in or leave the island. We discussed the situation.

She vomited the medication up, so he had to pour it right back down her as he didn't have any more available. This occurred several times while I stood there. I'm not sure why he wanted me there, but he did. I swallowed hard and took a couple of deep breaths. I talked with her in between the EMT's attempts to get the medicine down her. He told me she had reportedly taken sixty of her mother's prescription, twenty-two Tylenol, six other pills, and one aspirin. He was concerned about the Tylenol.

That evening I got quite an education on Tylenol, liver damage, and taking too much that could result in death. I also learned that Tylenol had a cumulative effect on the liver, so at some future time an individual who had ingested a large amount could take a couple of pills and drop dead. Maybe that's an exaggeration, but that's how I understood it. To this day I don't take Tylenol if I can avoid it which is a silly reaction, I suppose, but I just don't take it.

The EMT was finally able to get the girl stabilized. That evening and the next two days we discussed options for getting her to the emergency room at the hospital in Nome, and getting more medicine for her to counteract the cumulative effects of the Tylenol. He spoke with the hospital emergency personnel by phone.

Various scenarios included an air drop of meds, but then where would the plane drop it as fog covered the whole area. Another possibility was contacting Russian authorities and seeing if something could be done getting medication from Big Diomede— and this was before Russia and the U.S. were on good diplomatic terms back in the 80s. It would have probably caused an international incident. Besides the supplies on Big Diomede I suspected weren't much better than where we were. Mainly, it was used as a training area for Russian soldiers—their movements could be seen by teachers from time to time according to the stories I had heard.

In the meantime, my five days were up but I couldn't fly out either. I called the Alaska Airlines terminal in Nome daily to tell them I couldn't make the flight because I couldn't get off the island. We became quite friendly over the phone as they knew the situation and just kept rebooking me for the next flight out for which I was thankful.

Finally, one of the small bush planes was going to make a try for it as the fog had lifted a little and the island was marginally visible. The pack ice, however, was thinner than it should be for carving out a landing strip. Not too much thinner, or the pilot wouldn't have risked it, I reasoned.

We were going to try it. The plane arrived, and we raced out of the building. I had packed my supplies and sleeping bag for the hurried exit. A limited breakfast resulted in my grabbing a chicken sandwich in the cafeteria. I held on to that as if it were the most important thing in my life. The EMT, the girl, and I rode on snow machines across the ice to the plane. Baggage had been hastily thrown in the sleds attached to the snow goes.

The pilot never shut the engine down. This plane was not delivering supplies. It was a pick-up-and-go operation. We threw our gear in while he inched forward on the sea ice. We jumped in one by one, closed the door and with that the pilot pushed the throttle forward as far as it would go. We shot across the ice.

I munched on my sandwich as the plane gained speed. It was one of the bumpiest rides I have ever experienced before we were finally airborne. It's an understatement to say a sigh of relief washed over me as we gained altitude.

The rest of the flight was uneventful. We reached Nome a little more than an hour later. The girl along with the EMT went directly to the emergency room of the local hospital while I headed to the Alaska Airlines counter. I never saw nor heard from the EMT or the girl nor would I get a chance to visit Little Diomede again. I never learned what happened to her, but knew once she reached the hospital she would receive excellent care.

I reached Seattle and then Vashon Island that evening. My boss later sent me a bouquet of flowers as she knew part of the story—that was the only time that ever happened.

CHAPTER 41

The End? No Way! But Rather, Beginnings

When I look at what I did in retrospect, I get tired just thinking of all the miles I put on my body and mind during the latter part of 1985 beginning with a "marathon." The Fall of that year ended quite suddenly work-wise for me when a life-threatening situation developed because of complications from surgery resulting in a blood clot. It was late November when I ended up in the hospital for surgery for something totally unrelated to travel and work.

I was grounded by my doctor for the first two months of 1986 and had lots of time to think while I sat at home. Being grounded was probably the best thing that could have happened and helped me build up my reserves but it also changed the course of my life.

I knew then that I wanted to share my life with children, their heartaches, their joys, their growing up years, and adulthood. I didn't want to grow old alone as I had seen so many people do. Since Bob was 22 years older than me, the likelihood of my outliving him was a distinct possibility. His own two boys were already grown and away from home. I liked both of them and got along well with them I thought. Once my doctor gave me the okay to return to work, I headed back north to finish my contract for the school year.

During my recovery period at home Bob and I decided to adopt a girl. At the end of the 1985-86 school year I told my boss I was leaving SERRC to become a mother. Twyla was shocked, but very supportive.

Bob and I went to Peru between mid-November 1986 and the first part of January 1987, and adopted not one but two children—siblings, an 11-year old boy, Jhon, soon to turn 12 and his 10-year old sister, Natalia. That's another book (*Adoption in Peru*). The two months we were there brought constant complaints on Bob's part. One minute he was supportive of me and the next he said I didn't know what I was doing as children were a lot of work. His position on the subject of adopting children was negative. It became quite clear that he did not want to share me with a child, or with work, or anything else. He wanted to control me, have me all to himself, and I wasn't going to let that happen. But, despite his negativism, he signed all the paperwork.

Before I even returned from Peru to Vashon Island I had a call from Twyla—would I "make a short trip to Barrow, Alaska, to do some assessments as the psychologist up there was in desperate need of help." It was only a week-long trip. Yes, of course, I would go. I knew at that moment I would continue to go to Alaska as long as I had the opportunities. I also knew I would be there for the kids whenever they needed me. I had fallen in love with them from the first moment I met them.

The next few years I made more of those occasional trips north commuting from Vashon and traveling by commercial jet out of Seattle to Alaska. Bob was diagnosed with prostate cancer two months after our return from Peru. He became totally consumed in his fight with it. He blamed me. Irrational, yes, but he decided it was my fault. He wanted someone to blame. His anger smoldered. I realized how important it was for me to maintain my certification, medical insurance that not only covered me and the kids but most of Bob's medical bills, and my ability to support myself.

Bob's retirement in 1981 was at the end of his career. I was just beginning mine. In the first few years of our marriage we had many adventures. Flying to Alaska was a big part of them, as well as flying down to Mexico, and going to the east coast several times for two weeks for Bob's Army reserve time in the Pentagon. All these trips were made in the Bonanza. We had also made a number of trips during the summer months on our 32-foot motor sailor, a Monterey Clipper that we purchased in November of 1980, going to Alaska. It had been built in 1975. We renamed it the *H.M.S. Glenfiddich*. The *H.M.S.* stood for "Highland Malt Scotch" although the Canadians interpreted it as "Her Majesty's Ship" and one of their own military cruisers when we had radio communications with them in Canadian waters. It had a draft of four and a half feet. Its beam was ten feet-three inches while its displacement was 18,000 pounds.

Mini boat trips up to and around the San Juan Islands as far north as Desolation Sound were a natural. Once school was out with temperatures warming up and spring turning into summer, the four of us decided to make some little exploratory trips. The dachshunds joined us. Jhon became quite adept with the oars rowing ashore daily in our Avon dinghy. He soon learned, however, that the dinghy wasn't built for transporting all of us at the same time. When we landed on Clark Island, no one else was around so we had the shore to ourselves. It had taken two "ship to shore" trips to get us all on the beach. My camera was out as I snapped picture after picture of the kids while they chased the dachshunds and the dachshunds chased them.

Time to go back to the boat Jhon leaped in grabbing the oars while our six remaining dachshunds followed (Otto had passed away in mid-July). Bob and Natalia jumped in the back after pushing it out from the shore. The dachshunds followed them right into the boat. Jhon didn't weigh enough to counterbalance their weight and was sitting in the middle to make it worse. Water quickly came over the gunnels and found its way into the dinghy. It sank with all on board.

Fortunately, they were still in shallow water. The dogs were excellent swimmers and headed right back to me when I called. Both kids and Bob waded back to shore dripping wet. The dinghy was retrieved, and more attention was paid to balance the second time a trip back to the *Glenfiddich* was attempted and all trips thereafter.

We visited Friday Harbor's whale museum on that trip and also several other islands as well. We made several other local trips during the summer months in Puget Sound that included Blake Island, another island a mile from our home. The kids seemed to like boating, and were sorry when the summer ended and they headed back to school but excited to get back with all their friends. They were now in the sixth grade.

I made more and more trips to Alaska only this time I was commuting from Seattle and also working some in the State of Washington for a couple of districts on the Kitsap Peninsula.

Bob was still well enough to fly his beloved Bonanza around the world in 1990 and take part in the Vintage Air Rally between London, England, and Brisbane, Australia. He spent most of the previous year planning the trip. The kids and the dogs stayed home; however, I joined him. Friendships were developed during that trip starting March 25, 1990 at White Waltham Airfield in England and ending May 5, 1990 in Brisbane, Australia. The rally attracted not only would-be flight enthusiasts and adventurers including the two of us but also commercial pilots from several different airlines. After all it was the flight of a lifetime! And that's another story. There were 21 other single-engine pre-1950 airplanes with only about half of them completing the trip. The air rally was to commemorate the 70th anniversary of mail service between the two countries. After that my husband and I continued on to Papua New Guinea and then Guam where I caught a jet home, and Bob continued on around the world.

Our family including Natalia and Jhon flew commercially to New Zealand and Australia visiting the organizer of the rally who lived in Brisbane a month before Bob left in his plane from Vashon's airport. His younger son Mark flew with him to London then flew home. I met Bob in London and accompanied him on the rally then on to Papua New Guinea and Guam. From there I flew home commercially through Japan while Bob crossed the Pacific Ocean in the Bonanza.

Bob didn't always follow the rules on the trip. I noted a few situations in which was in the wrong. He flew into restricted air space in Italy to the extent a couple of Italian military jets flew up to check us out. The airport authorities in Southern France questioned him, checking his pilot's license and other documents before we took off, again because of flying into restricted area. The Australian equivalent of the FAA in the U.S gave him a stern reprimand when we were about to leave Alice Springs. He had violated landing procedures. He also flew into a restricted zone in Egypt although no one was the wiser on that occasion except me.

The following year found us flying to the Dominican Republic where we met several of the pilots who had taken part in the air rally. Flying home from that trip I became very aware that Bob was making serious errors in his judgments while flying. Other red flags were also observed.

Bob lost his beloved Bonanza in the spring of 1991 when he crashed landed on the California-Oregon border in the Siskiyou Mountains. It happened the end of March. He had had to re-license the plane and was forced to replace the wobble pump against his wishes. The mechanics doing the work put the wrong lubricant on it, so when Bob went to switch gas tanks the pump was frozen and didn't pump gas from the reserve tank into the main tank leading to the engine. He ran out of gas and was barely able to crash land near the main interstate highway into a rocky hillside. There is no doubt in my mind that his skill in flying probably saved his life; he walked away unscratched.

He ended up buying one of the other Bonanzas that had been a part of the air rally in 1990 using the insurance money from mechanic's insurance after an aviation inspector determined cause of crash.

After our trip to the Dominican Republic I was afraid for the kids to fly with him, and I always found excuses for them not to go on flights. I avoided flying with him as well. One of the FAA inspectors contacted our home after a flight he made by himself to Juneau. I talked with them briefly. Before the FAA could pull his license, he basically stopped flying. His older son Rob started flying him. I was glad to see that.

Bob was finally diagnosed with dementia, but not before he legally did everything he could to ruin me financially after his death. Such was the end of an almost-20-year marriage, short six weeks, when he passed away in June of 1995.

The kids were in college by the time Bob died. As for me, I was very happy to be reinstated as one of the regular school psychologists for Southeast Regional Resource Center.

CHAPTER 42

A Summer Family Trip

By the spring of 1988 the kids had been in the United States for well over a year. I wanted to introduce them to Alaska, although they had spent three weeks with the Andrews who were teaching in Klukwan when Bob and I made a trip to Norway that had been planned long before our trip to Peru. We talked about it, planned ahead and decided Bob was to take the boat to Ketchikan with one of his friends. The kids and I would fly to Ketchikan about three weeks later when they were out of school and meet him.

It was May 21st when Bob headed north. Jhon had gone with him to help load the boat at the marina and then the two of them brought it around the island to the front of our house. Bob left Vashon the next day and headed north mostly by himself except for three of our dachshunds, Duff, Baron, and Moose, and Kodi, our golden retriever. By this time we had lost MacDuff to cancer.

Initially, he started out with a friend of his. Phil left him a couple of days later in the San Juan Islands because of "all the confusion" and the "lack of luxury." I wondered what he expected, but was sorry for Bob's sake in that he would be making the trip with only the dogs for company. Phil's departure was almost like a premonition of a long list of events that were most unpleasant.

Jhon, Natalia, two guitars, our remaining three dachshunds

(Schnapsie, Charlie, and Schultz), and I arrived at the Ketchikan Airport with excess baggage on the tenth of June where Bob and the rest of the dogs met us.

The next morning we purchased groceries and fishing licenses, filled the boat's fresh water tank, and took off on a gray and sullen day. It definitely wasn't the kind of day I envisioned for a summer full of fun on the water, but it was what it was.

I sat in the stern some of the time reading Bob's entries in the logbook describing his trip between Vashon and Ketchikan. Troubles had begun almost immediately. The fathometer initially started acting up. I was surprised that he didn't ground the boat, although he did scrape a few sandbars in route. There were several entries in the log about a "whistling noise" coming from the engine compartment. Then he mentioned the bilge pump that had stopped working and needed replacing. A water hose for fresh water had a leak in it as well. Bob had bypassed the cutoff but failed to put the switch in the pump hole with the result of the cabin flooding. That must have happened in the first day or two of the trip. No wonder Phil abandoned "ship". Bob had everything torn up in the cabin from his notes with the comment that he thought that had finished Phil. It was the next morning when Phil had gone up town in Friday Harbor and returned saying he was bothered by all the confusion and was catching the ferry home. It was Monday morning the 24th of May.

Bob's later notes indicated he was having problems towing the dinghy. He also mentioned the autopilot becoming "flakey", and knowing Bob and his reliance on the autopilot, I figured he was more than upset.

Another entry indicated Moose disappeared but was soon found a half hour later. Rough weather didn't help any of the dogs, especially Duff. His entries indicated there was nowhere to stop to take them ashore. I could only imagine what it must have been like aboard the boat with sick dogs!

Following Canada's rough coastline, he connected with several people he had met before and also stopped at harbors we had visited in summers past before the kids arrived. Moose got his act together and was beginning to endear himself to Bob. Baron slept at Bob's feet as he steered. Continued problems with the water pump necessitated buying a new one which Bob was able to hook up. But its motor wouldn't run for more than five minutes.

Someone at one of the stops overnight told him to take it apart. He discovered that the pump had sat too long without grease. That was a simple fix; adding grease worked.

Further log entries mentioned a rough passage across Queen Charlotte Sound with the dogs terrified. Bob hit his ear on the door lock resulting in blood all over the cabin. He had bad weather with 15 to 25 knot winds, hurricane warnings on the radio, and the autopilot going completely out! The notation that he wished his son Rob were with him (Rob had helped him bring the boat back the summer of 1981), was penciled in at the bottom of the page.

His worst day sounded like a nightmare! It included cleaning out the boat, Kodi eating all the dachshunds' food while he was pulling up the anchor in fog, Moose disappearing a second time on the boat, fixing zincs on the engine, the refrigerator shutting down, with a final comment that it was "almost constant work solving one problem after another." Bob was stubborn and persevered!

Then there were those notations about having a drink or two with people he met as well as a "good night snort" before he went to bed. References to being tired were made; at one point he wrote "exhausted" and "going back to bed". I also ran across his comments about some people he met on another boat with a black and white cat named Scrimshaw. The cat boarded the *Glenfiddich* and "drove the dachshunds wild." Bob could have used more than an extra hand on that occasion.

As I read Bob's entries in the log, I was amazed he and the dogs had made it to Ketchikan alive, and was thankful that neither Natalia nor Jhon knew about the problems he had endured. They would have abandoned ship or we would have had a mutiny, I'm sure. Not a good trip, I thought to myself—not good at all! I closed the log book and said a little prayer as I put it back on the shelf. Those entries should have been a warning of more to come, but I ignored them. After all, what else could happen?

Once the kids were aboard, we headed for Lyman's Anchorage but overshot it and then couldn't find it as we backtracked, so we crossed Clarence Strait a second time and went into Myers Chuck. Jhon and Natalia's school principal lived there during the summer months but wouldn't be there until July. Too bad, as I knew it would have been fun for the kids to visit him at his summer residence.

Myers Chuck had metal grates everywhere. Jhon helped with the dogs as the grates were hard on their feet. Natalia worked on the cabin, which definitely needed a lot of help. She scrubbed and scrubbed and scrubbed; she had it spotless in no time! I was not sure how a summer aboard the boat was going to go with them. I was a little worried as a matter of fact, because they had never been on the water for long periods of time since our previous summer had been all short trips.

Both kids had their recorders and practiced. Jhon tried tuning his guitar with no luck. Both had been taking guitar lessons the previous year. I couldn't help him on this as I had never played a stringed instrument. I also introduced Natalia to cross stitching. She seemed to enjoy it, and I figured it would help with fine motor coordination—the educational psychologist in me was surfacing.

I should add that we no longer had the small rubber dinghy that we had the previous year, as we had invested in a sturdy wooden one capable of holding all of us at once.

Leaving Myers Chuck put us back in the main channel. We were barely there when we spotted a Black Bear ambling along the shore. It was a good sized one and I think both kids were properly impressed.

That evening we anchored and went fishing while Natalia and Jhon did a little exploring on their own. As luck would have it, they found two halves of a beaver skull. The next day we tried cleaning it by boiling the head, which made a most unpleasant smell. Cleaning the pot afterwards proved to be an even worse chore, but sea water, Pine Sol, Bon Ami, and Ivory soap in various amounts proved successful. It wasn't as if there weren't things to see and do.

We headed for Anan Creek in Humpback Bay, hiked in about a half a mile on a U.S. Forest Service trail to the falls and observatory. Lots of bear tracks and "spoor" were visible. No bears! Back on the boat we fished using our new $150 downriggers that had been in storage for three years. They should have brought us some luck—they didn't.

Heading up Blake Channel through the Narrows we passed the Wrangell Airport. We came around and docked at the marina, did a quick run through the totem poles on Shakes Island and headed for the Marine Bar and pizza. Neither Natalia nor Jhon seemed to mind the lateness of the hour or the pizza for supper.

After all, it had been a very full day!

Heading for Petersburg we had to pass the Wrangell Narrows at the right time or risk getting stuck. We hit a couple of small sand bars, waited a few minutes and with the rising tide continued on our way. Bob spent much of his time at working on the bilge pump.

Up at 6:30 the next morning all of us walked the dogs. Back on board a gentle wind blew us right into the dock where we had been for the night. We had to push the bow out and I ended up jumping onto two fishing boats in order to push our bow sprit out of the way. Finally, with combined effort we made it. We could relax and since it was June 14th and Natalia's 12th birthday, I brought out her birthday present.

"Happy Birthday, Natalia." One of the guitars was her birthday present. She didn't connect to the fact that we were carrying two guitar cases on the plane, one being Jhon's so was very surprised when I handed her the second case. A big smile erupted.

It was a beautiful day with glassy water when we arrived in Petersburg. I don't know what the kids thought of this Norwegian fishing community other than being curious, but the food was good. Years later, I ended up working in Petersburg going there three-four times a year, but that was in in the future.

We made a late start the next morning eating well, and left the harbor with yummy cinnamon rolls and bread from a deli. We had met Chuck the previous evening. He was someone Bob had met earlier in Canada and since he was going the same direction we were, we headed for Thomas Bay and Sunny Cove where we would join him for dinner. Once there I went into the cove staying aboard the boat while Bob and the kids went with Chuck to set crab pots. Bob tried fishing and had some little trout-like fish following his line but none would bite. I think the kids were secretly happy.

The crabs weren't tempted by our bait either. When we checked the next morning, the pot was empty. Then it happened. The fishing poles were out, and it looked like something was on mine. Of course, my line was knotted so I had to pull it in by hand. I landed a nice 20-pound white King salmon. It was a true miracle that I didn't lose it as it had also tangled with Bob's line. He pulled his line in by hand and had a small halibut on the end.

Chuck came over to our boat for dinner and brought a beautiful fruit salad. Did it ever go well with the white King! I wondered what the kids thought with their parents catching dinner, and meeting a stranger on the high seas who brought over a fruit salad. They only ate fish when nothing else was available. The first chance they had both kids would order fried chicken. Chuck left the cove much earlier than we did. We didn't see him again on the trip.

We continued north visiting Haines and Skagway. We took the train up the mountain to White Pass where Jhon and Natalia encountered their first snow. I felt good all over when I saw them make snow balls. I even got a snowball or two in the air as we waited for the train to take us back down to Skagway.

I wanted them to see Glacier Bay and remembered how special the trip we had taken with the Calvins nine years earlier. I had several days of work scheduled so flew to Juneau from Skagway while the rest of the crew went to Haines. From there they worked their way to Glacier Bay where I joined them at the lodge three days later—just in time for a great dinner. It was fried chicken for the kids. Bob and I had halibut—smile!

Once in Glacier Bay National Park we headed for Sandy Cove, then visited several glaciers. Three crabs found our pot, but one was put back into the water as it was too small. The other two provided lunch. Campers were there, so after taking the dogs ashore we decided to pull up our anchor and move to a "less crowded" spot. The major hoist was done from the cabin with Bob at the controls. Once at the water line, I took over to secure the heavy anchor just behind the bow sprit.

I remembered how much fun hiking in the Glacier Bay area had been. I guess I was trying to recreate our trip on the *Morning Mist* as it had been so enjoyable. We hiked above in the hills about two miles as there was a lot of open country and a small lake near where we anchored. Moose signs were present as well as evidence of other small critters. Four of the dachshunds didn't want to behave so were on leashes. Good thing because we found a tern's nest with three eggs in it. The eggs looked just like rocks. I took some great pictures as the sun was just beginning to set. The kids swam across small glacial lakes. Not me! But then the water was probably pretty warm as the lakes were shallow and had lots of sunlight to heat them up.

Rain joined us the following day. It was cold and wet outside, so I treated myself to hot buttered rum while Bob and the kids took the dogs ashore in the rain. It had to have been a good half mile row in the dinghy. That day we went to Margerie Glacier where the Sea Princess, a cruise ship, was anchored, so we left and headed for Johns Hopkins Glacier.

We maneuvered our boat into the ice and just drifted with it for about an hour in Johns Hopkins Inlet. The morning had been gloomy and oppressive but the rain finally stopped. I took picture after picture of seals. The sun came out from hiding as I snapped photos of yet more seals, and every now and then a picture of either Natalia or Jhon. From there we motored over to Reid Glacier where we found an abandoned cabin. Indian Paintbrush was just beginning to make its appearance. There was none to be seen in the rest of Glacier Bay as it was still too early for the plants to start blooming.

We anchored at Blue Mouse Cove. Bob worked on zincs in the engine. The old zinc had eroded so badly that he had to use an auxiliary generator in order to use the electric drill to remove it. It was midnight before he resolved the problem. The next day the starter wouldn't work.

I began to get creative in the kitchen as we were running out of basic food supplies. It was tuna fish spaghetti with two-bean salad for supper. I didn't have a can of a third bean. Yummy! We did replenish our ice supply at the glaciers. The dachshunds got into a fight over Kodi's food, with Duff getting bit. We were forced to leave under sail as the motor froze. We tacked our way out but then the wind died. We drifted, sometimes sailing when a breeze came up however short-lived. A large flock of terns greeted us at Willoughby Island. They were successfully fishing.

Problems continued to follow us. Finally, in desperation we dropped our anchor in 108 feet of water as we were drifting right out of the cove. No wind! And, of course, the engine still wasn't working! The anchor was no help either, so we hauled it back up.

Once the anchor was secured on the boat, the current pulled us toward shore and that's when chaos really descended upon us. Jhon jumped into the dinghy with oars and a tow line. Straining with the oars he pulled the bow away from the shore but didn't make much headway.

H.M.S. Glenfiddich in front of Margerie Glacier

Bob jumped in and continued Jhon's efforts to stay off the shore and finally made it into the channel and continued our drift. We put up our sail and let the Park Service know by radio our whereabouts. They told us not to worry about our park permit expiring. And, I thought to myself, I wanted to re-create our trip through Glacier Bay made in 1979 aboard the *Morning Mist.* Ha!

When we passed Strawberry Island, we were caught in the current and a rip tide. We ended up going by the island a second time and then passed it again several more times as the current carried us backwards despite the fact we were under full sail. That's when it started to rain seriously. We called the Park Service again as we were in the middle of the channel. They came out with what was called a Sérac and towed us back to Bartlett Cove where the lodge was located and was technically out of the park.

A repairman from the Park Service fixed our starter for $85.00. Bob complained of not feeling well, which was very unusual. I wondered if the stress from the trip so far was too much for him. He had been diagnosed with prostate cancer over a year previously and was fighting that, but had not had any problems with it.

We saw another fabulous slide show on bears in the park that evening. It was more fried chicken for the kids, while Bob and I had seafood. Walking out of the lodge to our dinghy we started rowing to where our boat was moored. There on the beach was a very large Black Bear walking along the shore without a concern in the world. I was amazed at the quiet way he passed into the tall grass and just disappeared.

We left Glacier Bay on the third of July and loaded up with fresh water. Bob was feeling a little better but still not good. Moose fell into the water on a short trip to shore. Jhon was ready to dive in after him but Moose not to be left behind started swimming when Bob called him.

The next day Bob was again feeling very poorly, so we headed for Auke Bay just north of Juneau instead of heading south. He planned to go to the Emergency Room at the local hospital once there. I steered most of the way and just east of Shelter Island saw a number of Humpback whales about half mile away. We entered Auke Bay's new harbor, and just as we pulled into the berth, the engine quit.

Linda from SERRC and her husband Greg met us and took Bob to the hospital in Juneau. He later returned to the boat feeling a little better but not good.

All in all we were in Auke Bay for nine days. The kids became very acquainted with the area during the time. The engine was finally repaired with replacement of a new cylinder that was shipped from New Jersey but without a head gasket causing a further delay. We tried to go north to Haines when the thermostat heated up so returned to Auke Bay. Another repairman we knew came out and worked on it. Still aboard the boat when we left, we dropped him off at the breakwater and then turned towards Haines.

This time we spotted about a dozen sea lions at Benjamin Island as well as a few porpoises. We stayed at Haines until the 24th of July with the boat, while Bob flew to Seattle for appointments with his doctors. It turned out he had shingles. I couldn't just leave the boat and fly down with him at the time. There was no question in my mind that staying in Haines with the boat, the kids, and the six dachshunds, and one golden retriever was what I needed to do. Bob and Margaret Andrews, the teachers I met from Freshwater Bay, were there and in a position to help me after Bob left. Natalia and Jhon had stayed with them in the early spring of 1987 in Klukwan for three weeks. It was a good time for them to get reacquainted. I stayed aboard the boat with the dogs.

After Bob returned from Seattle and we finally left, it was about eight minutes before the gill net opening so we dodged nets all the way down Lynn Canal.

We anchored in William Henry Bay, where a couple of men gave us a 35-pound halibut. I suspected they were over their limit, but it tasted excellent all the same. They told me the halibut were feeding off spawning salmon.

The next day was overcast. Surprise, the autopilot was also misbehaving as well. Bob, however, was able to fix it.

We ended up at Pavlof Harbor, which was full of boats. We met people from the *E Z Rider* and also from *Raccoon III*. We knew them from our trip two years previous. We also ran into Glenda and Bob Hutton, teachers I knew from Hoonah, in their boat, *Ragtime*. They were heading for Anacortes, so I figured we would see them again along the way. Sure enough, the next evening they were already at Baranof Hot Springs when we arrived!

After dinner Jhon and Bob went up to the lake, while Natalia entertained everyone with her new guitar. Bob Hutton, who was the music teacher from the school, tuned both Natalia and Jhon's guitars. We had a hot bath at the springs which turned out to be a cattle water trough. "Gross!" was Natalia's comment. Gross or not, it felt wonderful!

Kodi met a beautiful golden retriever and fell in love, and then met the boyfriend, which was followed by a fight. We retrieved Kodi without any injuries except for his pride.

The following evening it was dark and rainy when we found our anchorage. I was on the bow yelling directions to Jhon and Natalia who relayed them to Bob while he called out depths. We were finally secure in a small bite next to one that Bob and Rob had been in when they returned to Vashon from Alaska on our 1981 trip. An East wind came up and jammed the anchor chain in the lock. Fortunately, the anchor was already on the bottom and the wind set it firmly. We let out more chain and ended up swinging around on the anchor all night.

Mark, Bob's younger natural son, met us at the Petersburg Airport. We also picked up a new Suzuki motor for the dinghy while there. Mark convinced Jhon and Natalia to pick enough blueberries to make a pie by saying, "Marilyn makes a great blueberry pie." He was with us for about a week before he flew back to Seattle from Ketchikan. The day before he left, Mark caught a very nice salmon and before breakfast nonetheless. We ate well on his last night aboard the boat.

Once Mark left we went to the downtown dock in Ketchikan and took off in different directions with me checking a bookstore to see if they wanted any more of my books. It looked like I was the last one to arrive back at the dock. Excitement was high despite the light rain. I untied the mooring lines and pushed off leaping onto the boat at the last minute. Jhon helped me push off. Our boat was the only one at the dock. Bob headed for the middle of the channel. I went downstairs to the main cabin, but only saw the dogs. "Where's Natalia?"

Bob looked confused, saying "downstairs."

"No, she's not."

I checked the bow that was nothing more than a big bed that went wall to wall and the bathroom just in case she was hiding. She wasn't. The boat was only 29 feet long at the water line with very few hiding places. Slowly, we made a wide 180 degree turn in the middle of the channel and headed back. Long before we got there I could see Natalia dressed in jeans and a float jacket standing at the very edge of the dock following us with her eyes. She later said she had walked down the ramp to the dock and suddenly realized there was no boat.

We faced an eleven-hour run to Prince Rupert the next morning. The weather was iffy as a "low" was building out in the Aleutians. We cleared customs once at Prince Rupert. It was full of boats from the fishing fleet when we arrived. Unfortunately, the next morning the engine turned over once followed by a "clunk." We sat at the dock for the remainder of the day and were finally towed to Kello Marine. The engine had to be removed. What to do? It was going to take at least ten days to get another engine. We couldn't stay aboard the boat with the dogs while it was being repaired. Much discussion followed.

We drove home in a rented car, then returned on the 26th of August. The four of us along with our dogs boarded the *Glenfiddich* and left Prince Rupert after Bob made a trial run with the mechanic. Very late the night of September 5th we tied up at the buoy in front of our house on Vashon. The replacement engine had cost us approximately $6,200 Canadian dollars.

Natalia and Jhon rowing back from shore

Natalia made an entry into the log book dated a year later (August 18, 1989). She wrote: "I looked inside of the boat and it was pretty dirty but not that bad so I took my radio and put it full blast. I listened to songs while I was cleaning the boat. Dad said it was marvelous. We went to Tacoma to fill it with gas (diesel fuel) and on the way back a guy yelled and said 'It's still floating?' I said 'yes' and then he said 'Yeah, because I'm the guy that built it.' Got back to harbor and mom said the boat looked marvelous too. I'm so proud."

Reading Natalia's entry in the log book I was surprised to hear they ran into the boat builder. I thought to myself little did he know his comment about "still floating" was not just a casual remark to be taken lightly.

Our boating adventures, the kids' experiences that summer, and meeting friends we had in Alaska were a good background for Natalia who later got a summer job on the Victoria Clipper as a deck hand that took tourists back and forth between Seattle and Victoria, British Columbia.

When they went to college, both kids worked in Skagway during the summer months—Natalia for two summers in a gift shop, and Jhon for one summer in the same gift shop. Then Jhon ended up for a second summer in False Pass in the Aleutians working for the manager of the store who also owned a fishing boat. He was going to fish all summer, but after one trip in which they caught 5,000 pounds of salmon the fishing slowed down to not being profitable enough to take the boat out. On that trip Jhon almost went overboard when they delivered their fish to a larger tender. I'd like to think that his quick thinking along with his experiences on our boat allowed him to hang on. The rest of the summer Jhon spent working in the grocery store in False Pass.

CHAPTER 43

A Mini Tour

There were occasions when I traveled all over the map in a two and sometimes three-week period of time. I could tell what village I was in by just knowing the day. One such period was at the end of January in 1988 when I flew roughly 7,040 miles in a two-week period. After leaving Seattle I flew to Fairbanks. I was weathered out of Fort Yukon so spent a comfortable night in Fairbanks and left the next morning on a twin Piper Navajo only to get to the district office and wait for the Special Education director to arrive.

She finally returned and had me stay at the Sourdough Inn for the one night. I would be in Fort Yukon. It was the first and last time I stayed in that hotel! The walls were paper thin and the night was very cold. I could hear the village dogs barking, snow machines roaring outside, and creaks in the old building anytime someone moved across its floors. Even with all my clothes on and curled up inside my down sleeping bag I think it was one of the coldest nights I have ever spent in a hotel! I later learned the Sourdough had been moved to Fort Yukon from Circle in three sections on the river in 1926—previously it had served as an Army barracks. It eventually burned down.

The old Sourdough Inn—Fort Yukon
(Photo by Marylu Martin)

Some of my later trips found me staying in the District's accounting office upstairs and surrounded by files. Other overnights included a district-owned house on the corner about a block from the office, and a couple of times in private homes with school personnel. But mostly I went out to the dormitory that was about a mile from the district office more or less. More about that later!

It turned out there was only one child for me to see at the Fort. So, at 11 the next morning I found myself in a Super Cub on skis headed to Birch Creek where I was to meet and test three kids. It was a charter flight and the pilot was to pick me up the next day.

Birch Creek is a very small village along none other than Birch Creek (a river that flows east and then north from near the Steese Highway just past Twelvemile Summit, and eventually reaches the Yukon). The village is about 26 miles southwest of Fort Yukon. The first and only time I visited the community was at the same time the itinerant Special Education teacher was also visiting. She told me she worked in five of the district's schools, and in order to save transporting personal belongings from school to school she had purchased five hair dryers, five coffee pots, five cooking pans, and five bottles of shampoo plus a few other things all "in fives". In other words, she had five of everything she would need, and placed one set in each school that she served. Birch Creek was one of her schools. I thought to myself she was a true itinerant teacher. Hauling 83 plus pounds of equipment around with me gave me an understanding of why she did that.

I saw two of students that afternoon, followed by spending the night in a hot school building on the floor in my sleeping bag. I saw a third student the following morning. As I remember there was only one classroom. The outhouse was just that; it was outside!

I visited one boy's grandparents with the Special Education teacher that evening. The grandfather, I decided, had to be the oldest Indian man I had ever seen. The creases in his face were absolutely amazing. I tried not to stare. Their kitchen, living room, and one bed were crammed into the one large room with everything else. A wood-burning stove in the center heated the home.

To describe the room as "crowded" would have been an understatement. It was appallingly overcrowded! A television was playing. The couple appeared happy and content. I saw bulk tea, a microwave oven, two kittens named Shadow and Bandit chasing each other underneath chairs, and a table cluttered with all manner of things on it. The floor probably had never seen a broom! There wasn't much space left for the people. I concentrated on talking about the boy and lost track of my surroundings. The itinerant teacher and I walked back to the school. It was 40 degrees below outside.

While I was at the school she gave the kids a lesson in making applesauce. They enjoyed her and seemed to be paying attention to her words and the applesauce they would soon taste. It was a highly successful lesson.

My flight was cancelled the next morning due to cold weather—they don't fly below 45 degrees and it was minus 46 degrees in Fort Yukon I learned. That afternoon, however, I heard a plane fly over but was reassured by the regular teacher there that it wasn't mine—he was wrong. The pilot actually walked over to the school's door and got me since no one came out to meet the plane. He helped me carry my baggage back to the plane.

Around three in the afternoon I arrived in Circle where I tested a 17-year old girl. Circle was actually the end of the road as further driving was blocked by the Yukon River. My stay there was a quick in-and-out visit. From Circle I rode in a pick-up truck with one of the local residents and headed for Central thirty-six miles away. Shortly after we crossed Birch Creek, we met a Ford Falcon that took me to the Far North School in Central.

I was told by the teacher in Central all of the kids were in the "gifted range". I didn't argue. I did not see any Native kids at the school. We did discuss an upcoming field trip, actually going out of state. It seemed incredible and well planned. That fit right in with the workshop on talented and gifted students that I presented.

My overnight this time was at the Steese Roadhouse, which was an historic building that my husband Bob and I had occasion to visit on the trip in 1973. I looked for our names on the beams in the bar where we had written them along with hundreds of other visitors, but couldn't find them. While there we had encountered some of the most vicious mosquitoes I have met but during this trip mosquitoes were the least of my concerns. I heard nearby the temperatures were minus 29 degrees! I had a very good dinner and despite the cold was drawn to the outdoor hot springs.

I didn't have my swimming suit, but the hotel had one available for visitors and I didn't see any reason not to "try" the pool. I changed, headed for the water and jumped right in. Once there I began thinking about how I was going to get out. The couple of steps leaving the pool had "metal" railings. Click! In the temperatures reported I knew my hands would freeze right to the metal if I grabbed hold of them. So, I sat in the pool for the better part of a half hour debating on how I was going to get out without leaving part of my fingers attached to the railings. With the hot steam from the water, frozen fingers probably would not have resulted but I didn't want to chance it!

Finally, I reasoned, I could throw hot steaming water onto the metal rails, grab hold quickly and pull myself up and out. "Quickly" was the operating word for success!

Once out of the pool I scampered to the changing room and quickly returned to my winter attire. Going into the pool in the first place had to be one of the dumber things I think I had done. But, on the brighter side, the steaming water was invigorating. I went straight to bed after my little adventure and had a wonderful night's sleep!

Central wasn't finished with me yet. I left for the airport around four in the afternoon and found the pilot with a "stalled"

Cessna 206. In trying to start the plane, he ran the battery down. Three of us got out and started to walk when I spotted construction "houses" next to the airport with a running car outside, so I figured there had to be people there with a phone. After calls to the air service and a one and half hour wait, a beautiful Beech Bonanza flew in and picked us up. I felt the pilot was more competent than the one who ran the battery down but then I guess it could have happened to anyone.

I arrived in Fairbanks but by the time I got to the west side of the airport where the jets parked I had missed my flight to Anchorage. Worse, I missed the 8 pm closure for food on the grill so sat hungry until the 12:34 am flight to Anchorage!

Bob and my daughter Natalia were flying a "space A" military flight up from Seattle to meet me in Anchorage, but they didn't make it until the next day. Bob as a retired Army colonel could fly along with his family when space was available. Waiting for that possibility sometimes meant sitting for hours or even days although flights to and from McChord Air Force Base to Elmendorf in Anchorage were fairly easy to find space on. There were fewer seats available on the return trip. We went ice skating that evening. Bob and Natalia, however, were stuck waiting for another military flight south until the following Thursday. I couldn't stay as I had to go to another site in western Alaska.

Arriving in Bethel I spent eight more days including a one-day trip "up river" to Kwethluk, a small village on the Kuskokwim River. I was scheduled to go there by river taxi, but the driver was running his dogs instead of driving cab that day. Instead I flew on another charter flight out of Bethel, saw three kids there, and returned by charter with the sixth-grade teacher who told me some horror stories involving torturing animals. I was glad to see the schools in Bethel had signs made by the kids to the effect not to starve, torture, or hurt animals. I believed it was a very important lesson to teach that concept to those kids early in life!

While there I was able to visit the small museum as well as go to the Moravian bookstore where I purchased a small Eskimo print. Sunday, I went ice fishing on the Kuskokwim River with the Guinns, a family I had met in 1980. We didn't catch anything but had a great time!

Monday, I headed for Mountain Village, where I gave the second gifted and talented workshop in an all-day presentation. It went well and I returned to Bethel the following morning and boarded the jet home.

All in all, I spent two and a half weeks on my little "tour" of Alaska, and arrived home with 25 reports to write. My time on Vashon was going to be very busy working on reports. I knew the special education teachers wanted them as soon as possible.

The following morning, I was scheduled to work in Central Kitsap District. I had contracted for work in both Bremerton and Central Kitsap school districts on the Peninsula, so returned to work on the 11th of February. I was working a few days in Washington during the first couple of years after the kids were adopted in addition to making a few trips to Alaska. Those northern trips grew in number once Natalia and Jhon went to high school.

Part of DEW (Distance Early Warning) Line Radar
Towers in Fort Yukon
(Photo by Marylu Martin)

CHAPTER 44

Spots and Taylor

My first visit to Cold Bay had been in 1980 with Bob when I was collecting data for my dissertation project. We stayed in a Quonset hut left over from World War II. It was an extension of the Weathered Inn that consisted of eight rooms with a six-room bunk house a few steps away. The dachshunds had found a mouse near the building we were in but no rats. The mouse escaped through a hole underneath, and not being suicidal, didn't return while we were there!

When I returned there to work in the school, I stayed in the same Quonset hut Bob and I had stayed in with the dachshunds. No mice this time! Later trips, however, found me in one of the rooms in the main hotel. The local store was attached to the hotel as well as a bar and there was a place to eat across the parking lot. I visited the school for twelve-or-more years from the early-to-mid 1980s until the late 1990s, well after Bob had passed away. I always enjoyed my trips to this area.

The school's population declined considerably from my first visit when there was lots of activity with kids and several teachers including a special education teacher and a principal until my very last trip when there was only one teacher. Eventually, with only four to nine students three years in a row, the Aleutians East Borough School District closed Cold Bay School's doors, but that was long after I left.

I found Cold Bay's history interesting. There was evidence of prehistoric occupation by the Aleuts and later Russian encampments. But its American history began with the Japanese invasion of the Aleutians in World War II. Bob had been stationed on Amchitka Island further out on the Chain when he was in the Army in the 1940s. Cold Bay was actually part of the Aleutian Peninsula, and considered a "gateway" to the islands. I saw evidence of rusted gun emplacements and the footprints readily visible from the air of Quonset huts whose structures had long since disappeared. The same war ghosts were present in much of the rest of the area I visited particularly in Dutch Harbor when I was on my way to Akutan.

Control of the airfield passed to civil authorities in later decades. They maintained it as a useful location for fueling and emergency landing needs on the great circle flights from the west coast of the U.S. to eastern Asia. A Distant Early Warning or DEW Line station was established nearby and was later decommissioned. I would drive by it when I used the school's vehicle.

During the 1980s, deregulation of the airline industry caused many of the interests supporting the need for the community to evaporate. When I was there, Cold Bay served as a hub for traffic from Anchorage and Seattle to the small communities around it. It also had an excellent emergency runway for aircraft flying over the North Pacific.

The school let me borrow a land rover on my visits. After school found me driving to the Izembek National Wildlife Refuge on an old gravel road that saw little traffic. In fact, I never ran into other people! Nor did I meet any animals, although I knew bears frequented the area.

Those isolated moments provided a wonderfully exhilarating and refreshing "time out" for me to explore. I often got out of the vehicle and walked on the tundra. It was almost like walking on a springboard as the ground was soft and covered with millions of almost microscopic plants, single-flowered blooms, and tiny lichens woven into the ground cover. However, I never strayed very far from that land rover.

One time I managed to get stuck in deep snow when I tried to drive over a little dip in the road. I tried to back out by rocking the land rover back and forth but without success. I figured one or more of the teachers would miss me and come looking so staying in the vehicle made the most sense. Besides there were bears around, and the last thing I wanted to do was meet up with one on the lonely road without a vehicle for protection! Sure enough, a couple of teachers arrived within an hour and were able to pull me out of the snow with their vehicle.

My camera was always with me on those little exploratory adventures. I shot picture after picture of some of the tiny flowers. The refuge I visited encompassed several large lagoons that served as a food source and shelter for a large migratory bird population. At the end of the road was a small enclosure with windows on all sides. One could go inside and look out. I was never there for the major bird migrations, but I suspected it must be a spectacular sight to be inside the shelter and just watching. Again, the bears were out there as well as, but I never met up with any of them.

Memories from my later days working in Cold Bay included a couple of rats named Spots and Taylor. They came home with me on one of my trips. Spots was a white rat with black spots, and Taylor was a gray rat much like the basic generic rat that one might find in walls, a hidden corner in the garage, down by the docks, or any other place where rats hang out. These two were born in the school at Cold Bay.

No, the school was not overrun with rats. They were bred to be snake food as one of the teachers had a snake that she kept and raised rats to feed it. While I am all for scientific inquiry and viewing live critters in their natural habitat, I have never been fond of snakes. When I saw several rats in a cage and heard what their destiny was, it bothered me. The kids played with the rats making them quite tame. They readily adapted to life in the classroom and had become pets. The snake was an educational tool, but one I think could have been solved in other ways. I never saw the snake.

I enjoyed watching the rats play. One afternoon while I was in the room, I decided to rescue a couple of them. There was one beautiful white one with black spots that I particularly took a liking to so I chose her. I wanted a second one for company because rats are social animals, but I also wanted another girl as I didn't want them to multiply. The teacher found me a cute little gray girl. The white one obviously was named Spots. But what does one call a gray rat! One of the Special Ed teacher's daughters was very much into playing with the rats. Her name was Taylor. I decided that was a great name for the second rat. Taylor and I talked about it, and she didn't mind at all. In fact, she thought it was kind of cool that the rat was named after her. Besides the names, Spots and Taylor, just went together!

When I left the school, we packed the rats into a nice little carrying box and tucked it into my carry-on bag. I checked the bag through at the Cold Bay Airport. One of the checkers who also worked at the school knew what I was doing. She was mainly interested in metal objects, guns, knives or anything that could be used as a weapon or blow up an airplane. I was cleared all the way through to Seattle with a transfer of planes in Anchorage.

The two rats and I boarded the plane with no problems as neither one of the rats nor I were wearing any metal objects. Spots and Taylor rode comfortably in Alaska Airlines first class cabin in the luggage rack above my head well contained in their little travel box as we headed for Seattle later that day.

Once home I kept the two "girls" in a nice container with toys and other items that rats enjoy. My kids were fascinated as were their friends when they came over to visit. The dogs and cats I had could not get into the cage, and the rats only came out of their cage when it was safe and when I was there to supervise.

The two lived a good life until Spots had a stroke almost three years later. She was completely paralyzed on one side when I found her. I took her to the vet and he confirmed what had happened, and euthanized her as there was nothing more that could be done. He told me she had lived a very long life for a rat. I tried to find another companion for Taylor but the pet store on Vashon had stopped selling pet rats. Three weeks later Taylor died of a broken heart.

CHAPTER 45

Where in the World is Kashunimuit

"Could you go to Kashunimuit for a week?" Twyla, my boss, asked over the phone. "They would like you there sometime in the next couple of weeks. Give the superintendent a call."

Where the devil was that I wondered? With some misgivings and a quick check of my schedule I said, "Yes!" I had the rest of the month available.

The name sounded Eskimo, but beyond that I had no clue. I began checking my school directory and the map.

I was quite surprised when I realized I had visited there in years past with Bob and before I started working for SERRC. I knew it by the name of the village, Chevak, not by the school district's name of Kashunimuit. We had been there during the late spring months after break up on one of the early flights when Bob was calling on customers. A man by the name of Peter Boyscout had ordered some building materials, and Bob wanted to meet him and see his business.

It was one of the more remote places I had experienced at the time. Chevak was located on a river inland from the Bering Sea. Hundreds of tiny lakes surrounded it. While it was summer time for all practical purposes I had felt chilly enough to wear a light jacket. Some of the Eskimo children, on the other hand, were running around naked as we landed.

I thought back to that early trip. I remembered the landing

strip was dirt, and Bob was very careful not to put the nose gear down until he had slowed the plane down as it appeared soft. He usually landed like a duck sitting on the water anyway, but tended to really exaggerate on strips like the one at Chevak. Once out of the plane I sank down with each step I took crossing the tundra. It was like a bog as it was very wet. The people greeted us on snow mobiles, which they used on the tundra, even without snow!

Yes, I thought, it would be interesting for me to go back, see the village, and meet the kids, their parents, and the teachers. We had not seen much of it on that early trip, only spending a little over an hour there at most. I was looking forward to the visit.

Chevak was located 17 miles east of Hooper Bay, on the West coast of Alaska, eight miles inland from the Bering Sea.

I set up my schedule to go first to Anchorage, then Bethel, followed the next morning by bush plane to Chevak. This time I stayed in a Bed and Breakfast. It was far more pleasant than the hotel. Nothing looked the same at Chevak when we landed. One of the biggest differences was snow. There would be no problem this trip sinking into wet tundra. The airstrip was hard packed snow. It was frozen solid.

When planes land in some of these remote communities, half the village—or so it seems—comes out to meet them. It was no different this time. I was picked up with my baggage and testing equipment and whisked off in a snow machine with a sled to carry my stuff. The school was only a short distance away.

I learned much later after working in Chevak for the Kashunimuit School District that there is a tri-language system in Chevak: English, Cup'ik, and a mixture of the two languages. I had always referred to the mixture as "village English" both in this village as well as throughout Alaska. The people in Chevak spoke a dialect of Central Yup'ik, namely Cup'ik, and identify themselves as Cup'ik people rather than Yup'ik. That unique identity allowed them to form a single-site school district rather than joining the neighboring Yup'ik school district.

I was to return to this district a number of times in the years that followed. That first visit after testing kids all day, I found a comfortable classroom and "camped out" on the floor after heating up a can of tuna fish and rice in the school's kitchen. Popcorn was another personal favorite. That's where I stayed for the remainder of the week. During that visit my sleeping bag sprang a leak resulting in feathers getting on the classroom floor where I slept. I picked them up, but some escaped. I'll bet one can still find a feather or two in that room probably wondering where they came from.

On one of my early visits I stayed with the female administrator. On later visits I had gotten to know some of the teachers and stayed with the high school English teacher and her dog Fynnigan (or Fynn for short) named for James Joyce's *Finnigan's Wake.* Kathleen was very supportive of my manuscript, *Adoption in Peru,* and had been the first one who read it in its final form. She visited me on Vashon years later after I built my log home. While visiting she met my son Jhon. Natalia was going to school in the Netherlands at the time, so didn't meet her.

I sometimes tried to find a piece of artwork while working in communities and knew Chevak was known for its dolls. One afternoon after school, a local woman came in with perhaps the ugliest doll I have ever seen! The doll was an old woman dressed in a blue "kuspuk" making a basket. She was sitting on a piece of some kind of skin with long strands of grass near her. The face was pinched up giving it an almost sinister look. She held a partially completed basket in her hands as she wove. The doll's hair was almost white and went down to her waist. I ended up buying the doll but never cared for it that much possibly because I was never into dolls. I only hoped the money I paid her maker wasn't going to buy booze. That was how some of the women supported their habit. I understood from one of the teachers this woman had two young children—one no more than an infant so it felt good that I had bought the doll.

Life "out there" was a different world! There's the endless tundra, the sweet cherub faces of the little ones, and the kindness of the elders. Leaving the village one particularly cold day I stood out by the airstrip waiting for the plane which was late. One other person stood there with me along with our baggage.

An older woman came out of her house and invited us inside to wait. I was bundled up with hat, gloves, inner mittens, scarf around my face along with my down jacket and was still cold. We gratefully accepted. Her house was nice and warm—toasty to be more accurate.

I undid the coat as the warmth took over, and then took off my hat and gloves when an indescribable odor hit me square in the face. I guessed it was a seal that was being processed. The seal I decided had been out of the water too long. I was reminded of the "meat hole" on Little Diomede Island made to ferment seals and walrus. I kept the scarf around my head especially my nose. I was almost to the point of gagging, but didn't want to offend this very kind and thoughtful woman who invited us into her home to wait for the plane.

Fortunately, we heard an airplane fly over about that time. Back outside I welcomed the brisk fresh air the cold provided and headed to the plane that had now landed. Relieved I saw that it was the air service from Bethel to pick us up.

CHAPTER 46

Venetie on the Chandalar River

Venetie brings back good memories along with sadness. It is located 45 miles northwest of Fort Yukon, and is on the north side of the Chandalar River. It is the southern point of the reservation with its northern boundaries being Arctic Village. I visited both of these villages numerous times. Both were part of the Yukon Flats School District. An aside is that I named one of my cats "Chandalar" after the river.

The airport separated the school from the main village although there were some houses on the east side along with the school. The airstrip was no more than 50 yards from the school's front door. Despite this someone always picked me up. Usually, it was Manual, who was the maintenance man. With all the testing equipment and personal baggage I carried, I needed help. While the principals changed from time to time, Manual was always there. He was just older each time I visited.

I didn't know it until I did a little reading that there was a gold rush in the Chandalar region in 1906-07 that brought a large number of miners. A mining camp of nearly 40 cabins was established upriver from Venetie in Caro. By 1910 the "Chandalar" as it was called was played out. Caro was completely abandoned. A side note is that I named one of my cats "Chandalar."

In 1943 the Venetie Indian Reservation was established to

protect their land for subsistence use. At about the same time a school was established at Venetie that encouraged additional families to settle in the village. Eventually an airstrip, post office, and store were built. During the 1950s and 60s, the use of seasonal camps declined. With the coming of the snow machine, however, Venetie residents renewed their use of areas that had traditionally been occupied seasonally. When the Alaska Native Claims Settlement Act (ANCSA) was passed in 1971, Venetie and Arctic Village opted for title to the 1.8 million acres of land in the former reservation, which they own as tenants in common through the Native Village of Venetie Tribal Government.

My early memories were of a Special Education aide, Cora Gundrum, who was a very special individual. For one thing she was in a wheel chair. It did not interfere with her ability to get around or work with the kids. She controlled even the most "acting out" child with considerable ease. One boy I remember, in particular, was probably eleven or twelve years of age, and diagnosed as fetal alcohol-affected. He was the kind of kid who, when one walked into a room, one would immediately be drawn to him. All the aide had to do was look at him and he stopped whatever he was doing and went back to work. She was a very kind woman, and I truly think she loved all the kids she worked with and they knew it.

Cora did fantastic bead work, so I asked her to make me a pair of "dancing slippers." One evening after school, I walked over to her house where she lived with her sister. The two women measured my feet and we talked through the entire process. People wore dancing slippers at the dances but not outside in the snow. Both men and women had them. They would arrive at the hall and put on their special dancing shoes for the evening. The slippers were soft and pliable and perfect for an evening of dancing and fun. Later I also had her make me several beaded key chains. I gave a couple of them away as gifts, but still have two that I use regularly. The leather she used was moose hide both for the slippers and the key chains. The moose skin had been smoke cured giving off a very pleasant odor.

She also told me she had been "a drunk Indian" when she was a fairly young girl and was on the back of a snow mobile when it crashed. It left her paralyzed and in a wheel chair. I initially visited Venetie beginning in the early years of working in northern

Alaska, but then I didn't go back for a period of time. When I returned, I learned that Cora had passed away. I was very sorry to find that out. Her picture is in the glass cabinet at the school as one enters the front door and features some of the elders who lived in Venetie.

Other memories of Venetie included the old couch in the library. I think everyone who ever visited Venetie slept on it, including me on numerous occasions. I'd put my sleeping bag down and that was it for the night! Early on during my stays I couldn't find the light switch to turn off the library's lights. I walked around the room several times searching with no luck. That night I sort of went to sleep in the fully lighted room. Later, after asking, I found the switch was hiding behind some books. I'd always get up fairly early because I didn't want someone walking in on me. The coffee pot was in a tiny room in a separate office in the library. The custodian always kept the doors closed until he knew I was up and about. The kitchen and lunch room separated the elementary school from the office and the high school.

I was going regularly to Venetie in 2004 when one morning in September arriving from the airport, I had a long-distance call from my daughter at our home on Vashon. My precious black and tan dachshund, Eiger, had come up missing. I was sick with worry. I so much wanted to be home where I could look for him and it was all I could do to finish testing there, fly to Arctic Village and finish another day and half of testing before I could fly home to look for my little dog. When I got home, I spent days looking for him in every conceivable place I could think of. Eiger was later found dead by my son. Devastated, I still think of him every time I look at the huge Maple tree under which he is buried.

CHAPTER 47

Trapped—at 55 Below Zero

Sooner or later I knew it would occur, and after seven years and four months of travel all over Alaska the inevitable happened! The bottom dropped out of the thermometer while I was working at a remote site. I was at Koyukuk, a village at the mouth of the Koyukuk River where it meets the Yukon River. I was only 15 minutes away by plane from Galena with its long runway capable of handling jets, but I might as well have been in Outer Mongolia for all practical purposes!

Earlier in the week I had been at Kaltag also on the Yukon River. Both villages were in the Yukon/Koyukuk School District. The river was frozen, although underneath the ice, a current raged. Water seeped above the ice in places, and drifting snow hid holes. Travel on the river could mean sudden death. Despite this, drunks would venture out on snow machines. Others wanting to tempt fate would also venture onto the ice. Some came back with slush covering their machines, while others were never heard from again. I understood two men went through the ice during the past spring; one had been the father of the six-year old boy I had just tested.

I was told that not far from the village there was a natural opening in the river, perhaps an acre or larger in area. It created steam when the cold air hit the warmer water. When the temperature dropped to extremes, ice fog formed. Polluting smoke from the nearby villagers' wood stoves joined it to cover the land obscuring the airport, which didn't have runway lights.

I had been lucky to leave Kaltag when I had and before the planes stopped flying. Planes stopped when there was a combination of ice fog and below 40-degree temperatures. That kind of combination played havoc on travel. They also stopped flying in really cold weather because it was hard on the engines.

The temperature dropped again but I was already at the next school in Koyukuk. Someone told me the recorded temperature was 50 degrees below zero, and had been like that for almost two days. At night it dropped to 55 below. The previous day, it had "warmed" up to 45 below zero.

The weather map showed another high coming in and that meant more freezing weather. The barometer was still going up and that was also a bad sign. I remembered two years previously the temperatures remained down in the minus 50s and 60s for over three weeks in Interior Alaska at a time I had been scheduled to go. The school district's director had called me and cancelled my trips until the weather warmed up. It was over a month before I was able to travel back there.

This particular trip I was scheduled to go to a third village but had to cancel as it was usually ten degrees colder than Koyukuk. Instead I made reservations to fly home and hoped for the best. I had a seat on the jet on their 7:00 am flight out of Fairbanks. But getting to Fairbanks was a big question mark! I had a day and a half to finish the trip, and spent it in an upstairs classroom working on reports. I had to concentrate to just keep the kids whose parent or aunt or uncle had committed suicide straight from those who had lost a close relative because of a murder or alcohol poisoning.

There was, however, one student out of the seven I had tested in Kaltag who didn't fit either circumstance. He had recently been in a plane crash with three fatalities. It was his second plane crash. Needless to say, he was a little traumatized! I doubted the test results would be accurate and needed to qualify any statements I made in his report. He also had a number of bandages because of the burns from his neck to his feet due to the crash. The violence in this part of the world was unreal, although a plane crash could happen anywhere.

I had flown to Koyukuk when a small window of opportunity had presented itself just about the time the temperatures started to drop. The pilots who flew regularly in this area were alert and kept excellent track of changing weather patterns. Both Kaltag and Koyukuk schools were in the Yukon/Koyukuk School District. Weather reports suggested the low temperatures would last for more than just a few days. I finished testing in the evening. I wondered if I was going to make my flight out of Fairbanks.

A couple of people from the village came over to the school and asked if I could talk, or rather "counsel" a young woman who was "suicidal" in their words. She wasn't a student nor was she connected with the school in any way, and I wasn't licensed or certified to talk to local villagers in a counseling role. I gave a few suggestions to them strongly advising that someone be with her physically all the time until an appropriate counselor could meet with her. I also gave them telephone numbers of who to call for help.

While I was a certified counselor for school kids, I could not see adults in that capacity. Legally, I could only work with school-related issues and knew I had to stay out of village problems. Both the special education teacher and principal concurred.

With the temperatures outside and planes not flying, I was beginning to feel trapped.

After lunch the next day I was told one more plane was coming through to pick up stranded travelers like myself in spite of the 55 below degree temperatures. I was ready at a moment's notice to leave and hoped the news was true.

The thermometer climbed slightly upward in the late afternoon. Could it be? Overhead I heard a bush plane's whine as it buzzed the village. I grabbed my testing equipment and jumped on the waiting snow machine throwing my back pack, sleeping bag and testing kit onto the sled behind.

The driver, a Native woman, smiled as I tucked myself down behind her body—clinging on to her as the machine roared down the road and out of the village towards the airport. The trick was to stay on the back in order not to be thrown off because some of the Natives found it great sport to dump a stranger! I had hugged more Natives for dear life over the years as a result, and today was no exception as I clung to the woman. Of course, I didn't want to delay for fear the pilot would land, not find anyone waiting, and take off again.

We shot down the half mile or so of road arriving at the airport just about the time the plane's engine shut down! The pilot hurriedly jumped out of the plane to get me loaded up! I tossed my belongings in front of the open hatch for loading and a big smile crossed my face as I climbed aboard. I was getting up in the air and flying at least as far as Galena where I knew people! Galena, I might add, was a separate City School District. I had also worked there on occasion, although I never worked in the charter school at Galena where years later I learned that my friend Marylu Martin had worked probably at the same times I was there.

Our small plane climbed up and out of Koyukuk and minutes later landed on Galena's long paved runway. From there I caught a larger twin-engine plane that flew directly to Fairbanks. Relieved, I knew I was going to be on that 7:00 am jet to Seattle the next morning.

CHAPTER 48

Yukon and Koyukuk River Villages

Kaltag and Koyukuk were not the only villages I visited in the Yukon/Koyukuk School District. I had visited all of them at one time or another with the exception of Bettles, although I had flown over it several times. The district headquarters was located in Fairbanks.

It was the end of April in 1991. I had been in the Aleutians the previous week, and in Anchorage on the 25th of April when the first earthquake hit at 10:19 in the evening followed by all the lights going out in the hotel. It was a bit scary. It was a 5.1 quake on the Richter Scale. The next day I was scheduled to do an in-service, and also test a kindergartener from Ruby who was visiting Palmer (outside of Anchorage). She was brought to the hotel where I tested her. She was being considered for the Gifted/Talented Program. I found her bright, outgoing and fun to meet.

I left Anchorage for Fairbanks the next day by car, and along the way spotted a mama moose and two babies feeding next to the highway. Of course, I stopped, and started taking a number of pictures from the car. The moose didn't seem to mind at all. I kept the engine running the entire time just in case mama changed her mind and charged. She didn't. From there I drove to Denali Park but could only drive about 12 miles as the rest of it was closed because of snow. Stepping out of the car I immediately became aware of the lack of noise except for ptarmigan talking with one another and the wind blowing snow. The vastness of the area was overwhelming. I stood absolutely still for several minutes before returning to the vehicle.

I was chilled but had to go to the bathroom so took a side road with a scenic view. No one was anywhere around so once again got out, then squatted down. About that time a large truck took the same side road and was rapidly coming from the other direction. I leapt back into the car with my pants still down. He created one big snow storm as he passed me, but once past I could at least get out and button up my pants. I had probably surprised the driver as much as he did me.

All in all, I spent a couple of hours in the park before I headed to Fairbanks.

May 1, 1991 found me airborne between Fairbanks and Allakaket. Before we took off a second earthquake centered somewhere south of Denali Park was felt. It was 6.6 on the Richter Scale, and was the strongest one in three decades. The next day I was almost left in Allakaket. I'm not sure if it was because of the earthquake or something else. I quickly walked over to the store and called Frontier Air. They diverted their plane in Hughes back to Allakaket and picked me up. It was the end of a two-week trip.

The next fall I was to return to the Yukon/Koyukuk School District. My first stop was Hughes where I met Buddy. He's a miniature dachshund and a delight, but then any dachshund catches my attention particularly in a remote village. I took lots of pictures in the classroom. I showed the kids some slides of my own dachshunds. They ended up carrying my bags out to the plane. Later I learned that Buddy snapped at a child because he was being teased. The result was that Buddy was banned from attending class for the rest of the year. I was sorry to hear that.

From there I went to Huslia. It was a closed village to white visitors; one had to have a very specific invitation to go there. I did. It was also a very clean village. I ended up testing ten kids in Huslia including one high school girl, and hoped I made a small difference in her life as she was distressed about testing in general. We spent some time talking about test phobias. I also gave a slide show on my dachshund book; the kids seemed to enjoy it.

Flying that morning on the plane I thought I was going to die before I got to the school as I had drunk too much tea, hot chocolate, cider and grapefruit juice. Getting on a snow go once we landed with a full bladder was not fun, but I made it.

Once in Allakaket I found kids from Minto were there to play basketball. I managed to have one end of school closed off and locked, and snagged a wrestling mat before any of the visitors got them. I didn't feel bad about grabbing one of the mats for myself as I figured the kids could handle the hard floor better than I could. My body needed some cushion between it and the floor.

I watched the next morning as fog rose up from the river bank (Koyukuk River). The water had not yet frozen solid. Chunks of ice, however, floated around carried by the river's current. Thousands of tiny ice crystals had formed into each piece reflecting light in all directions. Overhead a moon stared hard and cold. Wisps of fog floated past it. It was 9 o'clock in the morning on the 26th of October, and the following week was Halloween.

Dogs howled. These villagers have had dog mushing and racing for years. Their yaps and barks rise up along the river ban, and bounce across to the cliff then back finding their way through the sleepy log cabins. Smoke curled up from fires and mingled with the fog. Now and then a black raven broke the stillness with its flight above the snow whitened trees.

Witches, ghosts, all sorts of goblins hung from the classroom walls. There were orange pumpkins, black cats and orange cats, green and pink witches with orange hands and green yarn for their hair strewn around.

There were several bee's nest—I wondered if these were from wild bees nearby, and what happened to them in the winter. A snow machine raced by the school. Inside the gym kids played another visiting team from Minto—the bouncing ball hitting the floor continuously. Computers lined one wall, an American flag hung from another—a reminder that this was still a part of the United States.

By 11:10 in the morning the moon was still at about a 45-degree angle above the earth. A woman pulled an orange sled with bundles on it and headed past the school.

I remember Allakaket, a village along the Koyukuk River, fondly. I only visited it twice.

CHAPTER 49

Not All Was Work in Nome

I headed straight to the Leonard Seppala Alternative High School from the airport on my first official work trip to Nome's City School District. Richard Burmeister was the Special Education Director and also the acting principal for the alternative program. He wanted to know how many kids I could test in a day and how long would it take me for each student. Later I learned that he had asked Marsha Buck, my current supervisor in Juneau at the time, the same questions and her response was that I was Nome's "employee" for the five days I was there so it was up to them and me.

I quickly went to work in one of the back rooms. Richard kept me busy assessing kids on that trip and all succeeding ones I might add. The driving force was his secretary Jenny who had students lined up for me—when I finished one, she had another one right there. My testing chair never got cold. Once school was out, Richard talked about flying, dogs, and the Iditarod. Of course, I encouraged him. That first night I went back to the hotel exhausted but was ready for another round of kids the following day.

Richard was a dog musher, had his own team, and was also part of the Iditarod Air Force. Until that point I had never heard of the latter. He said he was one of the pilots who donated time, talents, and a ski equipped bush plane to support "The Last Great

Race". As I listened I learned that it would have been impossible for the 1049-mile race to exist without this lifeline, network, or support system.

Nome was located on the southern Seward Peninsula coast on Norton Sound of the Bering Sea. It had an elementary school in town and Nome-Beltz Junior/Senior High School located out of town in addition to the alternative program within walking distance of the elementary school.

The five years I worked in the district I attended every one of the Iditarod banquets, met some of the mushers, and watched some of the dog teams arrive at the finish line. I scheduled my week in Nome at the beginning of the race in Anchorage and then stayed the following week on my own time for a week of vacation as there was no school during Iditarod week. The front runners took nine or ten days. That way I saw some of the mushers come in and attended the banquet the following Saturday night, although I never saw the lead team finish as school was still in session and I was testing.

Jhon and Natalia made the trip with me one year along with one of their high school friends using some of my air miles that I had accumulated from Alaska Airline flights. I arranged for them to spend a day in the high school there. Later I understood they caused quite a stir among some of the local kids as they were obviously not from Alaska. I wanted to introduce them to different experiences while there including walking out onto the frozen Norton Sound—walking on the ocean was not on one's usual entertainment list!

We stayed at June's B&B. June Engstrom was a retired reading teacher, who had been a gold miner's daughter in Nome's early days. Her sourdough pancakes were to die for! We had become friends after I discovered Nome had a B&B. I know she enjoyed meeting the kids and went out of her way to help them. When Natalia went flying out the front door and landed on her bottom because of the ice, June immediately pulled out a pair of boots with traction that Natalia used for the rest of her time in Nome.

Before the B&B, I had stayed in a hotel in town. I remember watching the beginning of Desert Storm on television in one of the hotels down by the beach. I also spent some nights at the dormitory that had once housed boarding students from villages and communities without high schools before the Molly Hootch case was settled in October 1976. After that land-mark court decision high schools were built in all the villages with ten or more school-age children. As a result, the kids from other villages who had attended the boarding school in Nome no longer did so but stayed in their home village. I don't ever remember anyone else staying at the dorm while I was there.

When I stayed out at the dorm next to the high school, it meant a taxi cab ride back to town four miles away in order to eat in the evening. It was fun riding around the town in those taxis—I got to meet some of the drunks that way and believe me they were there. I would add that the taxi service was excellent. I needed to put on my hat, gloves, coat and anything else I was taking before I called the cab because they were right there.

One night I remember getting into the cab with one fellow in front and some ancient-looking individual in the middle seat (I couldn't tell for sure if it was a man or woman) although the cab driver referred to them as "two fellows". I assumed it was a man. The older one was wheezing and dripping from the nose and mouth. He was carrying a cane. The younger one appeared to be a relative or friend, who knows, and the two of them went into the liquor store. We waited until a purchase was made and the two came back to the cab speaking in a native tongue. It sounded like "*muk tuk yuk tuk muk*". Another man named Philip, returned with them and got into the car as well with his bag of beer. After the three were delivered to where they were going, the driver took me to Beltz High School and the dorm where I was staying.

The dorm was attached to the high school by a long tunnel maybe 100 feet or more in length. At the end of the tunnel there was a surveillance camera. I used to wonder about it as I walked to the high school. Some very green paint that had been peeling for a long time covered the walls. Melted snow seeping down through cracks had left a few puddles of water along the walk and strange fluorescent lights flickered making it almost other-worldly. Midway through the tunnel was an exit to the gym and at the far end were the stairs to the cafeteria and school. I was completely protected from the weather and sometimes spent days indoors.

Getting to the dorm from the airport was a different matter. On one occasion I managed to sink down in a soft snow drift once I stepped out of the van that dropped me off. I was trying to take a short cut to the front door. The snow was piled high against the building so much so that the driver had to get out and pull me out of the snow so I could make it into the dorm's front entrance that was only a few feet away.

The superintendent lived in an apartment connected to the dorm. At times I tested in the fairly large open room just outside his door. Jenny would line kids up so when one returned to her office for a pass to re-enter class, she would send another one. She didn't miss a beat. But once the school day ended, that was it. There was no testing of kids after hours. Both Richard, the Special Education Director, and his secretary Jenny had their office at the high school by the second year I worked Nome.

Jenny's husband was on the police force so she kept me posted on where drug houses were located as well as the seamier side of Nome. Jenny also had a hip replacement shortly before I did, and was a great help when I arrived after my surgery. She instigated a wheel chair to meet me at the jet, along with the special education bus at the airport to drive me to school and access to a wheel chair in the school, which I really didn't need.

When I stayed in town rather than out at the dorm, Jenny often picked me up on her way to work eliminating the need for me to catch a taxi cab. I enjoyed our visits on those rides out to the high school and learned a great deal about what was going one in Nome.

Too many FAE (fetal alcohol-affected) kids were turning up. They were delayed, presented behavior problems, and in need of something besides a regular classroom program. A number of FAE kids were already in the Special Education program as well as one teenage boy with fairly severe physical deformities. I spent a considerable number of reading hours studying the syndrome as a result of him and others I met.

A blizzard was predicted for the next day on one wintery trip I made. I remember the following morning there was a lot of blowing, but the "blizzard" never materialized. I found the snow like grains of sand. It sparkled, almost like Fool's Gold, and crunched when I stepped in it. I found it really cold.

The dorm rooms were warm and somewhat okay, other than the fly corpses lying around all over. There were dozens of them particularly on the window sill, plus several dying flies every time I walked into the room. The main problem with staying in the dorm out of town, however, was costing a small fortune; I didn't mind paying because I would be reimbursed, but the cash flow out of my pocket became a problem as I didn't carry much cash with me.

Another psychologist, Robert Healey, was hired to work full time the third or fourth year I was there. He had retired from a school district on the East Coast, in upper New York, I think, and wanted the "Alaskan experience". He and his wife Claudia were both in Nome the first year and then he stayed on for a second and final year. He did counseling and follow up with many of the kids I tested.

The importance of connections in the bush was paramount to success and often led to lasting friendships. We became good friends and often had dinner together at the roadhouse on the first night of my visit in order for me to catch up on what was going on in the school. He mainly worked with the elementary staff and kids. I still get Christmas greetings from him and his wife. The two of them drove as far west as Sandpoint, Idaho, in the fall of 2004 long after they left Nome. I drove over to meet them. We had a good visit reminiscing.

When one high school girl told me that she talked with her imaginary friend who ran laps with her around the gym as well as other times during the day, I was thankful there was a psychiatrist in town, and hoped her family would take her for treatment. Her friend wasn't imaginary to her. I had tested this girl long before Robert was hired.

Laurie Knutson, an occupational therapist and also from SERRC, was contracted to work at Nome the year after I started going there. We shared other districts as well, but didn't really run into each other that much. I visited Laurie and her husband one weekend in the Kenai where he taught at a later time. On another weekend in the early fall both of us were in Nome at the same time. We rented a van on Saturday morning and headed out on the one road that went north, namely, Taylor Road.

Laurie and I didn't know it at the time but there were actually three gravel "highways" out of Nome. We might have chosen one of the other roads for our over-night camping trip. Each road was around 75 miles long. They went through tundra, mountains, coastline, rivers, and valleys and were littered with abandoned gold dredges (44 in all) and railroads. I only saw five or six of the dredges. I had been on the Council Road to see the "train to nowhere" with Bob in 1980 while I was doing my dissertation research.

As for the third road, the Teller Road, I only had one occasion to drive just a few miles on it to a river bed where I found a few rocks with specks of commercial grade garnets that someone had told me about. I brought several small rocks home with me.

The van was nice to drive after working in the school all week. Laurie and I stopped at a roadhouse of sorts on the way, walked around, visited an old church, then drove on for a total of about 65 miles to a very rocky, eight-mile detour that led us to Pilgrim Hot Springs. We took the detour, and of course, we went into the water. It actually was more like a hot tub rather than what I think of as a hot spring, but the water was wonderful and it was heated by the natural springs.

On our return to Nome we stopped at Mile 38 at the Salmon Lake Campground. It was the perfect place to camp overnight. Up went the tent, which by the next morning was covered with frost as was everything else! We soon discovered some tiny blueberries frozen near the ground waiting to be picked. They were delicious straight off the bushes as well as in our cereal!

Over the years I visited Nome and I purchased several nice ivory pieces from the gift shops. They were carved by natives living in the area. Walrus were a staple food source for the natives. Every part of their body was used even including the whiskers for toothpicks. I have one really nice walrus tusk that was originally used as a sled runner, and later figures of an Eskimo man and his team of dogs were carved into it. The dogs were pulling a freight sled across a broken patch in a river with one dog having fallen into the water. Nome is a big tourist area and in addition, native art was well represented in this area. I have these pieces in my collection reminding me of the years I spent in Nome. I also have a couple of those rocks with garnets in them down by my greenhouse.

Gold Dredge near Nome

CHAPTER 50

Beneath the Northern Lights

Not all of my sightings of the Aurora Borealis happened in the Far North. One of the most spectacular viewings was in the cockpit of an Alaska Airlines jet between Ketchikan and Juneau.

While I lived aboard our boat for the first three years working in Alaska, the remaining years I commuted between Seattle and Alaska on a commercial jet—usually Alaska Airlines—to wherever I was scheduled to work or at least to a central airport where I caught a "bush" plane to my job site.

September 16, 1992, I was on an evening flight from Seattle to Juneau with a stopover in Ketchikan. I boarded the plane in Seattle and promptly fell asleep, something I often did in the early morning hours or when I caught a night flight.

We made a brief stop in Ketchikan. I stayed aboard half asleep as I knew it would be a quick stop. Soon the plane was loaded and the door was closed. The seat belt sign went on, and the usual announcements were made to the passengers. I was comfortably sitting in my seat when I heard the flight attendant announce the names of the pilot and co-pilot. Oh! My gosh! I could hardly believe it. The pilot was Jim Durkin, one of the pilots I had met on the Vintage Air Rally two years earlier. He along with another Alaskan Airline pilot became friends with Bob and me on the trip. I thought the least I could do was to say "hello."

I quickly pulled out one of my business cards and handed it

to the stewardess with instructions to give it to the pilot for me, and tell him "hi". She took my card. Shortly thereafter she returned a little surprised and said, "I don't know who you are but you get to go up to the cockpit. Follow me." I dropped the book I was reading, stunned. I quickly got out of my seat and followed the woman forward. Wow! I thought. Wow!

I had never been in the cockpit of a commercial airplane in flight. I sat down in the seat behind the pilot after a brief greeting and fumbled with the seatbelt as I strapped myself in. It was an entirely different setup from what passengers wore. I couldn't believe my good luck. As for Jim, he looked about the same as he had the last time I saw him at the banquet in Brisbane, Australia, almost two and a half years earlier.

My eyes began examining the instrument panel. After an initial greeting neither the co-pilot nor Jim said anything further as they were concentrating on the flight. It's not very far between Ketchikan and Juneau for a jet. I continued scanning the inside of the cockpit and glanced up through the window ahead.

The Northern lights were shimmering in front of us. The ribbons of color were so close, closer than I had ever seen them before. They streamed through the sky dancing in silence. My whole being was drawn to the spectacle. It was almost as if I could reach out and touch them. I no longer looked up at them as I was part of the lights. Flying through space at that moment became magical.

We were sandwiched between the brilliant lights ahead and the recently dusted mountain tops that sparkled with fresh snow. The lights were putting on a show beyond all imagination. Reds, greens, and yellows flashed across the sky before me. They added light to the cockpit intensifying everything inside. Mesmerized, I sat very still barely breathing. Now and then the lights from a village winked at us far below but were quickly lost in the illumination around us.

All too soon we were cleared for landing in Juneau. Just as suddenly as the light display appeared, it disappeared. In place of the mystical display, I watched the red and yellow strobe lights showing the runway and guiding us down. We approached the runway at a much faster speed than I could have imagined. Once on the ground the strobe lights turned off and green lights took over marking the runway. We were much higher off the ground than when I had landed in small private airplanes. But, of course, we would be.

What a sensation, and what an unbelievable trip!

"Thank you," was about all the words I could get out as I left the jet's cabin.

CHAPTER 51

A Shaman but not in this Century

Kokhanok was located on the south shore of Lake Iliamna, 22 miles south of Iliamna and 88 miles northeast of King Salmon. I had never heard of it until I was sent there by the Special Education Director, although I had been to several of the other villages along the lake and in the Lake and Peninsula School District.

I was surprised to learn that Yup'ik Eskimos, Aleuts, Athabascan Indians, and Inupiaq people had jointly occupied the lake area for the past 6,000 years. Russian explorers came into the region during the late 1700s, followed by the first influx of non-native fishermen and cannery operations in the late 1800s. A flu epidemic in 1918 was tragic to the Native population there as it had been in other parts of Alaska. I was particularly reminded of Brevig Mission.

When my boss at SERRC had received a request for psychological services in the Lake and Penn District, she sent me. After all, I flew into King Salmon regularly to go to the nearby Bristol Bay School District in Naknek. It served the kids living in King Salmon. While the Lake and Penn's district offices were located in King Salmon, they handled all the other schools in the area except, of course, Naknek. Later in the early spring of 1998 I brought home two Griffon Pointer-mix puppies from one of the Chignik schools in Lake and Penn, but that's another chapter in my travels.

The Special Education Director for the district was a school psychologist but had considerable administrative duties, and was unable to do the testing needed for Special Education particularly the three-year re-evaluations required by law. That's when SERRC was called.

When I first met the director, he turned testing responsibilities over to me. Initially, he expressed concerns about how I tested, and asked what tests I used. He wanted to know my overall functioning as a school psychologist in the Bush. I was someone new to him, doing part of the job he had been doing, and I think he was reluctant to let go. We talked about it, and later became friends. After all he and his wife had a wire-haired dachshund named Nicky that I babysat for on several weekends while I was in King Salmon. They actually lived down the road in Naknek, which was about a 20-minute drive from King Salmon.

I first visited Kokhanok sometime in the mid-to-late 1990s. I was to fly into the 2,920-foot-long gravel strip several times with local air carriers when I visited the village, but never had occasion to fly into its seaplane base on the lake. I was curious, however, and walked down there on my first visit. It had an airplane dock and that was about it. During the fishing season I decided it probably saw a considerable amount of traffic.

The community of Kokhanok had a mixed Native population, primarily Aleut. Subsistence activities were the focal point of the culture and lifestyle. There were maybe 150 people living there or possibly a few more, which is typical of so many of the communities I had visited over the years. Saints Peter and Paul Russian Orthodox Church had served this village and was on the National Register of Historic Places.

The kids from the school left quite an impression on me the first time I visited there. I had been standing on the second floor above the kitchen and overlooking the gym before classes started in the morning. Small groups of high school students were below me quietly talking with each other. There was no yelling or rough housing behaviors. When the bell rang, they promptly walked quietly to their classes. It was so unlike many of the high schools I had worked in that I stood there for several minutes just staring in awe.

I had been asked to assess several kids in both the elementary and high school. One boy who was having difficulties in his classes immediately caught my attention when one of the teachers mentioned him as we walked to her house that afternoon. "People like him." She continued telling me that he was quiet and didn't cause any behavioral problems. Then she added a couple of comments that really got my attention. "He talks with the caribou and other wild animals. The animals are not afraid of him. They go right up to him." She added, "He's an animal whisperer."

That stopped me in my tracks. Being an animal lover myself I was immediately curious. So many of the people I met wanted to go out and hunt, shoot anything they could—although getting a caribou was a necessity if one wanted to have meat for the winter months. For these villagers living on the edge of the lake fishing was also a staple.

I reviewed his records as I always did with students I was testing, and found he had had trouble with a number of the classes over the years, reading being one of them, but in some areas he excelled. He had plenty of friends from what I observed. I was actually excited to meet him, and decided to do more than the usual test battery I administered for Special Education. I guess curiosity was more of a motivator for me to do extra testing than anything else. Besides I had more than enough time. He seemed to enjoy the interaction and didn't mind going through the various tests I had.

I was quite impressed by many of his insights and responses. I realized as I talked with him that he not only talked with animals, he communicated with them. He told me about a whole different world and I asked him to draw me pictures. What he drew was primitive but readily recognizable.

Surprised by his comments, I learned there were also people he communicated with who lived in the earth. I asked him to draw a picture. The result was like some of the Sasquatch or Big Foot drawings I had seen. People have claimed to have seen these very large, hairy, and humanlike creatures but this was the first person I had met who told me that he saw one. It became obvious he did not readily discuss this with people he knew.

I had grown up in the Pacific Northwest with stories about these creatures so was familiar with the concept. I always considered them mythical. But I have also felt that there are many things I don't know exist in the spiritual world and in other peoples' belief systems. I was interested in learning more.

This boy who sat in front of me was very sincere and obviously believed in what he was telling me. I sensed he was in touch with the spirit world. We spent a number of hours talking, questioning, as he told me about his life. In no way did I feel he was mentally unsound.

His scores on formal testing were low, while his insights were well above those of the average person. At the end of the testing I asked him if he would like to have a picture of my family of dogs. I gave him a picture post card I had advertising the books I wrote. The front of the card had my seven dachshunds in a canoe. He took it, studied it for a long time then thanked me and left.

I made a case for him later with the Special Education Director stating I did not think he was retarded but very definitely needed help in academic areas. I commented had he been born a hundred years earlier, he probably would have been a shaman or spiritual leader of the tribe. I don't know what the outcome was as far as what the director did with his qualifying label for Special Education services. I was sure; however, the boy would receive additional help in those areas in school that he needed. Being a behavior problem or mentally disturbed were not issues for him.

A year or so later I had occasion to fly back to Kokhanok. I asked one of the teachers who had been there the first time about the boy. She told me he carried the picture post card with the dachshunds on it under his cap all the time ever since I had left on the previous visit. I was amazed.

Later that afternoon I was walking up the school's stairs between classes when students were going up and down the steps, one boy stopped me. "I know you." He took his hat off and showed me the post card I had given to him so long ago. I didn't get a chance on that visit to talk with him more than my brief encounter in the stairwell. I was astounded that he even recognized me.

CHAPTER 52

Pribilof Islands

The Pribilof Islands—formerly known as the Northern Fur Seal Islands—are a group of four volcanic islands off the coast of mainland Alaska in the Bering Sea. The Siberian coast is roughly 500 miles northwest of these islands. They are about 200 miles north of Unalaska in the Aleutians. Only two of them have people living on them.

St. Paul on St. Paul Island contains the largest remaining Aleut settlement in Alaska and has about 570 residents while St. George Island is smaller with only about 100 people. Total area is about 77 square miles. I've been to both of them several times and found them covered with tundra, treeless, and mostly rocky. St. Paul is a bird watcher's paradise, so much so that regular tours are scheduled out of Anchorage during the summer months.

The school district office located in St. Paul was where I spent most of my time on that first visit. I met a number of the teachers as well as kids mainly at the high school level.

SERRC had been contracted to provide a school psychologist to the district, and the psychologist who had been there for a number of years requested the new person come out for a couple of days just to visit and meet teachers and kids. That was really amazing and pretty much unheard of but that was what was requested. Flights only went out on Tuesdays and Thursdays. Tuesday morning found me at the Anchorage Airport heading for the Pribilof Islands. I arrived but my bags didn't, so I did some scrambling to cancel them being sent out on the next plane two days later as I would be going back on that flight. I didn't have anything with me except my WISC-III kit (Wechsler Intelligence Test-Third edition), the clothes on my back and very little cash. Sallie Miller, the Special Education teacher, took me to the store where I did buy a tooth brush and a couple of other personal items while there. I also stayed with Sallie about a mile out of the village.

The superintendent of the schools met me once I landed. He told me he was on the outs with the school board and was leaving at the end of the year but didn't say why. He had been there some 14 or 15 years. Denver and his wife Pam were very genuine people and kind to me. He had wanted me to attend the school's evening potluck, and also there at the same time the out-going school psychologist was there. She had been principal there once, and was a professor at the University of Southern Alabama. Beyond that my instructions were vague—get to know the school, the faculty, and the island. I met Susan Tucker, the school psychologist, as well as the Special Education teacher at the potluck. Susan and I went into a closed-room where she showed me the files and asked what my background was. Once learning that I had worked in other native villages before she seemed relieved and that was about the end of the discussion except we toured the special ed room and looked at tests. We joked about what to do with outdated WISC tests—sending them out to sea tied to a brick or to the shredder.

I was introduced at the potluck. A fisheries biologist gave presentation on salmon streams on the Aleutian Chain complete with slides. The next day there was an all-day FAS/FAE/FADE conference and in-service. At noon the superintendent invited everyone attending including school staff from both St. Paul and St. George, to lunch at King Eider Restaurant. I ended up with the staff from St. George. Susan talked in the afternoon. She told me how much she appreciated me being there and attending her presentation. After the workshop everyone disbanded.

Sallie and I went to the City Building where the city clerk cashed a personal check for me so I purchased film, a tee shirt, and the book Libby about the first white woman to live on the Pribilofs. Roy, the maintenance man, took Sallie and me on a tour of the island. We visited several seal rookeries and the site of the sunken *Terminator*, a fishing boat that had run into the beach. The waters were alive with fur seals. The pups were all together on one beach. Anxious mothers herded them into the water to swim, but the youngsters followed them right back to land. Commercial harvesting of fur seals had been prohibited on St. George and St. Paul islands in 1985, and since 1986 harvesting had been allowed for subsistence purposes and only by Alaskan Natives. I was glad to hear this.

In 1997 I was planning to build my own log home on Vashon Island, obtaining plans and materials from Wilderness Log Homes in Wisconsin. I wanted to see a completed home, and was given the name of a couple living on St. Paul Island who had already built their home there having had the materials shipped from the Lower 48. Having a log home out there was unique since the Pribilof Islands were treeless. Since I was going out there, I looked the couple up.

They were delightful people full of information and very helpful. Roy, turned out to work for the school district doing maintenance work. His wife worked at the airport as an airline employee. Roy was also part of the agency involved in the protection of the wildlife refuge. They invited me to come see their home. Sure enough, it was very similar to what I was planning but had a completely different interior floorplan. I loved their open log stairwell and incorporated it into the plans for my home.

Roy gave me an extended tour of St. Paul Island including a high cliff wall, known as Ridge Wall that was well above the Bering Sea. I was truly excited to be given a private tour by someone who had grown up on the island.

We spent a little time at the seal rookeries and then headed for the cliffs. I understood that nearly three million birds, including some 220 species (including puffins, auklets, and kittiwakes), passed through the islands on their migratory paths. It was also the wrong time of year to see the millions on their annual migration, but there were quite enough to put me in a state of awe. I wished at the time that I had a set of binoculars with me, although I didn't really need them as I could see birds everywhere. During later months there would be many more birds visible than what I was seeing.

We drove to several other spots to view birds. The name of one of the ones we saw reminded me of swishing down a snow-covered slope by the way it was pronounced in Aleut. My private guide also told me about his boyhood. I thoroughly enjoyed the time I spent with him walking on the tundra and hearing the stories of his youth! He told me he and his friends used to climb down some of the cliffs after birds' eggs. One boy would be lowered down over the edge using the groups' belts as a rope and collect the eggs. I could envision kids lowering one of their own over the edge in order to gather a few eggs and not having a care in the world.

Roy took me to the airport. We talked about the luxury of my being there. I honestly don't believe he knew why I was there, and quite honestly I wasn't really sure why I was there either.

The islands, I learned, also had a wide array of other wildlife, which included reindeer, Arctic blue foxes, harbor seals, whales, salmon, and halibut. In 1984, they were made part of the Alaska Maritime National Wildlife Refuge. Driving around I have to admit that I had never seen so many foxes. Seemingly they were everywhere and seemed to be comfortable around people. The foxes were almost tame, but not quite. I wasn't surprised when Margaret Piggott, the physical therapist I worked with, told me about her encountered with a fox on St. George Island. I mentioned this incident in an earlier chapter when Margaret and I were working together in the southeastern part of Alaska.

It was unusual for two of us from SERRC to be there at the same time but we were. St. George did not have an airport until the 1980s. It was located on the roadway just west of the village. In the mid-1990s a larger runway was constructed at the west end of the island, and that's where we landed when I visited there.

Several years later on my way back to Anchorage from Dutch Harbor (Unalaska) the jet detoured by way of St. Paul and landed to pick up several passengers. I had been working at Akutan School, which was part of the Aleutians East Borough School District. When I went to that school, I always went through Dutch Harbor and sometimes overnighted at the main hotel in Unalaska before flying back to Anchorage. This time the flight detoured to St. Paul.

I stayed aboard the plane once it landed. While waiting for it to load, the wife of the man who had taken me on that wonderful tour of the seal rookeries and cliffs came aboard as part of her job with the airline. We recognized each other immediately and started talking for a few minutes. I asked her about her husband and was saddened to learn he had passed away earlier in the year from cancer. His story of climbing down the cliffs as a boy, dangling from a belt, and searching for eggs came to mind.

St. Paul was one of four places I actually got sick while traveling for the job. I ended up going to the local clinic and was given medication. Whatever had made me sick was short-lived and at the end of one of my visits out there. Considering the many years in which I traveled in Alaska, only getting sick on four occasions was astounding. Nome, Stevens Village, and the school in Manley Hot Springs were the other three schools, not counting the time I lost my voice in Savoonga and flew home early. None of the instances lasted for more than a twenty-four-hour period, but each incident stands out clearly in my memory. Professional medical help and medications were not readily available in most of the places I visited.

CHAPTER 53

The Big Girls

Chignik Lagoon or Chignik Lake—I don't remember in which village the girls were born. I visited both communities for the first and only time during my trip to Lake and Peninsula schools located on the Alaskan Peninsula. The furthest thing from my mind was to bring home more pets. I already had five dachshunds and a couple of cats, and was living in a rented beach cabin on Vashon Island for the winter months after my late husband died and his natural sons took over his house. I had just purchased some property of my own; my future home was to be built the following summer on that land.

The Special Education teacher had a purebred griffon pointer female that was in heat and she just let her out among the village dogs. DUH! The result was eight puppies—all needing a home! The school district's administrators told her she had to get rid of them by the following weekend and, of course, that's when I arrived.

The one child I was to see that day was gone, so I rescheduled myself to swing back through the village at the end of my tour of the local villages and see the boy then. I knew the Special Education director had particularly wanted me to see him so that was what I was trying to do. That was my undoing!

I stayed with the Special Education teacher on my return trip to the village. Let's face it: I was a patsy when I saw those pups—

then about eight weeks old. "I'll take two of them," I heard myself say. I knew what happened to unwanted village dogs, particularly in the winter months.

I didn't know a thing about griffon pointers, but the mom seemed a gentle enough soul. She was kind of brown all over and had whiskers or beard like several other varieties of dogs. I was fascinated. The pups all looked the same—black and white with white manes around the necks, spots on their legs and white on the tip of their tails. No one knew who the father was. Most, if not all, of the village dogs were Heinz 57 mutts with black Lab-like characteristics and probably were related.

Four of the pups were to fly to Anchorage to a pet store, one would go to a home in a nearby village, probably Chignik Lagoon, and one would remain in the village. And, my two puppies both girls—both girls—were packed in a cardboard box and flew out with me the last day I was there. The bush plane that carried us headed for King Salmon where we would connect with Alaska Airlines.

I chose the pick of the litter and the one the mother's owner wanted but the District Office told her "no more dogs." So, at the last minute I tried to decide which other one to take. Over in the corner one puppy made eye contact. She was the runt of the litter and the white mane she had didn't go all the way around her neck unlike her siblings. "What about that one?" I said pointing to the little girl. We loaded both girls into a cardboard box when I was ready to leave, and flew back to King Salmon.

The adjoining Bristol Bay School District located in Naknek was also a district in which I worked and had been doing so for a number of years so I knew the staff there. King Salmon Airport served the entire community, so I called ahead to the school in Naknek and explained my situation and asked if anyone had a crate I could borrow to carry two pups on my trip home to Seattle. The librarian had several crates.

The librarian at Bristol Bay School District came through with a dog crate, but when she saw the pups, she realized that it was too small for both. She was thinking smaller puppies. She called her husband who made an emergency run to the airport with a larger crate. Fortunately, the plane was a little late so I sat there on pins and needles wondering what to do if he didn't get there before I had to board. At the last possible minute the husband arrived with the bigger container. The puppies were quickly stuffed in and the crate was weighed.

Alaska Air personnel recognized me from my many earlier trips in and out of King Salmon, and were willing to work with me up to the last moment. They checked me in along with the crate at no charge since it would go in cargo as part of my "baggage". They checked us all the way to Seattle and I boarded with a huge sigh of relief!

Anchorage was a layover stop. I was sitting at the departure gate when an airline employee found me asking if I had two puppies in cargo. "YES!" Oh, oh! I thought. My heart sank.

He said the puppies had an accident in the crate and he had cleaned it out, fed them, and gave them some water. He had to throw away the bedding as it was really smelly and bad. He was very apologetic about that. At that moment I wondered what I had gotten myself in for. I thanked him and boarded the plane when it was announced.

I didn't see the pups until we arrived in Seattle. The Vashon Shuttle Service picked me up in the middle of the night, and we raced to catch the ferry. The driver was a retired police officer and also knew me from my frequent trips to and from Alaska. His wife always joked about him going on a "picnic" with me late at night— he usually had oranges, crackers, or some snack while we waited for the ferry. He also liked dogs, fortunately. We caught the last ferry. It wasn't the first time that I brought home some unusual baggage from Alaska, nor would it be the last.

I had plans to build a log house on my new property during the summer months but it was still the middle of winter at this point. My dachshunds were in a special area, fenced off. They had a good-sized run about fifty feet in length. My neighbor provided an aluminum garage door to shelter the two large dog houses so the dogs would be warm, dry, and safe. The cats could come and go to a greenhouse I had put up and to my neighbor's small miniature barn with straw in the top part. A pet service came by several times daily and fed my animals and played with them when I traveled. This was far from ideal to introduce two pups to, but it was the best I could do at the time.

Tosca, the one with the full mane, was easy to name, but I was at a loss as to what to call the smaller of the two. They both came to the name of "Tosca" when I called them. Then it came to me—Lucia! After all, I was an opera fan so why not name them after two soprano opera roles! Besides Donizetti's opera *Lucia di Lammermoor* was my favorite opera.

I flew back and forth to Alaska for the remaining months that spring. The pups grew bigger and bigger, and the pet sitter continued to stop by several times a day when I was out of town. The dachshunds trained the puppies, sort of, leading them mostly into all kinds of mischief. Can you imagine dachshunds doing the training?! I think it was their way of getting even with me for leaving them alone so much of the time.

The girls filled out and their legs grew. They began escaping the enclosure, leading the dachshunds and showing them how to climb the fence. The neighbor chased them down each time and returned them to their fenced-in living quarters. I only heard about it when I returned from each trip.

I moved to the property just before Memorial Day at the end of the school year. I lived in a tent under the huge Maple tree located next to the dog run while my house was being built. The girls were on a long line between the miniature barn my neighbor had and the tent that had been put up under the large Maple tree while the dachshunds slept inside with me. Best of all, I didn't travel during the summer months.

Meeting the puppies for the first time

Marilyn, Tosca, and Lucia
Then they grew and became the "Big Girls"

CHAPTER 54

Trips to the End of the Road

It was no secret. I loved to drive. There were only a few districts where I actually had access to a vehicle. I've mentioned my excursion to Mosquito Lake in an earlier chapter and my little after hour trips to Izembek National Wildlife Refuge near Cold Bay. Then there was the trip when Laurie and I discovered a road out of Nome and rented a van one weekend to go camping and exploring. I also had use of an old Ford truck in Fort Yukon to go back and forth between the school and the dormitory. More about that later.

Upon reflection there were two trips to Nenana both involving rental cars. One of those trips involved two days working there. I started the trip to Nenana in the early morning from Fairbanks having plugged the rental car in the night before in the parking lot of the hotel where I was staying. Unbeknownst to me the plug in wasn't connected to the electrical circuit, so when I went outside the next morning it didn't start due to freezing temperatures. That delayed my early departure. Fortunately, it wasn't one of the really bitter cold mornings and the auto repair service came over and soon had the car running for me.

The drive over to Nenana was pleasant enough, and since I had never been to Nenana, I was looking forward to being there. My job that time didn't involve testing but accounting for real time by teachers spent with kids versus time that had been claimed.

Rumors had it one of the teachers was "nipping at the bottle" during the school day and leaving an aid in charge of the class!

My other trip was in February of 1991 for the purpose of testing a girl from Hughes. Nine dog teams were running as part of the 75th celebration in Nenana. Unfortunately, I crossed the road about thirty minutes later so missed seeing the dogs sprint run.

When I returned the rental car to Arctic Car Rental in Fairbanks, however, the agent there told me an interesting story about a black cat with white socks and a white spot near her nose with the name of Ladybug. She had been owned by a miner who left her for a month at a time in his cabin with a box of litter and some dog food. He brought her into Fairbanks one day because she pooped in his cabin and began losing her fur. The owner of the car agency took Ladybug on, and after discussing it with the vet who agreed to split the cost, started feeding her good food and treating her like a real cat.

Ladybug lost all her fur, but grew a new, beautiful coat. She was less than one year old at the time. Four years had passed when I heard the story. I was told that she was hired out for $30.00 a shot. Her job was to catch mice in warehouses, and her income went towards the fee for spaying other cats. Her owner was involved with pet protectors.

Some of the best memories, however, were my road trips out of Fairbanks to Circle. Circle is 160 miles northeast of Fairbanks at the end of the Steese Highway and 36 miles beyond Central. At that point it was no more than a gravel road. The "highway" terminates at the Yukon River, which flows past Circle on its journey to the Bering Sea.

Several years after my original visit to Circle I was flown in on a charter flight from Birch Creek, the teacher I had met there retired. I was again scheduled to visit Circle. The two new teachers weren't new at all just transfers from Arctic Village. I knew both of them and had hitched a ride with them to Circle at the beginning of the school year after the district's Fall In-Service. That was my second visit.

I rode with Lynn in her car while Paula drove their motor home ahead of us. She reported a family of lynx on that occasion in the middle of the road near the Birch Creek Bridge just beyond Central. By the time Lynn and I arrived at the bridge the lynx were gone but not forgotten as I always invariably looked for them when I made later trips by myself and drove over the bridge. Unfortunately, I never saw not one lynx!!

Future trips to the end of the road were often driven by me in a rental car from Fairbanks, although I occasionally flew and sometimes caught a ride back to Fairbanks if someone was going into town. The driving took several hours and went over Eagle Summit, some 3,624 feet in altitude. I did see a moose or two on a couple of those trips, one near Fairbanks with a calf beside her, and the other beyond the bridge at Central standing in the middle of the road at dusk. I held back until he ambled off the road and into the woods. I knew moose would attack a car if they were provoked and sometimes it didn't take much to provoke them. Cars that had moose encounters didn't fare well and the one I saw was a bull moose sporting a very large rack.

Usually in the time it would take for me to go over the pass I might see one or two other vehicles. It wasn't a well-traveled road during the winter. Several times I saw groups of caribou at the higher elevations. A few wandered down to the road. As I had never been that close to a caribou in the wild, I found it down right exciting!

A Threesome of Caribou on the Pass

Most of the time I drove over the pass with snow on it and that proved to be a challenge on occasion. I followed the tire tracks that some other vehicle had made ahead of me and made sure my tires stayed in those tracks. I also said a few prayers the car I had rented would hold up! I joked about driving a "sewing machine" for a vehicle as the cars I rented did not have much "guts" in them and were not what one would chose to go over a pass in the middle of the winter. They were neither four-wheel drive vehicles nor did they have chains. Beyond the pass the road dropped down into Central. All wasn't easy driving on the road even at the lower altitude. Carla Sheive, who was superintendent at that time, slid into the ditch on one of her trips between the two communities. She wasn't hurt, but had to be towed out.

The area along the road around the two communities of Circle and Central had burned during the summer wild fires. Driving through the area one late morning I looked over the frozen landscape of blackened tree stumps, charred snags, and little pockets of snow and could see smoke and steam wafting up from the ground. I realized there were still tree roots burning underneath. It was an eerie sight causing me to stop and take a few pictures.

If the pass was closed, a road block went up, namely a gate across the road much like a railroad crossing and cars would line up to wait for it to open at the east end. On these occasions there might be three or four vehicles. I was one of those cars only once. Anyone driving usually checked at Central before leaving for the pass to go to Fairbanks, to learn if it would be a brief wait before the road was cleared on the pass they would drive to the gate. That's what I did. A railroad-like crossing was also at the west end a considerable distance from the pass. If the road was closed and I was still in Fairbanks, I just didn't go. Yes, I dearly loved those little trips!

I was delighted to learn I would be working with Lynn and Paula when I heard of their transfer to Circle. Both excelled in the classroom. Lynn Mooney was a special education teacher and also taught the high school kids. She had total control of those classes, at least, when I visited them. She later became the Special Education Teacher of Record for several of the other schools in the district so we worked together on some difficult situations in both Arctic Village and Beaver in later years.

Paula Noel was a specialist in early childhood education and taught the younger children. There were a couple of other teachers as well including one man who had a dachshund dog. Knowing he had a dachshund was a nice reminder of my dachshunds at home. He lived in Fairbanks with his wife, spent the week days in Circle teaching, and drove home for the weekends.

Lynn and Paula used to take the kids out on some interesting school outings including an ice-skating trip to Fairbanks one of the times I happened to be there. I joined them on that trip but sat on the sidelines as far as skating was concerned. I didn't think my hip would fare too well if I fell on the ice. Outdoor ski trips, overnight camping trips, and a variety of other activities were also reported. Paula was also the school bus driver. On one occasion I rode with her and the kids into Fairbanks on the bus. It was a much smaller bus than the traditional ones I saw in the Lower 48. On that trip we stopped along the way to dig up a couple of little birch trees to take home. While they made it home, they didn't survive the following summer.

It was a treat for me to go to Circle despite some of the difficult and sad situations there. I was always well received by these two teachers and made to feel right at home. They used to cook some of the most fantastic meals when I arrived. They had a little dog named Chili. After the new school was built I tested kids in a special little room that had been designed for visiting itinerants. That was the only school I visited that actually had a room designed for testing and itinerants. Before that I used to test in the main office and sometimes in the preschool classroom when the kids weren't there.

Years later Lynn and Paula helped me celebrate my 75th birthday on Vashon Island long after I retired. I enjoyed working with them and their friendship.

CHAPTER 55

Down, But Not Out!

During the 1990s I had several incidents that left me at the mercy of the surgeon's scalpel. Most of them were not accidents just age and years of service creeping up on me. One exception was a ruptured quadriceps tendon resulting from tripping on a light cord on the bottom step of stairs in my own house over the Christmas break. I was in too big of a hurry when I came down the steps. It hurt! The recess allowed me enough time to heal in order to travel with crutches.

Non-accidents included several rotator cuff surgeries along with a hip replacement. I didn't let any of them stop me from working except taking enough time off for recovery. A set of metal tips for my crutches was my security blanket for not slipping on the ice. And, of course, the rotator cuff surgeries didn't involve crutches.

The Special Education secretary in the Nome School District had previously had a hip replacement a few months before mine so she was very aware of potential problems. We talked about it, and I decided to go to Nome with crutches. I had been there often enough to know I would have the support of the staff and would not be hampered while testing kids.

The Nome Airport did not have a ramp for passengers to walk out on and into the terminal. Instead when the jet's door opened, passengers walked out and down the steps onto the tarmac and into the building. I managed to get to the door of the plane and used the railing on the steps for support with the stewardess carrying my crutches down behind me. At the bottom I was pleasantly surprised to see a wheel chair standing by for me. I sat down and let them push me right into the passenger terminal and out to a small school bus used for kids who had physical handicaps. The secretary, one of the teachers, and the driver all greeted me with big smiles. Fortunately, all of my testing that trip was at the elementary school.

Once there I went to work. The staff had made sure there was a wheel chair available although I really didn't need it. I used it anyway to my advantage and wheeled around the school with the greatest of ease.

I went to both Nome and Saint Mary's on crutches. Nome's Special Education secretary had a sense of humor. She brought one student for me to test on one occasion and in a very serious voice told him that he had to behave. If he didn't I had a built-in club! I showed him my very colorful purple brace. His eyes grew large and he was one of the most cooperative kids I saw that day!

Saint Mary's District also had me visit fairly often. The superintendent usually picked me up at the airport and drove me down to the school. I stayed with Cath, the Special Education teacher, who lived in teacher housing that was twenty steps across a small courtyard from the back entrance to the school. So, there was no problem getting back and forth. Besides, as I mentioned above, I had metal tips on the bottoms of the crutches to keep me from sliding on icy stretches.

I had been to Saint Mary's a number of times including a visit after one of my rotator cuff surgeries. All of the kids in Cath's classes were most interested. It was not a usual experience for them to see a visitor wearing a sling. On my next visit when Cath told the students that I would be there the following day, they were expecting my arm to be wrapped up. When I walked in the door on crutches, one girl looked at me very surprised and said, "I thought it was your arm that was broke, but your leg is all bandaged up."

Casts were equated with broken bones in the girl's eyes. The rotator cuff surgery, of course, had long since healed up. Later I had another rotator cuff surgery on the other shoulder. That really confused them. Upon arriving in the classroom, another one of the kids yelled out, "I thought it was your left arm, not your right one."

After that whenever Cath told her students I was going to be there the following day or so, it became a guessing game for the kids to figure out what part of me would be bandaged up or in a cast. Maybe, I'd be walking in on crutches!

I thoroughly enjoyed those kids in Saint Mary's public school. The Catholic boarding school for high school students was no longer in operation. In fact, when I visited the village I had a hard time remembering where it had been located except down by the river. The tiny airport Bob and I had landed on so many years before was also long gone.

Cath had a couple of dogs. After school hours I often sat in her living room with one or the other's head in my lap. It was a good way to get my "dog fix" for the trip as I missed my own dogs. On one visit her basset hound sneaked into the bedroom where I was staying and managed to steal my toothbrush right out of my luggage! Fortunately, he didn't find the toothpaste. His intention, I think, was to eat it not brush his teeth.

Both of these communities I visited on crutches had a large airport, although Nome was by far the larger of the two. Jets regularly flew in and out as well as small planes. I would not have been able to travel to many of the smaller villages I frequented on crutches nor would I have attempted it. Getting in and out of cars was not a problem, but trying to manage the back of a snow mobile or some other winter vehicle would have been marginal at best.

Cath's home was in Wyoming. She was later married after I stopped going to Saint Mary's. Schultzie, one of my dachshunds and the only one I had at the time, and I drove to her wedding near Jackson Hole that late spring. It was fun introducing Cath to Schultzie after all the conversations we had had about him while I worked in Saint Mary's.

CHAPTER 56

Dormitory and an Old Ford Pickup

It was the beginning of the 1997-98 school year when I was asked to once again go back to Fort Yukon after not having worked in that district for several years. There were a lot of new people there when I arrived. In fact, I didn't recognize anyone! Getting off the plane that fall I learned the superintendent had just died rather unexpectedly. Carla Sheive (Carla Sigler), the assistant superintendent, ended up taking over his position. She was an extremely capable woman and someone I greatly admired over the following years.

I also met Marylu Martin on that trip. Marylu was the full-time itinerant counselor hired by the district the previous spring. During the winter months she stayed in Fort Yukon and traveled around the district. We became friends over the next few years and shared several misadventures.

Geographically, Fort Yukon was located at the confluence of the Yukon and the Porcupine Rivers, about 145 air miles northeast of Fairbanks. Historically, it was founded as a Canadian outpost in Russian territory and eventually became an important trade center for the Gwich'in (or Kutchin) Tribe. They lived in the lowlands of the Yukon Flats and River valleys. The Hudson Bay Company, a British trading company, operated at Fort Yukon from 1846 until 1869.

It always fascinated me to walk behind the school district's office into the cemetery and look at the large headstone with the words "Hudson Bay Company" inscribed on it as it represented some of the early white residents who had lived and died there. I remember being surprised the first time I saw the cemetery so close to the office. I wondered where the new cemetery was located. I learned it was out past the airport. I never visited it.

I understood that a mission school had been established in 1862, five years before Alaska was purchased by the United States. The fur trade of the 1800s, the whaling boom on the Arctic coast (1889-1904), and the Klondike gold rush spurred economic activity for the Natives, but with it major epidemics of introduced diseases struck Fort Yukon's population from 1860 to the 1920s. Then in 1949 a flood damaged or destroyed many of the homes in the community. Fort Yukon was finally incorporated as a city in 1959, the same year as Alaska's statehood.

The dormitory in Fort Yukon was a good-sized building that had a large central living room of sorts with a television set. There was an assortment of chairs together with a couple of couches scattered around the room. Two fairly large bedrooms with a hall way leading to each room was separated by a kitchen and two bathrooms one off each of the bedrooms.

The bedroom to the left as one walked into the building was for "boys" and the one to the right for "girls." Each of these bedrooms had six to eight bunk beds in them and nothing else. More importantly, it was nice and warm. Putting my sleeping bag on top of the mattress worked and was much better than sleeping on a floor in the school. I used my down jacket as a pillow. There was also a tiny bedroom off the central room as well and must have been used for the "housemother" when the dorm was in full operation before the high school was built. When I found the dorm empty, I slept in that tiny bedroom.

The kitchen was equipped with a stove and refrigerator together with a few non-descript dishes and pans. Sometimes there were a few pieces of silverware, and sometimes not. I never knew what I'd find in the refrigerator or how long it had been there. I really didn't want to think about it so avoided opening it most of the time. Behind the kitchen was a tiny room with a washer and dryer in it.

Thinking back a few years the very first night I spent in Fort Yukon was in the old historic hotel that later burned down. It was one of the coldest nights I remember in all my years of traveling. I welcomed staying at the dorm as it was kept warm, sometimes almost too hot. During my first year back in Fort Yukon I also sometimes slept on the floor in the District's accounting office. Then there was a district-owned house on the corner less than a block away from the office where I occasionally camped out, but for the most part I ended up out at the dormitory and had access to the blue Ford pickup truck in order to drive to and from work. It was kept busy by others during the day.

The pickup had very few miles on its odometer but was battered to look as if it had just been hauled out from the junk yard. Fort Yukon's winters had not been kind to the truck nor had some of its drivers. It had been left out in the weather every winter with temperatures dropping to 50 below zero. There was an electric plug in for the really cold nights. All sorts of people including both school personnel and visitors ended up driving it. Some individuals knew what they were doing when driving, and others didn't or if they did they didn't care. While the maintenance crew kept it full of gas and oil and whatever else they deemed necessary to get a little more out of it each year, it needed a lot more TLC.

I remember coming out of the dorm one morning, hauling my testing equipment to the truck, starting it and letting it run for ten minutes to warm up, only to find that when I put it in gear to go forward the tires had frozen to the ground. One of them was flat as well! It wouldn't budge as it was being held firmly in place by ice. Fortunately, there was a telephone inside the dorm. At that point I had to call Samson, the head of maintenance in the district office, and have him send someone out to rescue me and get me to the office so I could go to work. The pickup was back in operating condition by the end of the day.

I was the only person in the dorm most of the nights I stayed there. On occasion, there would be another person or two staying at the same time. I can remember a traveling police officer with his K-9 partner, a black Lab, being there for several nights. Another time there was a speech pathologist, and on occasion there were several others on district business. I understood that visiting basketball teams and other groups would also stay there but I never ran into any of them.

Marylu usually stayed in town at a small apartment and

sometimes in someone else's house, but also spent time in the dorm towards the end of when she worked up there. One night after dinner we decided to do laundry. Neither of us had a lot to wash, so we decided to put everything in one load and even then it wasn't a full load. But it definitely saved time. Once finished, we loaded everything into the dryer. Unbeknownst to Marylu and forgotten by me, I had left a tube of bright red lipstick in my pants pocket. I never carried a purse up there because it was something added to carry and lose if I wasn't careful so I tucked anything I had in various pockets or my backpack. Unfortunately, the lipstick went into a pants pocket.

The dryer worked fine. The clothes were nice and toasty warm when we decided to unload the dryer and call it a night. While the heavier outer garments had streaks of red here and there, red-streaked underwear greeted us as we pulled the items out. We soon discovered that red lipstick doesn't come out easily. In fact, it wasn't coming out at all. Worse, we had washed just about everything we had with us for the trip. I have since been told that WD-40 will get lipstick out that has gone through the dryer, although one has to spray it on, re-wash the article of clothing again and then send it back through the dryer a second time. I haven't tried it.

There had been a change in superintendents when Carla moved on. Also, a new Special Education administrator had been hired and wanted someone to help with the files. Marylu was no longer employed by the district at that time but had lots of knowledge and experience. I suggested that she be hired by the administrator as she had been in the district for several years as the counselor traveling to all of the villages and staying in Fort Yukon, and I knew she wanted to make one more trip north. She was living in Moses Lake, Washington, at the time.

Marylu was hired for a month's work, and in my estimation was far more than well-qualified for the job. Marylu was kept busy. Among other things she was to clean out the files of duplicate stuff and there was a lot of it. The administrator had informed parents that they could come in and check their child's file or their own in cases where they had been tested in years past and get copies of anything they wanted.

Getting copies of actual standardized tests was neither appropriate nor legal in terms of test company agreements with the district. Nor did it make sense to hand a person a nationally normed test complete with answers. Access to that kind of data was confidential and the test would no longer be a "test" if it was just handed out.

The administrator made her announcement and said "everything" should be available for review and copied if desired. Marylu and I quietly went through each file, left the cover sheet of test with scores, date of test, and other pertinent information required by law, and disposed of the actual questions that were also part of the test booklet. As a school psychologist I took testing and testing protocols very seriously. I had previously ordered test materials for the district and had signed my name that the test booklets would be kept confidential.

We loaded up the back of the old Ford pickup with several boxes of tests and drove out to the dump one late afternoon. The best way to permanently destroy normed tests was to burn them so out came the matches. There were a couple of other small fires at the dump when we arrived so another little blaze wasn't unusual.

Paper is hard to burn unless you separate it into individual sheets and burn one or two pieces at a time. That caused us considerable problems as we had to rip each test booklet apart into separate sheets and then burn the individual papers. We spent the better part of an hour burning old tests, freezing while we were doing so in spite of our little bonfire.

It was quite dark when we finished and getting colder by the minute in spite of our little fire. In the end we successfully purged the district of test questions and answers that had no business being available to anyone who wanted them. The important data had remained in the files but the test items were eliminated. We went back to the dorm afterwards and celebrated our mission accomplished.

Since our days in the "Flats", Marylu and I have gotten together several times. One late spring we took a road trip to Chicago, Illinois, along with Kiley, one of my dachshunds, for a dachshund picnic where I was autographing books. I think Marylu took pictures of every dachshund attending and more than several of Kiley

Fort Yukon

Two memorable experiences on that trip involved having the best buffalo burgers ever in Sturgis in the Black Hills and later going through the Badlands National Park in South Dakota. We arrived at the park quite late in the afternoon and managed to see wild turkeys, pronged horn antelope, deer, bighorn sheep with several lambs, and all sorts of other critters that even the park rangers were surprised to hear about as most visitors didn't see them. Marylu did her best to take some outstanding pictures but dusk did not provide the best lighting. Despite this she got some great shots.

CHAPTER 57

A Cold, Wintery Night in Fort Yukon

I felt the cold as it seeped in through the cracks, or so it seemed. Not just because of the temperature but because of the bad previous 24 hours in Fort Yukon. Another suicide had occurred the night before. A young man shot himself with his hunting rifle. His 10-year-old son along with the boy's cousin had found the body. The two boys then disappeared. It was much too cold for two young boys to be wandering outside.

Marylu Martin was still working for the district at that time as the district counselor. Both of us were there for a week, although I was scheduled to leave the following morning. Marylu followed up with counseling whenever a suicide occurred whether it was in Fort Yukon or in one of the other villages within the district. She had gone looking for the two boys during the day, but couldn't find them. No one had seen either one since the previous night after the discovery of the body. Marylu wanted to find them, make sure they had a safe place to stay, talk with them, as well as with the adult responsible for them. It was unclear as to whom they were staying with at the time.The two of us had talked about the kids and where they could be, but neither of us had a clue. We decided to work late that evening in the district office before going back to the dormitory where we were staying. Everyone else had gone home at five o'clock. The quiet office provided me with time to concentrate on my reports. Instead I found myself remembering earlier trips to this village.

Marylu's office was at the other end of the hall, while my office was near the main entrance of the building and next to the coffee pot. We had keys to the district's pickup since we were both staying at the dormitory. It was a little over a mile away. Unlike the old Sourdough Inn that had been further out of town than the dormitory, the dorm was warm. Usually, when I stayed in Fort Yukon I ended up with the old blue pickup for transportation. Tonight, however, we had the superintendent's new bright red pickup so we were traveling in style!

My mind wandered as I thought about those two little boys and the father. Why? Such a waste I thought to myself. I stood up deciding a cup of coffee might help me to focus. The pot was empty, but there was plenty of hot water in the other pot and tea bags. Fixing a cup of tea I returned to my desk. "Get back to work," I scolded myself.

I was flying out the next day and decided to check my schedule instead, and finish my reports tomorrow when I heard the outside door open and with that sound came a rush of cold air. That wasn't really unusual but at this time of night it was a little surprising. Then I heard kids' voices. I stood up and walked out of my office a second time. Frankly, I was kind of glad Marylu was at the other end of the building although I doubt she could have heard anyone coming in from her office. One never knew when a drunk might stumble in even though the village was "dry". Two little boys, poorly dressed especially for the weather outside, stood near the hot water pot. Their faces were red from the cold. Both were shivering and trying to warm up rubbing their hands together. I looked at them, and I knew the two little boys had been found. I didn't want to scare them or chase them away. My goal was to get them down to see Marylu. "Want a cup of hot chocolate?" I asked as I pulled out two cups and two packages of cocoa kept below the shelf holding the water. Their eyes lit up and two heads nodded as I put the chocolate into the cups and added some hot water. "I'm Marilyn. What are your names? It's awfully cold out there, why don't you stay in here until you warm up?" They seemed to relax as they started to sip the hot liquid. "I have a friend who has been looking for you. She's down the hall, and I know she wants to visit with you."

I pointed to her office at the end of the hall and motioned for them to follow me hoping they would. They did, holding onto their cups. "Marylu, here are a couple of boys that I know you want to meet. They just came in from the cold to warm up and I gave them some hot chocolate."I didn't know if she had met them before or not as she often worked in the elementary school at this site.

Marylu sized up the situation immediately, quickly stood up from her desk and handed them some snacks. "I'll be back in my office. Maybe we can drive them home when you're finished." I said and returned to my desk. Some time passed before Marylu and the two youngsters came to my office to get me. We went outside, locked the building up and went to the red truck. Both boys liked the idea of riding in the superintendent's new red pickup. It hadn't been in the village that long so was a real novelty. They directed us to a house in the village. We made sure there was an adult there when we dropped them off and then headed for the dormitory.

I left the next morning for another village but I knew Marylu was staying in Fort Yukon as she was a full-time district employee and would definitely follow up on the two kids.

Two or three years later when I was back in the district and this time in the small village of Chalkyitsik, only 67 miles from Fort Yukon, one of the student's names stood out as I read the list the teacher handed me of referred kids. I knew villagers traveled back and forth between the two villages on snow machines during the winter months. A couple of the teachers had just made the trip on the well-established winter trail to Fort Yukon and back over the weekend.

The ten-year old boy who had lost his father was now living in that village with less than a hundred people in it. His teacher, a male, reported that he was caught taking things from the teacher's living quarters. "He's staying here with a relative. Getting him to cooperate is going to be a challenge," the young teacher told me. "He is having a lot of behavior problems.""I know him," I said quietly. "I suspect he very much wants your attention."I had him come into the library that was also the computer room and the testing room while I was there. I looked at him directly in the eye and said, "We have met, you know, in Fort Yukon!"I reminded him of the visit he and his cousin had made to the district office. He smiled as he remembered me and the hostility left his face.

At the time I was doing some research testing with the Psychological Association Research Corporation in addition to assessing kids for Special Education services in the district. I thought about it, and asked him if he would like to be one of the subjects for the special project I was doing and told him I could pay him $10 for doing it.

"You don't have to do this additional testing as it's purely voluntary, but I have to do the other testing for the school and I can't pay you for that as it's part of your school work."He understood. I explained that the research testing would have to be after school hours, but the rest of the testing would be during class time. He readily agreed and worked hard on both tests. His reading and math scores were low. He would qualify for additional help.

I knew in my heart that the loss of his father at the age of ten had a significant impact on his education. I was hopeful that the situation could be turned around.

He told me he might return to Fort Yukon to live. "That would be great" I thought, as there was a good special education teacher on site in the larger school. There he would get regular help and more structure. In Chalkyitsik because of the size of the school there was only an itinerant special education teacher who visited often, but not every day and sometimes not even weekly. Later I met with the relative he was living with and discussed the testing results. I confirmed that the boy would be returning to Fort Yukon to live.I smiled as I thought about how amazing it was what one cup of hot chocolate could do for a youngster on a cold freezing night in the middle of winter.

Marilyn leaving Fort Yukon
(Photo by Marylu Martin)

CHAPTER 58

Chalkyitsik

Memories flooded back at the mention of a suicide in Fort Yukon followed by the man's son moving to Chalkyitsik. I made several trips back and forth to that village. There was a winter trail between the two communities as I mentioned in the earlier chapter. Teachers occasionally took it using a snow machine. I always flew, but would have loved to have gone on that trail.

I thought about Chalkyitsik and the first time I visited it. I remember getting out of the plane and meeting a couple of women who were state workers. I didn't know what agency they were from or what they were doing in the village. But they had been staying at the school for the past few days and were on their way out. Neither one of them was very happy about their experience and expressed fears. Both seemed quite anxious to get on the plane and leave.

While we were waiting for the pilot to unload my baggage and load up their belongings, the shorter of the two women asked me, "Have you been to this village before?"

"No!" I said, "Why?"

"There were workers staying in the school. One-night drunks from the village came up to the school with guns and started shooting." She went on, "They surrounded the school, and started firing."

Chalkyitsik Airport

I looked at the woman almost in disbelief. Both women appeared to be genuinely frightened, but I found the story hard to believe. I couldn't get a sense of when this alleged attack had occurred. Initially, I thought it might have happened to the two women because of their comments but then realized it had happened long before they had visited the village.

"Be careful! You just don't know what can happen. Everyone had to hide in the center part of the school as they were afraid they would be shot." The other woman added, "You might want to think about not staying here all night."

I listened, and wondered what I was getting myself into. The school district had not mentioned this, nor had I heard any other references to such an occurrence. I reasoned that had anyone been hurt, it would have been all over the news. That kind of a story with villagers shooting at a school would also make the rumor mill in a big hurry. With that the pilot told the women to climb aboard. I watched as the plane took off then started walking to the school when one of the teachers met me with a sled. The end of the airport was adjacent to the school, which stood at the top of a small hill with a road leading down to the village. Snow was everywhere.There was a cyclone fence around the back of the school and inside it several buildings that were teacher housing. I would be staying in one of these buildings that had two apartments

322

in it. One of the teachers lived in the other apartment. I suspected there may have been an incident but in the distant past. The state workers, however, were convinced that it was very real and could happen at any moment. Their fear had seemed genuine.Most of my memories were positive, but I was always glad to leave the community mainly because it was the last site I would visit before I would be on my way back to Seattle and home. I also rarely went down to the village and wonder if perhaps my initial exposure to those two women and their "story" colored my feelings.I never really seemed to connect with the teachers as one or another was always transferring in and out. It was a somewhat isolated community with very few students in it. The one main classroom was multi-graded. Kindergarten kids were taught in another small room behind the office.The village itself had maybe 80 people in it although it had been an important seasonal fishing site in the past. Archaeological excavations in the area had revealed use and occupancy of the region as early as 10,000 BC. Some of the village elders remembered a highly nomadic way of life in recent years. They described it as living at the headwaters of the Black River from autumn to spring and then floating downriver to fish in the summer months. I knew the summers were short, and could attest to the fact that the winters were long and bitterly cold.

On one trip I did get to know one of the teachers fairly well as she had a golden retriever mama dog with a litter of pups. They were purebred puppies and had AKC papers. One of the village girls spent a considerable amount of time with the puppies as well. I wanted to take one of those pups home in the worst way, but I resisted. I still missed the two golden retrievers I had back in the 1980s. In late February 2002 I was back in Chalkyitsik at the school and waiting for the plane to arrive. I had been traveling all around the district for the previous two weeks and was at the end of my trip. I was ready to go home.A telephone call came in for me. That in itself was somewhat unusual. I quickly answered figuring it must be the air service telling me they were delayed or had cancelled my trip. Instead a familiar voice was on the other end. "Aunt Marilyn, Janet finally succeeded. She killed herself." It was my nephew's wife, Misty, calling me from Oregon.

Her words stunned me. Misty went on to say that Janet, my sister, had overdosed with prescription pills. "I'm on my way home and should be there late tonight. I'll drive down tomorrow" was about all I got out.

Misty and my nephew Scott lived in Bend, Oregon, at the time. Janet was my only sibling and three and a half years younger than I was. She had exhibited mental problems for years and had made numerous attempts at suicide but always called resulting in someone rescuing her. I was to learn they hadn't even found her body until a week or more after she died. She would have turned 60 years old in another couple of weeks. I had never really connected with her, and now would never do so. She was an individual I had not gotten to know. We were as different as night was from day. Numb, I climbed into the twin-engine plane that had landed a few minutes later to pick me up. The pilot was a woman I had flown with a number of times. I sat up in the co-pilot's seat as per usual. We briefly talked on the way back to Fairbanks, and I told her what happened. I felt a need to share at that moment.

CHAPTER 59

Arctic Village

Arctic Village was a place I had never heard of before I stepped out of the Bonanza on its graveled air strip in 1973. Upon reflection, it was one of the few communities I visited over a span of almost thirty-three years. That first time occurred before the Molly Hootch decision had been reached in 1976.

After that high schools were built in the villages including Arctic Village. Its new school had opened in the Fall of 1980, a week after I was there to do interviews for my dissertation. The Arctic Village I remembered from my two earlier trips was no longer there when I returned. I couldn't identify the street that Bob and I had walked down on my first visit in 1973 nor could I find the place where I interviewed one of the women for my dissertation research project in 1980.

The new high school building I saw then was recognizable but it looked far from new. There had been a number of those little spruce trees near the building, but nothing else. The building was a tired and well-worn structure having survived a number of winters and several graduating classes of students. The students as well as the community as a whole had made their mark.

The building no longer stood out by itself on my next visit. There were other buildings and houses nearby. I had made several trips to Yukon Flats during the mid-1980s—on at least one of those I had visited Arctic Village. On that occasion, I remember a house where two teachers lived next to the high school; elementary kids must have had classes in it. Later it expanded into a square building of sorts that served as the elementary school. Two classrooms were in the building, one for younger kids, and a second multi-graded classroom for students who were older (fourth grade and up). A teacher's apartment was also part of the building, and across from it was a maintenance building.

The generator for the entire village was housed in maintenance building. Fortunately, the school had a backup generator. I never saw the inside of that building. One evening it burned down. I didn't see the fire, but I arrived a few days later and saw a lot of charred wood. One of the teachers had taken a video of the fire and shared it with me. She said that an individual could stand right next to the flames and not feel the heat as it went straight up because of the extreme cold. That I could believe.My first two trips I hiked into the village. Those early trips were in the summer months. Once I came back as a school psychologist for the district, the maintenance man drove out to the airport in a truck to pick me up—at least—most of the time. It was usually the same person. He just got older with each visit.

My baggage and testing equipment were piled into the back of the vehicle and we headed for the school where I would be dropped off at the front door. It was a good mile and not something I wanted to walk in the middle of the winter!On one occasion, however, my "taxi" was a dog sled pulled not by dogs but by a snow machine. I could have sat in the sled, but I opted to stand on the back of it holding on to the bar or rail in front of me the same way mushers do. I always traveled north with a down jacket, a double layer of warm pants and a hat covering my ears. But that time while I had heavy gloves on, I wasn't wearing the inside liners since I had been on the plane. The cold seeped in to where my hands and fingers were. I couldn't let go of the rail to protect my hands by putting them inside my jacket or I would have lost my balance and gone flying. I remember it being a very long mile.

We used to toss a cup of hot coffee up in the air outside the district office in Fort Yukon, and long before the liquid hit the ground it shattered into a million tiny frozen particles. That's about how cold I felt when I arrived at the school. Fortunately, I didn't shatter.

On one visit I went behind the high school after classes on the back of a snow machine to watch the caribou browse. It was late afternoon and caribou came right to the edge of the village near the school. I discovered this and wanted to get some pictures. A couple of us got on snow machines to find them, and sure enough they were browsing among the trees. A nearby stream separated the animals from where we were but the water was frozen solid. They were eating and didn't seem too concerned about people being there but a few moments after we arrived they had faded into the nearby brush and just disappeared.

To sleep at night, I chose the kindergarten room in most of the schools. This because it usually had a carpet on the floor. Sometimes, however, I had to find another room. In Arctic Village I usually slept in the computer room that was part of the high school and near the office. Unlike many of the districts I visited, the school had purchased some cots that could be set up quickly for itinerant visitors. I very much appreciated this and at night stretched out inside my sleeping bag on top of one of those cots. The room was off the one main high school classroom.

On the other side of the office was one additional room that high schoolers sometimes used, and where kids in Special Education were taught. I often tested there. The back of the building held the cafeteria at lunch time and served as the gym the rest of the time. The showers were off the kitchen and the gym. That was the layout of the school that I remembered seeing from the outside so many years before. Its footprint was a basic square.

One evening I went with one of the teachers to meet the parents of a preschool child. We were there to discuss the preschooler's program. It was in the middle of the winter, but then it was always in the middle of the winter when I was up there working or so it seemed. I walked into their small home that was toasty and warm, almost too warm. The room was close and without any air circulating.

I chanced a glance into the kitchen, and almost wished I hadn't. In and around the sink was part of a dead caribou. The leg bone complete with fur was propped up. Someone had been cutting it up for meat. I could only imagine how many germs were on the counter. But no one was sick. Everyone seemed healthy. The family just left it when we arrived and met with us in the main room. This was a larger house because in the back there was a bedroom. Some of the homes had a living room and a kitchen combined, and a bed off to the side and that was it.

Another time I was invited into one of the homes for supper. I felt honored that the woman felt comfortable enough to invite me. I liked her and had spent time in school meeting with her. She worked in the school. But still I was an outsider who flew in from the Lower 48.

When I arrived at her home there were at least three or four other people all sitting around in the main room watching television. I was handed a plate with food on it. The woman who had invited me also had a plate. We sat and visited. The food was good. I wondered if the rest of the family had eaten before we did. I was confused. We talked about school and my visit to the district as well as my testing.

At the end of the meal I returned the plate, which was then wiped off and filled with food for another member of the household, and that was repeated until everyone had eaten. Homes in Arctic Village did not have running water although the school did. That was also true of many of the other villages I visited throughout the state.

My original boss, Twyla Barnes, had left SERRC, moved to Vancouver, Washington and became Superintendent of the school system there. The spring of 2003 also brought about changes in SERRC as far as itinerant specialists were concerned, at least, that is what I was told. SERRC's Board wanted itinerants to live in Alaska. There had always been a comment or two about my traveling from Seattle. I was then told I would need to be interviewed for the job I had held in both a full-time capacity as well as part-time one for 20 years. That didn't sit well with me. I ended up leaving SERRC and working for the next three years independently against SERRC's administrators' wishes. I was very sorry to end my years with SERRC in that manner. No one even said goodbye.Carla Sigler, Yukon Flats superintendent, asked me to continue working for the district either as a school psychologist or as the Special Education coordinator. The pay was the same so that didn't influence me. I decided to work in the coordinator's position as it would give me something different to do. That meant I traveled to Fort Yukon on a monthly basis. Sometimes I stayed for a week or more and at least one time was only there for four days.

The Special Education teacher in Arctic Village had apparently wanted the coordinator's position and made things a bit difficult when I was given the position. She had it in for me as well as the district office. The assistant superintendent Harry White and I ended up going up there to work with her. She skipped out on the two of us, leaving a cup of hot coffee on her desk that we discovered when we arrived moments later after having been told she was home sick.

Fortunately, I had the support of both the superintendent and the assistant superintendent and was able to sort out her records.Later after Carla left the Yukon Flats schools, she became the superintendent of Yakutat School District, hiring me again to review records in the Special Education files. I had visited Yakutat in years past with Bob, but had never worked in the school district. I was delighted to be working with Carla again.

After Carla left I went back to my school psychologist position traveling all over the district including Arctic Village. I did that until the 2006-2007 school year when I retired.

CHAPTER 60

One More Trip

My last trip, but I didn't know it at the time, covered three separate districts including Naknek in Bristol Bay, the correspondence program in Juneau, and Yukon Flats. It had its ups and downs. Unlike previous trips this one began in Portland, Oregon. I had taken my dachshunds down for safe-keeping to stay with my friend Carol in Vancouver, Washington, and decided to fly to Alaska from Portland rather than drive back home then fly out of Sea-Tac.

I was anxious to get this trip over with as quickly as possible. I hated leaving my dachshunds, especially one of my ten-week old pups who had major health problems. She had stopped gaining weight and at ten weeks of age that was not good.

Fortunately, I arrived at Portland's airport half an hour before I needed to only to learn the flight had been cancelled at the last moment. What! The ticket agent quickly switched me to an earlier flight just before the gate closed. I dashed to the gate and made the direct flight to Seattle where I changed planes.

In Seattle I ran into a delay because of a mechanical problem. After a considerable wait we were invited to board a 737-400 series jet headed for Anchorage. The drunk sitting next to me kept getting up to "piss" in his words. Each time I graciously got up to let him out until we landed and were taxiing to the gate when he insisted on getting up again. I refused to stand up until the plane stopped and that annoyed him. Fortunately, before he became really nasty, the seat belt sign went off, so I shot up the aisle. Why the attendants ever served him more liquor on the flight was beyond me, but they did.

I went down the stairs instead of waiting for the elevator to Penn Air's check-in for the trip from Anchorage to King Salmon. I had made it despite my earlier delay. This time we flew in a Saab 324. The flight was uneventful. Since there was a lot of cloud cover I didn't even see Mt. Augustine blow off steam and belch its ash and molten rock, but I knew it was down there somewhere doing its thing.

One of the major caribou herds migrated through the King Salmon area; I remember one time I was lucky enough to see part of the migration. There were miles and miles of caribou in long lines below me all on the move.

My first impression of Naknek in 1983 was nothing but wind, rain, clouds, and sky that was all similar to the Aleutians, but I noted at the time that it also had a few trees, not many, but they were there. Surprisingly, I spent my coldest day in Alaska there when the thermometer dropped to 71 degrees below zero. That day they closed the school.

Phyllis, the Special Education teacher, met me at the airport and we drove to my favorite B&B in Naknek, a community less than a half hour away, just north of the river. The woman who ran the B&B had been the school's cook for years. She usually brought over special snacks for me when I arrived. I enjoyed staying there and visiting with her.

In my early years visiting the community I had stayed at both hotels at one time or another, and then I discovered the B&B that included a small cabin away from the other rooms. I looked longingly at the cabin I used to stay in but it was occupied so I went to my old room attached to the main house when Phyllis dropped me off.

Looking at the cabin reminded me of one late evening when I was staying in it. I had looked out the window and saw a very large mama bear. She was no more than ten feet from me as I sat motionless when I first saw her. She was closely followed by her cub. In no way did I want her to know I was in the cabin watching—the outside door was not that strong. She could probably have busted it down with one swipe. I was glad I didn't have any food in the cabin that might have attracted her.

After that incident I walked with a great deal of care the back way to and from the school. Most of the mornings, however, one of the teachers picked me up. On an earlier trip before I found the B&B there had been an incident of a bear rummaging around in the hotel's garbage where I was staying. I became a believer that there were bears in town.

Mount Augustine blowing off steam

During the summer months Naknek was filled with fishermen. After all, it's a fishing community. It's no wonder that they have a couple of good restaurants, and, of course there's the Red Dog, which I understood was a "wild bar". I didn't go there as I felt it was a little unsafe in the evening hours. I have had some fabulous meals, however, at the other restaurant; they made a mean pizza.

The main school building included both an elementary school and high school and was only a very short ways from the B&B. It was a pleasant walk except when bears were reported. Kids in the fourth grade and up flew over daily from South Naknek across the river. Those in the primary grades stayed on the south side. I rarely went over to the south side, but had on a few occasions in past years. Naknek (Bristol Bay School District) was one of those schools I had been going to the entire time I worked in Alaska since 1983. I had gone through several principals as well as a couple of special education teachers during my years there.

The trip went very smoothly in the school as no problems greeted me. Bristol Bay's personnel had always been good to me, reasonable, and above all else organized. There was never a time when I walked into the school but someone greeted me by name. The week went by uneventfully with me testing four kids, meeting parents and teachers, and, oh yes, answering those blamed email messages.

The district had me scheduled to come back in the spring, but I managed to finish all their three-year re-evaluations and there were no new referrals to do. The spring trip was cancelled.

All was not good back home, however, as my ten-week old puppy, named Cinnamon, died while I was in Naknek. I guess I knew she wasn't going to make it because of her multiple handicaps, and now she wasn't processing food. One of Carol's close friends carried her around in a neck sling until they could get her into the vet, who was surprised that I had been able to keep her alive for as long as I had. I left Naknek feeling empty inside.

I was not looking forward to the following week in Yukon Flats. The director just couldn't seem to get it together working with the individual schools. This trip she was convinced I would go to Fort Yukon first; then Cruikshank School in Beaver, which was fine with me except that the school in Beaver was on break. She knew it but insisted the teacher just bring in the kids. That wasn't going to happen.

The teacher finally told her in no uncertain terms the students would not be there at the end of the week since the school was closed. I suspected the teacher had already lined up another district in which to work the following year or she would not have been so direct.

My problems didn't end as I was told to also test a child from Stevens Village in Fairbanks at the hotel over the following weekend since that child wasn't in the village. I started digging around and made a couple of phone calls and discovered he had been escorted out of the village after threatening suicide. I realized she had deliberately misled me in relating the problems he had. I smiled when I learned the boy was in lockup and wasn't about to be released for school-related testing. I knew a psychiatrist would be seeing him, and thought under the circumstances it was far more appropriate.

I had also negotiated a little trip to Juneau with my friend Roxie Quick to test two kids in the Correspondence Program on Saturday. She was the director of the program. Friday, after two phone calls with Lynn Mooney, who lived in Circle but was also the Special Education Teacher of Record for Beaver, I was told by Lynn to go to Beaver at the beginning of the week when the kids were in school. I did just exactly that.

Well, Juneau was on, so I stayed all night at the Hampton Inn in Anchorage after flying back from King Salmon Friday night on another Saab, and didn't sleep a wink.

I boarded an almost empty 737-400 series Alaskan jet and was told I would need to sit towards the back because of weight and balance of the plane. And, yes, the plane was virtually empty. I heard someone call my name. I looked up to see Shirley, a Special Education teacher. I had worked with her both in Fort Yukon and a number of years ago in Klawock in Southeastern Alaska. She was flying to Yakutat, but decided to go via Juneau because even though it was farther it was shorter time-wise because the direct flight made the milk run between Anchorage and Yakutat. I sat down with her, and we had a great visit.

Once in Juneau I got off while Shirley continued on the flight that went back to Yakutat. My good friend Roxie, who had also worked in Fort Yukon when Shirley was there, and met me when I got off the plane. We went to breakfast then headed for the correspondence school. The kids came in like clockwork—two boys who were easy to test and friendly. Afterwards, Roxie and I headed for the Heritage coffee house and had a latte, then went shopping where I bought a warm hat and two pairs of wool socks. We met two of Roxie's fellow workers at the movie theater where we saw one very funny film, *Failure to Launch*. All of us howled. That was just what I needed.

Afterwards, we hit downtown Juneau, and a pizza place on the water front. A glass of wine and a pizza put me in a good mood. Roxie's fellow workers left and she took me over to Douglas Island where a woman did massages. Oh, my! Grapes and a cool glass of water accompanied me while I soaked 15 minutes in the mineral springs' hot bath with the water bubbling away. What heaven! That followed a massage with hot rocks that lasted for almost an hour. I could hardly negotiate my way out after that but managed to get back to Roxie's place and crashed. I still didn't sleep much because of dreading Monday because of having to deal with the director in Fort Yukon.

I flew back to Anchorage on a 7:22 am 737 Alaska jet. Again, the plane was almost empty! I went back to the rear of the plane as it was another weight and balance issue. I had about a two-hour wait before I caught another jet to Fairbanks. Again, I was greeted by an empty jet. No wonder Alaska Airlines was charging so much for their tickets. They had to make money somehow.

That night I spent at my favorite hotel in Fairbanks, Sophia's Station that was located near the airport. I finished the two reports on the kids from Juneau just about the time another friend, Carla, who had been superintendent both in Fort Yukon several years earlier and then in Yakutat, arrived. We went to the bar, had a drink together then she left, and I had dinner, watched one television program, and crashed. I finally was able to sleep.

Unfortunately, I ran into the director from Fort Yukon the next day at the airport. She wanted to give me "a heads up" that there was no paperwork completed in Beaver or so she thought and that I wasn't to test if nothing was done. The speech therapist last week had told her the teacher on site didn't have anything ready. It was a new speech pathologist who had not worked much in the Bush nor in the Yukon Flats District.

The "if" in the director's comments provided me with an out. Lynn, I knew was working behind the scenes with the teacher, had called her and told her what I needed. I figured when I finally met the teacher the next day, I would have to sit down with her, and see what she had.

Delays in Fairbanks meant I arrived at the school in Beaver at 3:45 in the afternoon by a snow machine that had picked me up at the airport. It was only about a block from the school but was very nice to get a ride to the building. The school was closed up. The maintenance man who picked me up had the keys and let me into the building. They knew I was coming.

C'est la vie. I have always been convinced that my escapes from bad situations meant God was watching over me. I've also been convinced that a team of guardian angels were ever present. They certainly were on this trip. I finished it in good stride meeting the teacher in Beaver and seeing some kids. I returned to Fort Yukon testing kids there as well. At that point I gave notice to the director that I would not be returning to Alaska after the current school year, and wanted to give her a "heads up" so she could find another school psychologist for the district. From what I later heard her contract was not renewed and she returned to the Lower 48 the following year.

I flew back to Fairbanks and on to Portland as I needed to pick up my dachshunds. I had a spring trip scheduled for Bristol Bay as I mentioned above, but it was cancelled when there were no kids who required testing. I was sorry about that as I was looking forward to flying back up there.

After 33 years of going to Alaska my trips ended very abruptly as has my story. I thought of the seven years beginning in 1973 of getting to know and love Alaska. That was followed by my six-week trip with my husband and our three dachshunds while I interviewed Native women and their changing roles since statehood. In 1983 I began 23 years working and being where I wanted to be. During those 33 years I met many wonderful people and lots of great kids.

I hope you, the reader, have a sense of what I did. I have enjoyed putting my adventures down so others can enjoy. I have a print in a prominent place in my office of five black ravens sitting on an old gray snag and entitled "The Social Club." A couple of them have a red berry in their mouth. It was done by JoAnn George, one of the Tlingit artists I met on one of my early visits to Angoon. I think of my trips over the years to Alaska as I look at those ravens, and yes, I want to go back for another visit. They are calling to me.

One of Angoon's Ravens

ABOUT THE AUTHOR

Dr. Marilyn Cochran Mosley is a retired educational psychologist and has worked with children and young adults since 1973. Prior to her career in school psychology she had been a counselor at the college level both at the University of Washington in Seattle and at Grinnell College in Grinnell, Iowa. She then returned to Seattle to complete her formal education and began working in the public-school system in Washington and later in Alaska. She lived in Alaska for three years traveling all over the State, then commuted to Alaska from Seattle for 20 years part-time before retiring in 2007. She was married to O.A. "Bob" Mosley for 20 years until he passed away in 1995. They adopted two pre-teenage children from Peru in 1986.

Marilyn is a third generation Oregonian. She grew up in the Pacific Northwest, and has traveled extensively throughout the world including a trip in a single-engine Beechcraft Bonanza between London, England, and Brisbane, Australia, in the World Vintage Air Rally in 1990.

She lives with her seven dachshunds on Vashon island in Washington. Her son and daughter live in nearby West Seattle. Outside her professional life, Marilyn is an avid photographer, and loves animals and the outdoors. She writes for fun, and has held both a scuba diver's certificate and a private pilot's license.

YUKON RIVER
(Photo by Marylu Martin)

Dachshunds on the Yukon

Made in the USA
San Bernardino, CA
13 January 2019